FAMILY CIRCLE

FAMILY CIRCLE

A Study of the Epworth Household in Relation to John and Charles Wesley

By
MALDWYN EDWARDS

WIPF & STOCK · Eugene, Oregon

Wipf and Stock Publishers
199 W 8th Ave, Suite 3
Eugene, OR 97401

Family Circle
A Study of the Epworth Household in Relation to John and Charles Wesley
By Edwards, Maldwyn
Copyright©1949 Epworth Press
ISBN 13: 978-1-60608-732-9
Publication date 4/27/2009
Previously published by Epworth Press, 1949

Copyright © Epworth Press 1949
First English edition 1949 by Epworth Press
This edition published by arrangement with Epworth Press

FOR
CAROL
WHO WILL ENJOY THE FAMILY GHOST

CONTENTS

PREFACE	. . . . . .	vii
1. A FIGHTER EVER	. . . .	1
2. THE FATHER AND HIS SONS	. . .	23
3. MRS. WESLEY	. . . . .	46
4. SUSANNA THE MOTHER	. . . .	57
5. THE FAMILY GHOST	. . . .	87
6. DEAR SAMMY	. . . . .	100
7. CHURCHMAN AND POET	. . .	115
8. THE WESLEY SISTERS	. . . .	132
9. HETTY	. . . . . .	154
10. THE FAMILY GROUP	. . . .	174
INDEX	. . . . . .	189

PREFACE

THIS book was written accidentally. I had set out to write a book on the subject of 'The Brothers' and meant to study John and Charles in relation to each other and their joint contribution to the Christian Church. To do that properly it was necessary to make a thorough investigation of their common antecedents. It is true that apart from family letters and such of the published works of Samuel the father and Samuel the son as I was able to study, there was not a great deal of primary material. Stevenson, Adam Clarke, and Luke Tyerman had all dealt with the subject in detail and there did not seem any fresh facts that would come to light. Nevertheless, the research proved an absorbing task, and so I set out to write the first chapter on the family from which the brothers came. But the chapter grew to an unconscionable length and still there was more to be said. So almost against inclination I came to see that the subject would demand not a chapter but a book.

Once that decision had been made the book shaped itself. First it was necessary to show that despite his imperfections Samuel Wesley, the father, was a great man. If he has suffered in the past by the uncritical adulation of his biographers, he has often suffered in the present by a too severe criticism that has lacked proper perspective. Susanna is much more generally appreciated, and it was only necessary to go rather more fully into her system of teaching and to discuss her own religious standpoint as expressed in her writings and her letters. Old Jeffrey could not be passed over silently because for a time at least he made so much noise. Even those who do not know the members of the family know of the family ghost, and it seemed worth while not only to go over the recorded facts again and daringly to essay an explanation, but also to show how permanent an impression the phenomena made on the mind of John.

It was a peculiar pleasure to write about Samuel the son, partly because he is not so well known as he deserves to be, and partly because he has his own important place in the family circle. It seemed necessary to speak not only of his life and scholarship, but of his poetic talent and his relationship to the other members of the family.

The sisters have a real if tragic interest. Justice has been done by earlier writers to the known details of their lives but not to their relations with John and Charles. It is too often assumed that once the brothers had left Oxford they also left their family behind. This is very far from the truth. As the brothers were devoted to their parents, so they were devoted to their sisters, and the exigencies of their work might indeed hinder, but could not destroy, the close contact they maintained with the surviving members of the family circle.

The story of Hetty is known to the world through the genius of Quiller-Couch but it seemed necessary, whilst accepting the main features of that portrait, to qualify certain judgements, and even here and there to retouch the canvas. Hetty certainly was not even a minor poet for the exact student to recall. But the fact that in such an age she wanted to write poetry, and that she could skilfully turn a line seemed worthy of illustrative and extended mention.

Finally it became necessary as the narrative unwound itself to speak of the relation which all the members of the family bore to one another, as well as their special relationship to John and Charles. One had set out knowing of the vexations and heartaches of the girls, and of the early departure of the boys from the Epworth nest. What one did not expect to find so fully was (despite the sickness, sorrows, and vicissitudes, despite separations and marital misfortunes) that the family should be so indissolubly united.

John and Charles do not appear except in relation to the others because the whole intention of the book is to show what sort of parents, what sisters, and what sort of a brother they possessed. It is only when one knows their family history that one can properly appreciate their inheritance, and realize in part why it was that they were matched with the hour.

As always in my various books on Methodism, I am indebted again to the painstaking care and advice of the Rev. F. F. Bretherton, B.A., who has so willingly read through the manuscript. I would like also to record my deep appreciation of the great help given to me by the Rev. Frank Baker, B.A., B.D., who has not only read through the book but has also allowed me to take advantage of certain unpublished letters of the Wesleys bearing upon the family life. I am greatly indebted to my mother who has given painstaking care to the correction of the manuscript.

Lastly, I want to say how much I owe to the kindly interest and great patience of Miss Gwenda Smith who has toiled cheerfully through the unenviable task of deciphering my writing and has typed the whole manuscript with uncanny accuracy. It is likewise a great joy to thank the Rev. George Lockett, a friend who has given himself willingly to the cheerless task of compiling the Index. The help of my wife has been a continual inspiration.

My debt to earlier and later writers who have worked in this field will be apparent to all who read the book.

MALDWYN EDWARDS

31st October 1949

Chapter One

A FIGHTER EVER

THE RECTOR of Epworth looked again at the letter he had written. This had been a moment to wait for—to relish—and in the long uncertain future to look back on as a high moment of ecstasy and fulfilment. Life had been chequered, but here surely the clouds had broken and the sun had shone in strength and splendour. The twelve pounds John required would mean a further straitening of resources, and then there would also be the repayment to his son, Samuel, of ten pounds lent to John. Charles might have to go up to the University without any monetary help from his father. And as for his family, from April until the harvest, they must exist on what five pounds could procure. But these were trifling matters. '*Sed passi graviora.* Wherever I am, my Jack is Fellow of Lincoln.'

The Rector gave himself up to reverie. This constant shadow of money troubles had darkened his life, but it had not broken his spirit. He could truthfully declare that despite all adversity he was a fighter still! Not that the fight had ever been easy. Poverty had not been the less grinding for being genteel. His father, John Wesley, son of the Rev. Bartholomew Wesley, had been prepared for the work of the ministry from earliest years. He had done more than ordinarily well at New Inn Hall, Oxford, and in due course had proceeded to the Master's degree. His great aptitude for Oriental languages did not prevent his desiring to be a preacher rather than to follow the more settled life of a scholar. In 1658, during the Commonwealth period, he had been approved by a Committee of Triers and appointed the Vicar of Winterborn Whitchurch in Dorset. But after four happy and useful years the Act of Uniformity (1662) fixed Bartholomew-tide as the day when all those in Church livings should use the 'new book' of Common Prayer or be ejected. On that sad day two thousand clergymen chose to be ejected rather than compromise with their consciences. Amongst them was John Wesley, who on 17th August 1662 confronted his people for the last time and tried to console a weeping, broken-hearted congregation as he preached from

Acts 20^{32}, 'And now brethren I commend you to God and the word of his grace'.

Henceforth there was to be much poverty and little comfort for the young minister, his wife, and his ever-increasing family. They moved rapidly from Melcombe to Ilminster, Bridgwater, Taunton, and so to Preston near Weymouth. In each place he preached as he had opportunity, running continual risk of imprisonment for the offence. For a time he even had charge of a small Dissenting congregation at Poole, but the passing of the Five Mile Act (1665) made his work more hazardous. At times he went into hiding, on other occasions he was caught and suffered short periods of imprisonment. The six months' confinement in the prison at Poole was the longest sentence, but no long detention in a seventeenth-century jail was required to undermine a man's health. There were indeed other factors. He could perhaps have endured alone the vicissitudes awaiting any Dissenting minister in the reign of Charles the Second, but he had the perpetual worry of having to commit his young wife and her babies to the same hard road. Some friends had died, others like himself were being persecuted; the true cause was in peril and the ungodly were rejoicing. Exhausted in body and spirit, John Wesley died when, as Dr. Calamy, his biographer, said 'he had not been much longer an inhabitant here below than his blessed Master was, whom he served with his whole heart, according to the best light he had'.

The Rector of Epworth smiled a little grimly as he thought of the family circumstances when his father had died so tragically. Four months before he was born his mother had gone out from the security of the Whitchurch Vicarage into an alien, inhospitable world. But somehow his parents had continued to send him to the Free School at Dorchester. Then his father had died and his mother had not only kept him a further twelve months at the Grammar School, but had sent her twelve-year-old son to a Dissenting academy in London (1678). How had it been done? It is true an Exhibition worth about thirty pounds a year had been granted him out of a Dissenters' fund. But this was not the complete solution. Samuel Wesley, accustomed beyond most men to wrestling with the demon of money, could not wholly give the answer. When he and Matthew the surgeon, his brother, were men, they had provided for all their mother's needs. On one occasion when her debts had brought her within sight of the debtor's prison he had found forty pounds to aid her, and always he had sent her ten pounds each year. In her long widowhood he had relieved her poverty out of his own. But at least she had contrived to keep him for over four years at the Academy and there had been laid the sound basis of his classical learning. He did not get on very well with the Dissenters in later life. He was civil and tolerant, but anything further was, in his view, inexpedient. For, as he was fond of saying, the Dissenters are 'a sort of people none of the best natured in the world'. He declared that he honoured some and pitied others, but hated none. And yet how closely interwoven his own life had been with the Dissenting sects. His father had gone out of the Church of England to become a Dissenting minister for conscience' sake. The Dissenters, debarred by law from the universities, had established academies that soon became famous for their high educational standard. From Mr. Veal's academy at Stepney, Samuel went on to the academy of Mr. Charles Morton at Newington Green. If he criticized the academies later it was not on the ground of scholarship, but as breeding places of disaffection and disloyalty.

It is one of the ironies of history that John Wesley should have left the Established Church and become a Dissenter at the dictation of conscience, whilst his son, Samuel, should, after an independent course of reading, conducted within a Dissenting academy, decide, for conscience' sake, to leave the Dissenters and enter the Established Church. When he set out from his London academy to go to Oxford (1683) he had, in his own words, 'to foot it'. His knapsack on his back contained his books and clothes and in his pocket was forty-five shillings—all his worldly wealth. But his spirit was unconquerable. He desired to serve the Church and he wanted an Oxford degree to that end. It meant a ceaseless fight against poverty, but that was a struggle to which he was well accustomed. He trudged the long miles with light heart, and in August 1683 was entered as servitor on the registers of Exeter College. This college had been founded by Walter Stapleton, Bishop of Exeter, in 1316, and in Samuel Wesley's time there were rather less than a hundred students. He entered as *pauper scholaris*, which was the lowest of the four conditions of membership, and as a 'servitor' his maintenance was provided by waiting on another student. Under such circumstances, he not only proceeded to his degree, but after five years' residence, had actually increased his savings to one hundred and fifteen shillings. In a letter to his brother, Matthew, he said that he lived in Oxford, 'without any preferment or assistance except one crown'. How then had he managed not only to live, but to save? Doubtless, in addition to his duties as servitor, he taught other students not so advanced. He would also economize in coals, in food, and in clothes. But he received at least a small sum of money from another source. The eccentric John Dunton, who published Samuel Wesley's first book,[1] written during his Oxford days, said that the Rector of Epworth got his bread by the *Maggots*. This was the curious title Samuel Wesley chose for a book of poems which on the first page beneath his portrait contained the ingenuous and disarming lines,

> *In his own defence the author writes*
> *Because when this foul maggot bites*
> *He ne'er can rest in quiet:*
> *Which makes him make so sad a face*
> *He'd beg your worship or your grace*
> *Unsight, unseen, to buy it.*

He anticipated the objection that it was 'light vain and frothy' by saying that if the objector would lend him a handful of beard and he had the charge of grafting it on, he would promise to reform with speed and thoroughness. He also pleaded that time ought to be allowed for diversion as well as toil, and that nothing in the poems would make the reader blush.

Many of the pieces were directed against contemporary vices, but some were concerned with homelier matters. From his poem on the 'tobacco pipe' we learn that even at Oxford he had learnt to find comfort in his pipe, a consolation that never failed through the exigencies of a chequered life. He could almost have said with Charles Lamb that he had managed to emit so much smoke because he had toiled after it as other men after virtue. This was not pleasing to his sons, and it was most distressing to Adam Clarke with his violently expressed antipathy to tobacco. Even the excellent Luke Tyerman speaks of 'the unfortunate habit'. But it is good to know that Samuel, who had to deprive himself of so much, did not in his frugal existence deny himself the satisfaction of his pipe. Indeed, on his own admission he often sought

---

[1] *Maggots: or Poems on Several Subjects never before Handled. By a Scholar.* London. Printed for John Dunton at the sign of the Black Raven at the corner of Princes Street near the Royal Exchange, 1685.

comfort on cold mornings in his cheerless room with its unlit fire, by stretching out his hand for tobacco.

> *In these raw mornings, when I'm freezing ripe,*
> *What can compare with a tobacco pipe?*
> *Primed, cock'd and touch't, 'twould better heat a man*
> *Than ten Bath faggots or Scotch warming-pan.*

It is possible that when Pope wrote in the *Dunciad*:

> *Maggots half form'd, in rhyme, exactly meet*
> *And learn to crawl upon poetic feet!*

he was referring to Samuel Wesley, his later friend. The point in any case is not important because no one desires to defend the literary merit of the poems. The real significance of the book is that it showed another side of the poverty-pressed, hard-working student. It offered a parallel to the Oxford idyll of his famous sons with their lovely ladies in the quiet of the Cotswold hills. This was a witty, companionable Samuel Wesley!

In another respect his Oxford residence compares with his sons'. It was during his stay at Oxford that James the Second ascended the throne and proceeded at once to secure the appointment of *Romanists* at Oxford Colleges. At Samuel's own college James had demanded that Father Petre (descendant of Sir William Petre, founder of the fellowships) should nominate seven Fellows of Exeter College. This right, however, had passed out of the Petre family for seventy years, and the University resisted the King's demands. But James was still more arbitrary in his demand that the Fellows of Magdalen College should elect a papist. They refused and elected a man of their own choice. Whereupon James the Second called on them to elect a turncoat prelate named Parker. When they again refused, James, in great indignation, came to Oxford in the summer of 1687, and harangued the Fellows who had been summoned into his presence. For some reason not stated Samuel Wesley was a fascinated witness of the scene. 'To home get you gone! I am King! I will be obeyed. Go to your chapel this instant and admit the Bishop of Oxford. Let those who refuse look to it—they shall feel the whole weight of my hand: they shall know what it is to incur the displeasure of their sovereign.' It is reported (though not credibly) that Samuel Wesley afterwards remarked, 'I saw he was a tyrant'. Certainly the sentiment was right. What we do know is that the following year, when the Prince of Wales was born, a volume of congratulatory poems was written by members of Oxford University and amongst the poems was a most flattering adulatory composition from Samuel Wesley. The truth is that throughout his life he had a high conception of a king's office and the strongest veneration for his person.

It affected his normal judgement just as it did in the case of his sons. Beyond any question it was the main reason why he decided to become a member of the Church of England. Dissenters always seemed to him uncertain in their grasp of a subject's duty to the monarch. When he left Oxford (1688) he was firmly bound to Church and King.

His deacon's orders gave him a title that in monetary value was worth twenty-eight pounds a year, but twelve days after William and Mary had come to the throne, Samuel was ordained priest (24th February 1689) by the Bishop of London. Had he only desired money and security, he would have held his first appointment longer. He was appointed chaplain on a man-of-war at seventy pounds a year with leisure for indulging his restless pen, and he hoped for relative affluence. But within the twelve months he had resigned and was a curate in London striving to live on thirty pounds a year. The one totally sufficient reason for this hasty move is that he had now become a married man. Susanna Annesley was the daughter of Dr. Annesley. In him great learning, preaching ability, and moral courage were combined. He had taken the degree of LL.D. at Queen's College, Oxford; and had held important posts including a lectureship at St. Paul's and the living of St. Giles's, Cripplegate. When he was ejected by the Act of Uniformity and with two thousand other ministers went out 'not knowing whither he went', he had forfeited an income of possibly £700 a year. But his subsequent lot was not as hard as that of many because he became a natural leader of Nonconformist Churches in London and a friend and teacher of ministers in their poverty and distress. When Samuel married Susanna, Dr. Annesley was in charge of a meeting-house in St. Helen's Place, Bishopsgate, and so continued in great peace until his death in 1696.

When the good Doctor was asked by Dunton, the publisher who had married one of his daughters, what was the precise size of his family, he replied with a somewhat puzzled air that it was either two dozen or a quarter of a hundred. Where twenty-five children are concerned, one less or more in computation would hardly seem important. But that twenty-fifth child mattered a great deal for she was Samuel's bride and the mother of the Wesleys. Susanna received much from her father and the goodly stock from which he sprung. He was the nephew of the first Earl of Anglesey.[1] Her mother's father, John White, had been an eminent lawyer and for many years was Member of Parliament for Southwark. He had been appointed chairman of a House of Commons Committee to inquire into 'the scandalous immoralities of the clergy'. The findings in 1643 were so shocking to the Royalists that he was violently attacked. In defence he published his *First Century of Scandalous Malignant Priests*. He did not live long enough to advance to his second hundred names, but he had already shown that a grave state of affairs existed. Clarendon said that White was 'a grave lawyer but notoriously disaffected to the Church'. Such a warning even from so staunch an Anglican was necessary, for White was willing to abolish the office of 'deacons, chancellors, vicars, surrogates, and registrars' as being of human origin and of no service to the Church. For the office of bishop, he cared still less. But White till his death in January 1644 was esteemed for his absolute integrity of character. He was buried in the Temple Church and the marble tombstone above his grave bore the inscription:

> Here lyeth a John, a burning, shining light,
> His name, life, actions, were all White.

Samuel had discovered a wife who had White's faculty of logical argument, Annesley's wit and culture and grace, and, if report be trusted, her mother's deep and natural piety. Eighteenth-century portraits were often flattering to the sitter but we have the supplementary evidence of contemporaries which confirms this fact that in her youth she had a slim figure and undeniably good looks. Eliza Clarke, who had close association with friends of Charles Wesley's widow and children, was bold to say that she was very pretty and 'retained her good looks and symmetry of figure to old age'. When Sir Peter Lely had painted the portrait of her lovely sister, Judith, a friend of both remarked that

---

[1] Luke Tyerman pointed out the curious fact that the father of Samuel Wesley's mother, and the father of Susanna Wesley's mother, were both John White by name.

'beautiful as Miss Annesley appears, she was far from being as beautiful as Mrs. Wesley'.

With his young wife, Samuel settled down with a good heart to a curacy in London. It was worth thirty pounds a year but he had an itch to write and his scribblings doubled his income. It is probable that much of his literary gleanings came from his share in the *Athenian Gazette*. This was a penny paper published thrice weekly by John Dunton, who was assisted in the venture (1690) not only by Samuel Wesley but by a certain Richard Sault whose particular skill was in mathematics. The curious title was chosen by Dunton from Acts 17^{21}: 'For all the Athenians and strangers which were there spent their time in nothing else but either to tell or to hear some new thing.' The express design of the paper was to receive and answer all questions in all departments of literature. Adam Clarke hazarded the quite likely conjecture that Samuel's part was to answer questions in divinity, Church history, and philosophy. The paper has some importance in the history of the periodical in England. It was one of the earliest to be concerned with literature in its broadest sense. Certainly it attracted immediate attention. Coffee Houses clamoured for it, and leading writers and men of affairs including Defoe, Nahum Tate (the poet laureate), the Marquis of Halifax, Sir William Temple, and Dean Swift contributed to its pages. In 1692 the three indefatigable writers responsible for the *Gazette* had published *The Young Students' Library*. Samuel Wesley's most important contribution was a long essay on 'The Points, Vowels, and Accents in the Hebrew Bible'. Before this ambitious undertaking had been published, he had, through the influence of the Marquis of Normanby, taken the living of South Ormsby in Lincolnshire (1691).

South Ormsby was a pleasant village and the young rector had pastoral charge of about three hundred people. It could not have been a very welcome change for Susanna, now the mother of a growing family. Wesley wrote of the rectory as one in which every consolation must be found elsewhere.

In a mean cot, composed of reeds and clay
Wasting in sighs the uncomfortable day;
Near where the inhospitable Humber roars,
Devouring by degrees, the neighbouring shores.
Let earth go where it will, I'll not repine,
Nor can unhappy be, while heaven is mine.

It is true unhappily that many of the country clergymen of the late seventeenth and eighteenth centuries were coarse and ignorant and lazy. This criticism has, however, been overstated by writers who see everything black or white. Samuel Wesley said that with few exceptions the clergy in his diocese were men of piety, learning, and devotion to their work. Samuel himself had breeding, learning, and immense industry. He could easily have vegetated, but he chose to give himself more completely to literary labours. He still took some part in the *Athenian Gazette* until it ceased publication in February 1696. In 1693 appeared *The Life of our Blessed Lord and Saviour Jesus Christ: An Heroic Poem*; 'dedicated to Her Most Sacred Majesty, In Ten Books'. With the poem appeared verses of extravagant and fulsome flattery written by the egregious Nahum Tate. He even dared to say 'Milton's noble work is now complete'. But if John Wesley is to be credited, Samuel himself knew better. With a nice terseness he said, 'The cuts are good; the notes pretty good, and the verses so-so'. Samuel Wesley, junior, was a most loyal son but he could only praise it in most guarded terms.

> *Whate'er his strains still glorious was his end,*
> *Faith to assert and virtue to defend.*
> *He sung how God his Saviour deigned to expire,*
> *With Vida's piety though not his fire.*

John Wesley in a letter to Thomas Carlill said that there were many excellent lines in the poem but they must be taken in conjunction with the rest. Consequently he could not print the poem. This 'curate's egg' verdict by a fastidious critic shows how very unequal the son judged the work to be.

Samuel Wesley could only plead guilty to Dunton's charge that he wrote too much by two-thirds. It would have been some extenuation if like his son, John, he had been willing to revise and prune and polish his work. But that was not his nature. Adam Clarke's charge did not relate so much to the halting rhymes, as to the liberty Wesley had taken with the life of Christ as recorded by the four evangelists. 'The attempt to do it is almost impious, and in the execution how many words are attributed to God which he never spoke, and acts which he never did.' Nevertheless, despite its faults the poem went through a second edition in 1697, 'revised and improved with the addition of a large map of the Holy Land'. There were two further editions in the nineteenth century, one edited by Dr. Thomas Coke.

The poem was written in the close-rhymed couplets, which, already made popular by Dryden, were to be used with such masterly effect by Pope, and were still to be employed by the great Dr. Johnson half a century later. It had other characteristics of the Augustan age in the preponderance of words with Latin rather than Anglo-Saxon roots. These have a sonorous, but in the end, somewhat chilling effect. But the chief defect of all such writing is the sense of artificiality produced. This does not matter in the satires of Dryden and Pope. It was used with happy effect by Pope in his later translations; in the abstract philosophizing of the *Essay on Man*; and it provided a perfect medium for that masterpiece in mock epics, *The Rape of the Lock*. But the Augustan style was only a reflection of the somewhat stilted and artificial life of the age. The coffee-houses rang with political gossip and social scandal, but life outside the middle and upper classes of the towns was not sought and hardly known. If we want to know how the poor lived we must go, not to the poets, but to the cartoons of Hogarth. Nature was uncouth and barbarous. Mountains and deep valleys did not fit into the tidy, ordered scheme of things. In such an age there could be no real interest in the simple human day-to-day life of our Lord. The style doubtless is the man, but equally it is a reflection of the spirit of the age. Samuel Wesley may be blamed for his excessive haste and carelessness, for his halting rhymes and lack of true poetic spirit, but scarcely for his abstract treatment of his subject. Could the following description of our Lord's transfiguration have been written at any other time in English literature?

> *Unrivall'd beauties deck'd the Saviour's face,*
> *His dazzling form the circling glories grace;*
> *His seamless coat, than falling snows more white,*
> *Enclosed a pillar of transparent light.*
> *The two great prophets who beside Him stood*
> *Array'd in light their modest glories show'd;*
> *Thus stars appear, when twinkling, they display*
> *Their feeble lustre to the orb of day.*

The style is much better adapted to the discussion of philosophy and theology. He wrote nobly of God's being and attributes:

> *No mean succession His Duration knows*
> *That Spring of Being neither ebbs nor flows:*
> *No point can mortal Thought assign*
> *In His interminable line.*
> *Nor our short compass meet the circle all divine.*
> *Whatever was, was God, ere time or place;*
> *Endless duration He, and boundless space,*
> *Fill'd with Himself, wherever Thought can pierce,*
> *He fill'd, himself alone, the Universe.*
> *One undissolv'd: nor ceases to be One*
> *Tho' with him ever reigns the eternal Son!*

Samuel's pen during these years was still busily scratching out answers for the *Athenian Gazette*. After his contributions to the *Young Student's Library*, he continued to write more verse. Amongst his poems were two highly flown elegies on the death of Queen Mary and of Tillotson, Archbishop of Canterbury. In his fulsome eulogy of Mary there were three lines that might go into any anthology of bad verse. Queen Mary had her coronation prepared in Heaven by angels using 'more than usual art and care' Another, meantime had been growing restless:

> *And first mankind's great mother rose,*
> *'Give way, ye crowding souls', said she,*
> *'That I the second of my race, may see'.*

It is on John Wesley's authority that we have the story of how Samuel came to leave South Ormsby. The Marquis of Normanby had advanced to favour in the court of Charles the Second and had learnt his morals from his royal master. Samuel Wesley must often have felt distinctly uncomfortable as his chaplain. A question and answer in the *Athenian Gazette* doubtless refers to his own condition. 'I am forced to see misses, drinking and gaming and dare not open my mouth against them.' The Marquis kept a woman in his house at South Ormsby, and this woman visited Mrs. Wesley, who received her civilly on many occasions. But one day when Samuel Wesley entered and found the lady sitting at ease by his own fireside 'he took her by the hand and very fairly handed her out'. Samuel Wesley never lacked moral courage and the incident accords with his character, but on other grounds it would seem John Wesley's memory was at fault. The Marquis and Samuel were on good terms. Had he not recommended his chaplain for an Irish bishopric to the ill-concealed disgust of

Tillotson? When Wesley left South Ormsby he still remained chaplain to the Marquis, and in 1701 dedicated his *History of the Old and New Testament* to him. He had also at this time (1701) received financial help from the Marquis in his dire distress. The woman so peremptorily ejected by Samuel was probably a mistress of Lord Castleton who rented the Hall and lived a notoriously dissolute life. If John's version be accepted the possibility is that the Marquis, conscious that Samuel had only acted according to his principles, hastened Samuel's removal without breaking the friendship.

Samuel thought that he had been presented to the living at Epworth still in Lincolnshire at the express wish of the Queen. This belief is not altogether easy to credit since the Queen had died two years before. What may have happened is that she expressed a wish for this to happen before she died. The circumstances are obscure. No one knows when precisely he took up residence. It can only be said with certainty that he, his wife, and their young children were there by the end of 1696 or at the beginning of 1697.[1] In this parish he was to labour fruitfully for thirty-nine years. His rectory was to become more famous than any in England. To some, Haworth Parsonage on the edge of the desolate moors might appear to have the more romantic interest. In both houses shone brightly the pure light of genius, but even in human interest the tragic story of the beautiful and gifted daughters at Epworth offers a lively parallel with the sorrow in another setting of Patrick Brontë's children. In its effect upon the life of England Epworth Rectory stands alone.

To understand the greatness of the children, the share of Samuel Wesley in the shaping of their characters must be fully understood. Even before he came to Epworth his courage had enabled him, despite poverty and hardship, to work his way through school and academy to university, and so to Holy Orders. He owed something to others, but it was on himself that he had chiefly to rely. Difficulties sufficient to overwhelm a lesser man only sharpened his native resolution. Courage, physical and moral, argue a man of personality and decided opinions. Samuel Wesley in an age more productive of outstanding men than our own more stereotyped society, was a 'character'. He had breeding, wit, and considerable learning, but in the holding of convictions at which he had

[1] Frank Baker has now discovered from the records that he was instituted to the living on 23rd April 1695. He did not, however, take up residence until 1697. He was presented to the living by the King.

finally arrived, he showed all the massive qualities of a bull-dog. Paradoxically enough, it is only in this way we can account for the flattering encomiums of royalty and great personages which in a different type of man would at once be regarded as sycophancy. In this respect John was strangely like his father. They both had so ingrained a reverence for monarchy that they wrote in terms of unbounded and uncritical praise. Samuel spoke of William and Mary with precisely the same adulatory strain that John Wesley used of George the Second and George the Third. When George the Second died he asked when would England have a better prince, and of George the Third he said that he was one of the best of princes. Neither father nor son could ever be accused of toadying, but both had their blind spots. It is just because they both held strong convictions that they rarely saw people in half-lights, but painted them either black or white. And the white was always dazzling when their affections and respect were engaged!

Another distinguishing trait of Samuel Wesley was his indefatigable industry. It is a part answer to those who would indiscriminatingly censure the manners and morals of eighteenth-century clergymen that in country rectories there were men like Samuel Wesley devoted to the interests of their flock, wholly persuaded of the truths of the Christian religion, and living simple and blameless lives. But Samuel Wesley was not only a zealous Churchman, he never ceased to put his learning at the service of his pen. If he had attempted less, he would have achieved more. He might not have been capable of writing such devotional works such as those of William Law, but had the inclination been present he could have written in the same strain as Hervey, William Melmoth, Robert Nelson, and Mary Astill. These forgotten writers wrote for a public with voracious appetite and their simple devotional books had a staggering sale. But Samuel Wesley was more ambitious. The titles of his greatest works, the *Life of Christ*, the *History of the Old and New Testament* and the Latin dissertations on the Book of Job, reveal the largeness of his conception! He would attempt only the greatest themes. It is true he failed, but it was a gallant failure—and more impressive than the minor successes of other men.

The people of Epworth knew not the time of their visitation. They were strangely honoured when the thirty-four year old rector and his wife came to live and labour in their midst. He, on his part, needed all his courage, convictions, and tireless energy to face the particular problems of his parish. He had first to contend with the intractable nature of the countryside. Axholme, eighteen miles long and four broad, was, in the seventeenth century, little more than a swamp, but many years before Wesley's arrival it had been drained and gradually it has become rich and fertile. But the district was low lying and liable in greater or lesser degree to be flooded by the surrounding rivers, the Trent, the Don, and the Idle. When Dr. Adam Clarke visited Epworth in 1821 he said that even at that date there was no road on leaving Epworth 'for upwards of forty miles, but fields of corn, wheat, rye, potatoes, barley, and turnips which were often crushed under the carriage wheels'. Samuel Wesley, farmer as well as rector, had more than once to look out on Nature in a bleak, inhospitable aspect, and to suffer injury at her hands.

But the people were far more intractable than the land they cultivated. Living on the Isle of Axholme meant that they had little contact with the larger life of England. This insularity made them suspicious of outsiders and resentful of interference. Samuel Wesley took his duties too seriously for their liking. They hated both his plain speaking and his attempt to reform their morals. And Samuel was never the most tactful of men. John Wesley told Henry Moore that on one occasion his father found a farmer cutting the ears of corn from his tithe sheaves and putting them into a bag. The Rector marched the farmer back into the Epworth market-place and, turning out the contents of the bag before the astonished people, he told them of the farmer's petty pilfering. Then he left the discomforted man to the judgement of his neighbours and with the most complete sangfroid went back to the rectory! It was characteristically brave, but was it wise? These men made violent enemies. In the previous century the Fenmen had been known to burn the crops of their opponents and to kill their cattle. In 1697 a much-hated landowner, Nathaniel Reading, had his house burnt down and there were indications that his enemies intended him and his family to perish with the house.

Already in 1702 Samuel Wesley had suffered the loss of two-thirds of his parsonage by fire. Again in 1704 fire destroyed all his flax. But the fire on the midnight of 9th February 1709 is the best remembered incident connected with the old rectory. There can be few Methodists who have not seen the picture of the rectory ablaze, and the little John Wesley being dramatically rescued from the flames. It was indeed a very narrow escape. Some of the children had escaped, but until a cry was heard from the nursery, the Rector did not realize that John was missing. The little boy mounted a chest near the window and so was seen. There was no time to fetch a ladder. One man gallantly stood under the wall and a lighter man, climbing on to his shoulders, rescued the child. At that moment the roof collapsed with a heavy crash, but since it fell inwards, no one was hurt. In a more than ordinary sense, John Wesley later described himself as a 'brand plucked out of the burning'. Knowing the character of many of his father's enemies, John Wesley had no hesitation in supposing the fire to be deliberately intended. This is, however, by no means certain. The earlier malevolence had softened, and it was possibly due to a certain carelessness on the part of the Rector. It was a fearful blow but the Rector was not thus to be broken. 'Come, neighbours', he called out, 'let us kneel down! Let us give thanks to God! He has given me all my eight children, let the house go, I am rich enough!'

But the strictest discipline of spirit was needed, not against the unfriendly country and its peasantry, but against the constant pressure of poverty. Although Samuel earned a certain amount from his writings, his professional income for the first eleven years of his married life had not averaged more than fifty to sixty pounds a year when necessary expenses had been paid. These expenses included furniture, the Broad Seal, taxes, his mother's debt and a fifty pounds repayment of a loan. Out of this income he had to provide food and clothes for a family which regularly increased each year. Ten children were born in those years and five of them died. His living at Epworth was far better financially than many, but it was insufficient and so the scholar and poet turned farmer.[1] This meant the borrowing of capital and the paying of interest on it. But he had neither inclination nor aptitude for his self-imposed task. Nor was he a man of affairs. Samuel Annesley when in India had asked Wesley to attend to some of his transactions, and he complained bitterly that the Rector was 'not fit for worldly business'. Susanna readily assented and she was most qualified to speak. 'I must own', she said, 'I was mistaken when I thought him fit for business. My own experience hath since convinced me that he is one of those who, our Saviour saith, are not so wise in their generation as the children of this world.' The condition of his finances cannot wholly be attributed to the provision for his numerous family. If he was not idle nor extravagant, he was, to

---

[1] This was quite a normal procedure at that time.

speak kindly, not far-seeing in the management of his finances. But his difficulties were real enough! In a letter which must have been painful to write he described to Archbishop Sharpe the position in which he found himself:

> EPWORTH
> *December 30th, 1700.*
>
> MY LORD, I have lived on the thought of your Grace's generous offer ever since I was at Bishopthorpe, and the hope I have of seeing some end, or at least mitigation, of my troubles, makes me pass through them with much more ease than I should otherwise have done. I can now make a shift to be dunned, with some patience; and to be affronted, because I want the virtue of riches, by those who scarce think there is any other virtue.
>
> I must own, I was ashamed, when at Bishopthorpe, to confess that I was £300 in debt, when I have a living of which I have made £200 per annum, though I could hardly let it now for eightscore.
>
> I doubt not but one reason of my being sunk so far is my not understanding worldly affairs, and my aversion to law, which my people have always known but too well. But, I think, I can give a tolerable account of my affairs, and satisfy any equal judge that a better husband than myself might have been in debt, though perhaps not so deeply, had he been in the same circumstances, and met with the same misfortunes.
>
> 'Twill be no great wonder that, when I had but £50 per annum for six or seven years together, nothing to begin the world with, one child at least per annum, and my wife sick for half that time, that I should run £150 behindhand, especially when about £100 of it had been expended in goods, without doors and within.
>
> When I had the rectory of Epworth given me, my Lord of Sarum was so generous as to pass his word to his goldsmith [banker] for £100 which I borrowed of him. It cost me very little less than £50 of this in my journey to London, and in getting into my living, for the Broad Seal, etc.; and with the other £50 I stopped the mouths of my most importunate creditors.
>
> When I removed to Epworth, I was forced to take up £50 more, for setting up a little husbandry, when I took the tithes into my own hand, and for buying some part of what was necessary toward furnishing my house, which was larger, as well as my family, than what I had on the other side of the country.
>
> The next year my barn fell, which cost me £40 in rebuilding (thanks to your Grace for part of it); and, having an aged mother, who must have gone to prison if I had not assisted her, she cost me upwards of £40 more, which obliged me to take up another £50. I have had but three children born since I came hither, about three

years since; but another is coming, and my wife is incapable of any business in my family, as she has been for almost a quarter of a year; yet we have but one maid-servant, in order to retrench all possible expenses.

My first-fruits came to about £28; my tenths are near £3 per annum. I pay a yearly pension of £3, out of my rectory, to John of Jerusalem. My taxes came to upward of £20 per annum, but they are now retrenched to about half. My collection to the poor comes to £5 per annum; besides which, they have lately bestowed an apprentice upon me, whom, I suppose, I must teach to beat rhyme. Ten pounds a year I allow my mother, to help to keep her from starving. I wish I could give as good an account for some charities, which I am now satisfied have been imprudent, considering my circumstances.

Fifty pounds interest and principal I have paid my Lord of Sarum's goldsmith. All which together keeps me necessitous, especially since interest-money begins to pinch me; and I am always called upon for money before I make it, and must buy everything at the worst hand; whereas, could I be so happy as to get on the right side of my income I should not fear, by God's help, to live honestly in the world, and to leave a little to my children after me. I think, as it is, I could perhaps work it out in time, in half a dozen or half a score years, if my heart should hold so long; but for that, God's will be done.

Humbly asking pardon for this tedious trouble, I am, your Grace's most obliged and most humble servant.

S. WESLEY.

The Archbishop of York must have been much moved by the letter because he not only sent money himself but prevailed on some of his friends to help Samuel in his distress. In particular the Countess of Northampton sent £20. The Rector was naturally grateful but the two letters he sent in acknowledgement are not obsequious, nor fawning in their compliments, but the plain-spoken gratitude of a man partly relieved of a heavy burden, which of necessity he had had to carry.

These rays of light might break the clouds but could not disperse them. When a man walks however carefully on the poverty line, sickness or sudden disaster can so easily pull him below it. The Rector imprudently sent a friend a letter he had written against the Dissenters. This was published in 1703 under the title, *A Letter from a Country Divine to his Friend in London Concerning the Education of the Dissenters, in their Private Academies in several parts of this Nation. Humbly offered to the consideration of the Grand Committee of Parliament for Religion now sitting. London MDCCIII.* In a second pamphlet, *Defence of a Letter concerning the Education of Dissenters,* 1704, Wesley claimed that he had no idea it would be published and it was done without his consent. This is strange indeed, but it does not excuse the fact that he wrote it nor the matter it contained. It was hard that one who owed so much to the Dissenting interest and received his education at their academies should have disparaged them so strongly. The utmost he could say about Dissenters themselves is that he 'honoured some, pitied others, but hated none'. Samuel Palmer wrote two able pamphlets against Wesley's work and he was joined by the great Daniel Defoe himself. Palmer reasoned, but Defoe used a cudgel: 'If I should say that a mercenary renegade was hired to expose the private academies of the Dissenters, as nurseries of rebellious principles, I should say nothing but what is in too many mouths to remain a secret.'

But so far as Epworth was concerned, it was his part in the incredibly violent general election of 1705 that raised hot fury against him. Burnet, a dull but usually a trustworthy historian, declared that a great number of pamphlets were written on the theme that Bishops were betraying the Church and that 'the Court would sell it to the Dissenters'. The cry that throughout the country made men shudder was 'The Church is in danger'. In Lincoln the contest for the county seats was unusually severe. The old members, Sir John Thorold and 'Champion' Dymoke, were joined by two newcomers, Colonel Whichcott and Mr. Bertie, as candidates for Parliament. Samuel Wesley, before he realized the true state of affairs, promised Thorold not to oppose him, but he refused to help Dymoke. Whichcott, on the other hand, was a friend and neighbour and he freely promised him his vote. But on returning from a short visit to London he found that the contest was raging and that the safety of the Church was a foremost issue. Thorold and Dymoke had declared themselves wholly for King and Church. Whichcott and Bertie, though Churchmen, were friendly to Dissenters and critical of the Establishment. Wesley considered that altered conditions absolved him from his promise. It was a step that only a bold man would take, but Wesley never lacked courage. He threw himself into the strife and on the steps of his own Church was denounced as 'rascal and scoundrel'. On one occasion his very life was threatened, but he heard of the plot and returned home a different way. When he went to Lincoln to record his vote an unruly mob 'kept drumming, shouting, and firing off pistols' throughout the better part of the night, under the very window where Mrs. Wesley lay exhausted after her recent confinement. She had given the infant to a woman to nurse. This woman could not rest throughout the terrifying noises of the night and when the crowd had finally departed, she sank in heavy sleep and overlaid the child. Mrs. Wesley wakened to find a child cold and dead being thrown into her arms, and a distracted woman escaping as fast as she could.

But Wesley's enemies had not finished with him yet; the two men he opposed were both elected and, coming out of his church some short time after the election was over, a certain Mr. Pinder, a friend and supporter of Colonel Whichcott, confronted him and demanded the immediate settlement of a debt bordering on £30. Samuel asked for a few hours' grace. There was furniture in the house and stock on the farm and the goodwill of his friends. But before anyone could come to his rescue he was hurried away to Lincoln Castle and lodged in the debtors' jail. Adversity teaches patience, and the Rector, two days after his confinement, wrote in philosophic mood to his friend the Archbishop of York. 'Now I am at rest, for I am come to the house where I've long expected to be.' He said that he had no great concern for himself and that he found much more civility and satisfaction than in *'brevibus gyaris'* of his own Epworth. His only expressed concern was the leaving of his 'poor lambs in the midst of so many wolves'. It is the latter half of this letter which throws light on the spirit and resolution of the fiery little man. In a short space of time he had obtained permission to read prayers every morning and afternoon and to preach on the Sunday. He was writing to the Society for the Propagation of Christian Knowledge for books to distribute among the prisoners; and he added with a touch of his pawky wit: 'I am getting acquainted with my brother jail-birds as fast as I can.' He told Archbishop Sharpe that he hoped to do more good in his new parish than he had in his old one.

In September 1705 his cup of bitterness seemed to be full. His enemies, insatiable in lust for vengeance, had maimed his animals so that the cows were 'all dried by it' and this, he said, had been the chief subsistence of his forlorn family. His dog who had made a 'huge noise indoors' was punished the next day but one by having a leg almost chopped off. Once again his native courage asserted itself. He had begun his letter by saying that he was glad the Archbishop had no ill opinion of him but happier still that he served a Master who could not be deceived and who would never forsake him. 'A jail is a paradise in comparison of the life I led before I came hither. No man has worked truer for bread than I have done, and few have lived harder or their families either. I am grown weary of vindicating myself: not, I thank God, that my spirits sink, or that I have not right on my side, but because I have almost a whole world against me, and shall in the main leave my cause to the righteous Judge.' A lesser man could have complained that almost the whole world was against him, but only a man of great spirit could have concluded the letter in Wesley's terms. 'Most of my friends advise me to leave Epworth, e'er I should get from hence. I confess I am not of that mind, because I may yet do good there and 'tis like a coward to desert my post because the enemy fire thick upon me. They have only wounded me yet, and I believe, *can't* kill me.' His friends, both clerical and lay, came to his rescue and before Christmas he was back at Epworth.

During Samuel's imprisonment the Archbishop, in conversation with Mrs. Wesley, directly asked her whether she had ever wanted bread. 'My lord,' Susanna replied, 'I will freely own to your Grace, that strictly speaking, I never did want bread. But then, I had so much care to get it, before it was eat, and to pay for it after, as has often made it very unpleasant to me. And I think to have bread on such terms is the next degree of wretchedness to having none at all.' To such a level of poverty was the family reduced!

The last great calamity which befell Samuel Wesley was the great fire which destroyed the rectory in 1709. Not only the house, but furniture, books, and manuscripts were lost. The children had to be lodged with friends and neighbours whilst the parents fended for themselves as they were able. Refusing to be overwhelmed by this fresh disaster, the Rector, helped by the Ecclesiastical Commissioners, caused the new parsonage to be built within the year. The old thatched building of lath and plaster gave place to a plain solid building of that red brick which was so generally used in Queen Anne's reign.

But the new house did not mean a new start. Poverty was still in constant attendance. In a long letter written to her brother in 1722, Susanna said that nearly thirteen years had elapsed since the rectory was burned yet it was still not half furnished, nor 'the wife and children half clothed to this day'. She proceeded to tell of the large debts still unpaid, of her own constant ill-health, and of the burden and expense involved by the children. Susanna was incapable of whining. The letter was a plain statement of fact. The little living at Wroot worth £50 a year was given to Wesley in 1724 and for some years the family actually lived in the Parsonage there rather than in the superior one at Epworth. But whilst the living brought a certain financial relief, it created its own problems. The country round was little more than a swamp, and in time of flood, the only way to reach Epworth was by boat. In one of his letters to John, written in 1727, the Rector describes laconically one such journey. 'I am ipped [sic] by my voyage and journey to and from Epworth last Sunday; being lamed with having my breeches too full of water, partly with a downfall from the thunder shower and partly from the wash over the boat. Yet, I thank God, I was able to preach here in the afternoon, and was as well this morning as ever, except a little pain and lameness, both of which I hope to wash off with an hair of the same dog this evening. I wish the rain had not reached us on this side of Lincoln; but we have it so continual that we have scarce one bank left, and I can't possibly have one quarter of oats in all the levels: but thanks be to God, the field-barley and rye are good.'

In the midst of this life of incessant struggle against poverty came the news that John had been elected to a Fellowship at Lincoln College. The Rector had full cause to rejoice when on 1st April 1726 he wrote his letter of congratulation. He looked down the long years of trouble, sorrow, hardship, and vexation of spirit. But at least they had not passed leaving him no recompense for his life of toil. In his children his work would go on and his name be perpetuated. His reverie was not unpleasant. If the years had brought their disappointments, they had also brought a harvest. This was the fulfilment of brightest hopes. And if this had happened, what else might the future hold of marvel and surprise? In very truth though the remaining years brought him increasing physical infirmity and though he was willing in 1734 to hand over the Wroot living to John Whitelamb, who had recently become his curate, they brought their recompense. In a letter to Samuel junior (28th February 1733) he was able to record an increase from twenty to above a hundred at the Communion Service. He thankfully declared that after nearly forty years' labour among them, his people grew better. When John Wesley preached in Epworth Churchyard (June 1742) he found 'a vast multitude gathered from all parts' and thinking of his father's forty years' work, he commented: 'Let none think his labour of love is lost because the fruit does not immediately appear.' He said that the seed sown so long since, had now sprung up, 'bringing forth repentance and remission of sins'. If the Rector had any grave disappointment in these years it was that neither Samuel nor John could be persuaded to accept the living at Epworth which he was so ready to resign to either of them. But whilst he might stare in bewilderment at their carefully stated reasons, it was enough that they and Charles were devout and scholarly men over whom any father might rejoice! It was entirely characteristic of so bonny a fighter that when all fighting was at an end and John asked him in those last hours if he was in pain, Samuel Wesley said with a smile lighting his face: 'God does chasten me with pain, yea, all my hours with strong pain; but I thank Him for all, I bless Him for all, I love Him for all!' After the son had commended his father's soul to God, Samuel, utterly composed, whispered: 'Now you have done all.' It is appropriate that when John Wesley described the 'serene and cheerful countenance' of the Rector in the hour of death, he wrote of that great struggler throughout an arduous life, that 'without one struggle', he fell on sleep.

Chapter Two

THE FATHER AND HIS SONS

THE FAULTS of Samuel Wesley are obvious but they have been exaggerated by many critics. Did he leave the sorely pressed Dissenters because he wanted the safety and greater prospects of the Established Church? The charge is inconsistent with his courage and independence of character. He early came to identify Dissent with disloyalty to the Crown; to such a true blue Tory as himself its liberalism of outlook seemed positively dangerous. And had he not been present at an anniversary festival of the Calves-head Club? These few dissenting political extremists only served to confirm him in his views. It is much to be regretted that he published a pamphlet against Dissenting academies but, unlike many contemporary pamphlets, it was not personal nor venomous in its attacks, but a lengthy expression of his fears that Dissenters might be an unsettling force in the nation. His love of King and Constitution was constant, deep, and genuine. He suffered grievously in his own parish for his attachment to the Tory party. His three principal works were dedicated to royalty. In the most famous quarrel of his marriage he would not suffer in silence the refusal of Susanna to say Amen after the family prayers for King William the Third. She would accept as a *fait accompli* the succession of the Prince of Orange, but he could not oust the Stuarts from her heart and prayers. 'Two Kings—two beds' was his ultimatum, but he had a wife whose unmovable stand on matters of conviction, was as strong as his own. She said: 'Whether the praying for a usurper, and vindicating his usurpations after he has the throne, be not participating in his sins, is easily determined.' He went off to London. As John explained he had in any case to attend the Convocation but the accession of Anne (1702) and perhaps anxiety for his wife's welfare brought him back to Epworth, forgiving and forgiven. Allied to this love of King was love of Church. When the nation was divided by the impeachment of Dr. Sacheverell into two camps, Samuel Wesley had no hesitation in standing alongside this strange divine whose wild, unbalanced sermons against Dissenters and Low Churchmen had brought him to the bar of

C

the House of Lords. John Wesley in his *History of England* declared that it was Samuel Wesley, his father, who prepared the written defence of Sacheverell. But it was in his patient, sustained, and faithful work at Epworth that his great love of the Church, her creeds, sacraments, and worship was most fully shown. Even after his heavy fall from his horse and wagon in 1731, he continued to visit his parishioners whose every name he knew. Adam Clarke said that he sifted their creed as well as their conduct, and allowed 'none to be corrupt without instruction or reproof'. For the curious there is a series of letters relating to two particular cases in which Samuel strove to discharge his duties according to canonical law. (Canon 109.) For if a churchwarden failed to bring evil livers to justice, then it was laid upon the clergyman of the parish. A person found guilty of adultery was commonly ordered to do public penance in the parish church or in the market-place and to stand in a white sheet barelegged and bareheaded. Then they confessed their crimes in a prescribed form of words.

Samuel Wesley wrote to a Mr. Perry in December 1730 to say he had 'two couples of sinners on his hands—the first very lean; the latter very fat'—whom he desired to bring to public justice. He did not want to be baffled in the matter because he said he looked on the exercise of discipline to defend the event. Samuel Wesley pursued these cases in correspondence with Mr. Chancellor Newell throughout the whole of 1731 until the matter was concluded.

If the Rector was so wholly devoted to the Church of England, its worship and its discipline, and if he had a strong attachment to the Tory interest in addition, it is easy to understand his break with Dissent and his opposition to its religious and political principles.

But if the charge against his attitude to Dissenters can be met, there is no such complete answer to his management of money. The living at Epworth, though actually only worth £130 a year according to Susanna, was still valuable. It is true that children arriving regularly year by year sometimes dismayed the Rector who only gasped when such generous measure was exceeded. 'My Lord', he said in one of his letters to the Archbishop (18th May 1701), 'Last night my wife brought me a few children. There are but two yet, a boy and a girl, and I think they are all at present. We have had four in two years and a day, three of which are living.' When his brother, Matthew Wesley, accused him of extravagance he tried in reply to present a balance sheet. Most certainly no such account could ever be audited. Some of the largest items of expenditure were left with a blank line. Indeed only four items were listed with their cost: Taking livings, repairing houses, £160; Rebuilding part of house first time, £60; Rebuilding whole house, £400; Attending the Convocation, £150. Following these items the quaint account sheet read as follows:

    Expended in sickness for above 40 years . . . ———
    Furnishing the (new) house . . . . . ———
    Eight children born and buried . . . . ———
    Ten (thank God) living, brought up and educated . ———
    Most of daughters put out to a way of living . . ———
    To three sons for the best education I could get them
      in England . . . . ———

Now this list makes a strong appeal to the heart, but not an equal appeal to the head. His wife and daughters had no illusions about his business management, and no one suspected him of being a good farmer. It was doubtless unjustifiable for a man who was hopelessly in debt to travel three times to London as an elected member of Convocation. £150 was a very heavy extra charge to bring on a family that could so ill afford even minor luxuries. It is true that to be elected a Proctor for the Diocese of Lincoln representing the diocese in this national assembly of the clergy was an honour. It is possible Samuel may have thought that in such attendance lay his one chance of preferment. It is certain that the life of the town must have been a great diversion and joy to a cultivated scholar who otherwise had no relief from the unending sameness of life in a country parish. Above all, for a man who so faithfully loved and served his Church the opportunity of attending Convocation must have seemed a duty and privilege on no account to be missed. But if these circumstances extenuate, they do not excuse the fastening of a halter still more firmly around the neck. Then there were items the Rector did not think fit to put down on his account. For example there was the cost of his books, though these might fairly be regarded as his tools of trade. In Samuel's case the cost was excessive because of the preparation of his monumental work on Job. But doubtless his answer would be that he hoped as in former days, not only to recoup his expenses, but to make money on the venture.

With no special pleading for Samuel Wesley, it may fairly be said that he was not reckless nor improvident and that his journeys and his books were his only real extravagances. But he never realized as fully as his wife was forced to do, the proper state of his finances, and he had not her particular skill in careful husbandry. The last charge against Samuel has no answer. He was tactless and on so many occasions he suffered for it. His critical faculties seemed to desert him when he espoused a cause that was dear to him, and in his judgement of people whom he liked. And he was not the most patient and reasonable of men! His temper in any circumstances would not have been even—but with continual births and deaths in the Rectory; with a wife ailing, as he said, the half of every year; with the shepherding of a boorish, obstinate, ill-disposed people; and with nature's calamities dogging his way, his temper grew shorter. It is an old adage that when poverty comes in at the door, love flies out of the window. There are those who suspect it was true of the Wesley household. Actually love still remained, it was only good temper that on occasion fled. In one of her letters written to John in 1735 towards the very end of her husband's life, Susanna confessed that it seemed 'an unhappiness almost peculiar to our family that your father and I seldom think alike'. The major disagreements we know, but who could estimate the smaller points of difference? Samuel at times must have been a sore trial to a long-suffering wife. Things might have been different had she been a cipher, but she possessed a spirit and mind of her own. If the Rectory often rang with loud words, it was because two strong personalities, unwilling for the mere sake of quiet, to yield ground, were evenly matched with each other. The strong tones were Samuel's and the quietly insistent voice was that of Susanna. In this respect truly, John in his quiet persistence coupled with admirable control of temper was his mother's son. The Rector was not unaware of John's habit of logical reasoning and at times he was half amused and half irritated by it. We have his oft-quoted remark: 'I protest, sweetheart. I think our Jack would not attend to the most pressing necessities of nature unless he could give a reason for it.' And thirty-five years after his father had died, John recalled one of his wise sayings: 'Child, you think to carry everything by dint of argument. But you will find by and by, how very little is ever done in the world by clear reason.' It took the hard knocks of incessant campaigning to convince John that his father was wholly right. Ruefully he said in a letter to Joseph Benson:

Against experience we believe;
We argue against demonstration;
Pleased while our reason we deceive;
And set our judgement by our passion.

Charles, on the other hand, impetuous, short tempered, and given to violent outbursts of feeling, was clearly Samuel's child. But both John and Charles inherited their father's trait of physical and moral courage. In Browning's phrase they were fighters ever, and neither allowed any obstacles to daunt them, nor any adversities to wear down their spirits. In this respect the sons had not only Samuel's spirit, but the constant inspiration of his example.

We are moulded not only by heredity but environment. Physical and mental traits were inherited from their father, but they had likewise the strong influence of his life and his strongly held convictions. How much was Charles confirmed in his uncritical and unwearying love of the Church of England by the memory of a father who once rejoiced that there was no Papist or Dissenter in his parish! And John, with deep filial affection and respect for Samuel, always refused to face the logic of his actions and protested his determination to live and die within the Established Church. All their early associations were bound up with the life of a country rectory and of parents wholly devoted to the principles and practice of the Church as by law established.

It was doubtless in this same fashion that John and Charles became Tories. They had early learnt that the Tories were the safeguard of the true interests of the Church and that Whiggism was too closely identified with Dissent; Dissenters, they understood, left the door open for republicanism and infidelity. The Tory party and the Church of England seemed to them the two walls of a harbour which was safe and deep for shipping.

It was not only in his general but in his particular views that the father influenced the sons.

In 1698 Samuel Wesley had preached before the Society for the Reformation of Manners on the text which John Wesley sixty-five years later was to choose when he preached before the same Society. 'Who will rise up for me against evil-doers? Who will stand up for me against the workers of iniquity?' (Psalm 94^{16}). The text sufficiently illustrates the purpose of the Society, though Daniel Defoe in his *Poor Man's Plea* complained that small flies were caught, but great ones broke through the cobwebs. In the next year Samuel Wesley wrote his *Letter concerning the Religious Societies* and thus showed his interest in two great contemporary movements. In his pamphlet he explained the difference between them. 'In the first place I find many persons are in the same mistake which you were once in, and confuse these religious societies with the societies for reformation, though they are quite different as to their institution and immediate ends, and for the most part as to the persons of which they are composed. The immediate business of the societies for reformation is to assist the civil magistrates in putting the laws in execution against profaneness and immorality and consists of sober persons . . . most of them of the Church of England: but religious societies . . . are composed of such as meet wholly upon a religious account to promote true piety in themselves and others, and are all of them strict members of the Church of England.'

Samuel proceeded to say that many belonged to both societies. He had shown his sympathy with the Society attacking public vice and now he warmly commended the religious societies as under the parish priest 'promoting the great ends for which he has dedicated himself to God'. In this way they would care for the sick and poor, give an account of the spiritual estate of themselves and others and engage in 'pious discourse'. It was these societies, begun in 1677, which were still lingering when John Wesley started his work. There are many references in the first volume of Wesley's *Works* to his attendances at these societies and his speaking at them. They gave him the model he wanted when he formed his united societies in 1739.

People came to Charles and himself for advice and comfort, and he advised them in these terms: 'Strengthen you one another—talk together as often as you can, and pray earnestly for one another that you may endure to the end and be saved.' They replied, 'We want you likewise to talk with us'. 'So I told them: "If you will all come together every Thursday evening, I will gladly spend some time with you in prayer, and give you the best advice I can." Thus', he adds, 'arose what afterwards was called a society, a very innocent name and very common in London, for any number of people associating themselves together.' They united in order to pray together, to receive the word of exhortation and to watch over one another in love that they might help each other to work out their salvation. Some days after the Society had been formed, some members expressed a determination to make a quarterly subscription to assist Wesley to pay for the lease of the Foundery. Then a steward was chosen to receive the money and very soon after the Society was divided into smaller companies called 'classes', consisting of twelve persons each. One of these persons was styled the leader.

If John Wesley was thus indebted to the religious societies, it was because of his father's interest and commendation that he was first drawn to them. When he used the laity to 'promote great ends' he was only doing what his father had urged in 1699, and the 'pious discourse' of Methodist classes was entirely in accord with what Samuel Wesley had sought.

A second great interest of Samuel, communicated later to his sons, was in the world-wide work of the Church. When he was still in his thirties the Rector would gladly have gone as missionary to India, China, or Abyssinia. In a scheme propounded to the Society for Propagating the Gospel in foreign parts, he offered to visit English settlements between St. Helena and China; to pierce into Abyssinia; or he would learn Hindostan [sic] and preach to the people of India in their native tongue. Whatever use was made of his services he made two conditions. He was to receive £140 of which £40 would pay for a curate at Epworth. In the case of his decease, proper provision was to be made for his wife and family. Whilst he lived they were to have the income of the Rectory. From the start he was one of the most enthusiastic supporters of Oglethorpe's Georgia scheme and corresponded with him as early as 1732. Writing to him in 1734 he declared: 'I had always so dear a love of your colony that if it had been but ten years ago, I would gladly have devoted the remainder of my life and labours to that place and think I might before this time have conquered the language without which little can be done among the natives.' Since he could not go, he tried to persuade Oglethorpe to take his son-in-law, John Whitelamb, but for some unexplained reason this never happened. Instead, within twelve months of the Rector's death, his own two sons were on the high seas, full of hope at the prospect of preaching the Gospel and administering the sacraments in that new colony.

The Lincolnshire parsonage might have been set in a very straggling undersized country town, but its windows opened out on all the world. Apart from life the most precious thing salvaged from the fire in 1709 was the great hymn of Samuel Wesley on redemption. It anticipates the contrast between the universal and particular, the all and the one, which Charles Wesley delighted to employ. And as the first two verses so clearly show, the divine drama is enacted against a universal background.

> Behold the Saviour of mankind
> Nailed to the shameful tree!
> How vast the love that Him inclined
> To bleed and die for thee!
>
> Hark, how He groans! while nature shakes,
> And earth's strong pillars bend;
> The temple's veil in sunder breaks,
> The solid marbles rend.
>
> 'Tis done! the precious ransom's paid;
> Receive My soul! He cries:
> See where He bows His sacred head!
> He bows His head, and dies!
>
> But soon He'll break death's envious chain,
> And in full glory shine:
> O Lamb of God, was ever pain,
> Was ever love, like Thine?

John Wesley not only regarded the world as his parish, but drew upon the world for his reading, and the reading he selected for his followers. The *Christian Library* which he issued in fifty volumes is a notable illustration. Missionary hymns are not necessarily those with special reference to particular places, or climates, or peoples. The greatest missionary hymns are those which comprehend the whole world as the sphere of God's love and activity. That is why so very many of Charles Wesley's hymns are essentially missionary in outlook. Even when they were written polemically the result was the same. Not the few, nor the many, but all, the Saviour came to save. The sons followed a father's tradition.

Perhaps the greatest service Samuel Wesley rendered to John and Charles was by the precept and example of daily life. They grew up in the home of a scholar whose reading was wide and deep, who had a command of many languages and whose scholarship was always at their disposal. It is a thousand pities that, with abilities unequal to his conception, he set himself to produce a masterpiece in Latin on the Book of Job. For the last thirty years of his life it occupied much of his spare-time studies and doubtless it became at times a burden to the family. And yet the very titles of the fifty-three dissertations are a tribute to his vast learning and industry (*Dissertationes in Librum Jobi*). After the dissertations came the Hebrew text of the book of Job collated with the Chaldee paraphrase and with the Septuagint. There were also the comparison with the versions in Syriac and Arabic, and the Latin versions of Castellio, Montanus, St. Ambrose, Junius Tremellius, Piscator, and the Zurich divines. Then came the English version of Tyndale and the authorized version of 1611. Each verse was collated in all the versions and the variations were recorded. Probably the greatest orientalist in the first part of the nineteenth century was Dr. Adam Clarke and no one was more competent to assess the worth of Samuel Wesley's undertaking. He was one of the very few who could judge the relative worth of the versions that Samuel used, and his skill in the use of them. He said of Wesley's *Job*: 'It is one of the most complete things of the kind I have ever met with, and must be invaluable to any man who may wish to read the Book of Job critically.' John Wesley said dryly that his Father's Latin work on Job 'contained immense learning but of a kind which I do not admire'.

The Rector needed the patience of his hero to toil on with it through many years, more especially when with one hand paralysed he had to force himself to write with the other. Yet his courage did not fail him. He wrote in a letter to one of his subscribers (1732): 'though I have already lost the use of one hand in the service, yet, I thank God, *non defecit altera*, and I begin to put it to school this day to learn to write, in order to help its lame brother.'

But perhaps the valiant subscribers needed even more patience. When at last the volume came out, did many of them follow in their own way the example of Queen Caroline? Samuel had died with the work still unfinished, though it is likely, in assuagement of his disappointment, that he had heard of the Queen's willingness to accept the dedication. His elder son, Samuel Wesley, junior, completed the book, and six months after his father's death, John Wesley was appointed to present it in the name of his deceased parent. The Queen was romping with her maids of honour but she suspended her play, heard and received him graciously, commented on the fact that the book was 'very prettily bound' and then laid it down on a window seat without opening a leaf. What did the gallant James Oglethorpe do with the nine copies he ordered? Some of the 343 subscribers praised it, but Bishop Warburton indulged his wit. 'Poor Job! It was his eternal fate to be persecuted by his friends. His three comforters passed sentence of condemnation upon him, and he has been executed in effigy ever since. He was first bound to the stake by a long catena of Greek fathers: then tortured by Pineda; then strangled by Carryll and afterwards cut up by Wesley and anatomized by Garrit. He was ordained, I think, by a fate like Prometheus, to lie still upon his dunghill and have his brains sucked out by owls.' But where few could follow a learned work in Latin, and fewer still were interested in the contents of the book, it is obvious that the judgement of dullness can only be accepted if it comes from a sufficient number of those qualified to judge. A general chorus coming from non-readers of the book means nothing. Whatever merits the book possessed, it did not make sufficiently wide a public appeal, and so it was quickly forgotten. From a financial point of view, he would have been well advised to have written with a more modest aim. But he was neither hack nor hireling, and in the service of learning he was willing to pay heavy dues.

This scholarship lay easily upon him. He was no pedant, and he could not have been a recluse, had he tried. There are many stories which display the ready and easy talker, of shrewd sense and of lively wit. If he was no poet, he was a ready and often an able versifier till the end of his days. His gift in greater measure was transmitted to his sons and what was talent in him became genius in his son Charles. The daughters were not so readily appreciative of their father's gifts. Their life was hard, narrow, and uninteresting. Upon them fell as they grew older the task of assisting Susanna in the drudgery of household duties and the fight to maintain a brave front with insufficient means. They lived in a century that did not speak of 'careers for girls', and with all their native intelligence they had to give way to their brothers when the question of education was considered. They lived in a remote part of an inaccessible countryside with Lincoln as the only possible contact with the wider world of fashion and culture. They were surrounded by people socially and culturally inferior to themselves. Though they had many prospective suitors they could hardly hope to find any who would make suitable partners. It is no wonder that they do not speak of their father in the same terms of devotion and respect that their more fortunate brothers used. In the correspondence which has been preserved the Rector was 'guide, philosopher, counsellor, and friend' to his three sons. He told John which was the best commentary on the Bible, advised him to compare the Hebrew Bible, Vulgate, and Samaritan in the Polyglott in the morning, and each afternoon to make sure of an hour's walk in the fields (January 1725). He sent him a sober estimate of Thomas à Kempis, assessing his weakness and strength, and concluded that it was impossible to read him without desiring to imitate 'his heroic strains of humility, and piety, and devotion'. 'But most', he said, 'master St. Chrysostom, and the Articles, and the Form of Ordination' (July 1725). In another letter he confessed his admiration of John's powers of reasoning. But he added cautiously: 'He that believes and yet argues against reason is half a Papist or enthusiast. He that would make Revelation bend to his own shallow reason is either half a Deist or a lunatic. O my dear! Steer clear between this Scylla and Charybdis.' Still keeping a zealous eye on John's studies he disclosed to him a half-formed plan of his own.

'I have sometime since designed an edition of the Holy Bible in octavo, in the Hebrew, Chaldee, Septuagint, and Vulgate, and have made some progress in it. I have not time at present to give you the whole scheme of which scarce any soul knows except your brother, Sam. What I desire of you is first that you would immediately fall to work and read diligently the Hebrew text in the Polyglott and collate it exactly with the Vulgate, writing all, even the least, variations or differences between them. Second to these I would have you add the Samaritan text, which is the very same with the Hebrew, except in some very few places, differing only in the Samaritan character, which I think is the true old Hebrew. You may learn the Samaritan alphabet in a day, either from the Prolegomena in Walton's polyglott or from his grammar. In a twelvemonth's time, sticking close to it in the forenoons, you will get twice through the Pentateuch: for I have done it four times the last years, and am going over it the fifth and also collating the two Greek versions, the Alexandrian and the Vatican, with what I can get of Symmachus and Theodotian, etc.' (January 1726).

This lengthy extract is doubly interesting because it shows not only what he expected of his son, John, but the discipline to which he subjected himself. There is a touch of wry humour in a letter Samuel sent to John about the illness of Susanna Wesley (18th

July 1727): 'We received last post your compliments of condolence and congratulation to your mother on the supposition of her near approaching demise; to which your sister, Patty, will by no means subscribe, for she says she is not so good a philosopher as you are, and that she cannot spare her mother yet, if it please God, without great inconvenience.'

In a notable letter addressed both to John and Charles he said of their mode of life at Oxford: '*valde probo*.' He thanked God that he had two sons together at Oxford to whom had been given grace and courage to turn the war against the world and the devil. Now, argued the Rector, you have only the flesh to combat, and this can only be done by prayer and fasting. In a revealing section of the letter he speaks about their prison visitation.

'I am afraid lest the main objection you make against going on in the business with the prisoners may secretly proceed from flesh and blood. Go on, then, in God's name, in the path to which your Saviour has directed you, and that track wherein your father has gone before you! For when I was an undergraduate at Oxford, I visited those in the castle there, and reflect on it with great satisfaction to this day. Walk as prudently as you can, though not fearfully, and my heart and prayers are with you. Your first regular step is, to consult with him (if any such there be) who has a jurisdiction over the prisoners: and the next is to obtain the direction and approbation of your bishop.'

When one thinks of the father as an Oxford undergraduate writing his *Maggots*, and enjoying his snuff and tobacco, it is necessary to remember that long before his sons, he visited the prisoners and performed his acts of mercy and of love.

When his sons were rudely jolted because their prison visits and the monthly sermons to prisoners were laughed at and ridiculed by university members, they wrote in dismay to their father. He hastened to reassure them and to strengthen their resolve.

'I can scarce think so meanly of you as that you would be discouraged by "the crackling of thorns under a pot". Be not high minded, but fear. Preserve an equal temper of mind, under whatever treatment you meet from a not very just or well-natured world. Bear no more sail than is necessary, but steer steady. The less you value yourselves for these unfashionable duties, the more all good and wise men will value you, if they see your actions are of a piece; or what is infinitely more, He by whom actions and intentions are weighed will both accept, esteem, and reward you. I hear my son, John, has the honour of being styled "the Father of the Holy Club": if it be so, I must be the grandfather of it; and I need not say that I had rather any of my sons should be so dignified and distinguished than to have the title of His Holiness' (1st December 1730). The meetings of the brothers Wesley and their friends had been designated the 'Holy Club' in ridicule by their fellow students.

In a similar fashion the Rector had given counsel and advice to both Charles, and to Samuel. Writing to Charles he said: 'Between logic, grammar, and mathematics be idle if you can, and I give my blessing to your bishop for having tied you a little faster by obliging you to rub up your Arabic. A fixed and constant method will make all both easy and delightful to you' (29th January 1730). It was in one of his letters to Samuel that he revealed his perplexity and pain at John's refusal to succeed him in the living at Epworth. The Rector had already conducted a long and fruitless correspondence with John in which arguments on each side were raised and countered. Finding John to be immovable, the Rector roundly declared to his son Samuel, that he could not accept or understand John's position. John had said that where he could be most holy there he could best promote holiness in others, and Oxford was the place most fitted for his improvement. The aged father was willing to allow that it might be true if the acquiring of knowledge was the only end, but for the understanding of men and things, a wider stage was required. Lying behind his argument, however, was the desire to provide for Susanna after his death by securing her continued residence in the rectory. Besides, the Rector, conscious of his own greatly increasing infirmities, was fearful lest his forty years of honest labour would be lost. 'The vineyard which I have planted with no ignoble vine must soon be rooted up, and the fences of it broken down—for I am morally satisfied, if your brothers both slight it, Mr. P—— will be my successor.' There was no moaning or complaint in the letter and it ended on no note of bitterness. Samuel bade his eldest son do what he could with John and then concluded:

'While the anchor holds, I despair of nothing, but firmly believe that He who is best will do what is best, whether we earnestly will it or not. There I rest the whole matter, and leave it with Him, to whom I have committed all my concerns, without exception and without reserve for soul and body, estate and family, time and eternity.'

In a sense the most interesting letters between Samuel and his sons do not belong to this last decade of his life but to an earlier period. After his imprisonment in Lincoln Castle he addressed letters to Samuel, which show how he watched over the religious development of his sons, and tried to shape their thinking. Samuel was at this time a pupil at Westminster School and although addressed as 'child' in the letters, was sixteen years of age. His father urged him to think large thoughts of God; to maintain the habit of regular prayer, and to keep fixed hours for everything, 'not neglecting bodily exercise for the preservation of your health'. In another letter he gave free expression to his love of good music, and of the need for making the best use of public worship. Make sure, he said to his son, that you understand the cathedral service, for if you do, you will find Church music a great help to devotion. Some, he argued, have even been helped by the 'sorry Sternhold psalms', though these are infinitely inferior to cathedral music. It was only a poetically minded father who could suggest to his son that he might find pleasure and profit in translating portions of the Bible into verse. The Rector had attempted this himself in his *History of the Old and New Testament*, and Charles was later substantially to do it in his *Short Hymns on Select passages of the Holy Scriptures*.

He did not hesitate to advise his son on the use and abuse of love. 'Whoever expects to become anything in the world must guard against anti-platonic love in his youth, shut his eyes and heart against it, burn romances, have a care of plays, and keep himself fully employed in some honest exercise; and then, I think, he will be in no very great danger from it.' Thus love, but what of hatred? The Rector said he did not know how it was possible to have it in extremes against anyone. He confessed that he had much ado to hate the devil himself, though he had often pitied him. He told his son that Scripture passages which enjoined 'hating the wicked' refer chiefly to their vices. Anger, argued the Rector, is in a different category 'and I own to be more difficult to subdue', though it is too often compounded of pride or interest. And so, he pleaded, master yourself, for it is richly worth your labour. 'There was never a truly great man who could not bridle his passions.'

The letters between father and sons in school and university illustrate the warm relationship which existed between them. In their need they constantly wrote for advice and he on his part was always ready to offer his counsel. Even on his death-bed he had words for them which remained indelibly on their minds. To John, he said in terms which adumbrated the Methodist doctrine of Assurance: 'The inward witness, son, the inward witness; that is proof, the strongest proof of Christianity.' John quoted this saying in a letter to John Smith (Archbishop Secker) (22nd March 1748). To Charles he said prophetically: 'Be steady. The Christian faith will surely revive in the Kingdom: you shall see it though I shall not.' Never were words more swiftly and fully realized!

Perhaps the greatest proof of his influence over them lay in their acceptance of his sturdy orthodoxy. Samuel Wesley never wavered in his enthusiastic belief in the historic Creeds. The preface to his poem entitled *An Epistle to a Friend Concerning Poetry*[1] shows how strongly he resented the Deistic and sceptical tendencies of his age. He said he was concerned to denounce not only loose living but loose thinking. 'My quarrel is with those that rank themselves among atheists, and impudently defend and propagate the ridiculous opinion of the eternity of the world and of that fatal invincible chain of things which is now made use of to destroy the faith, as our lewd plays are to corrupt the morals of the nation; an opinion big with more absurdities than transubstantiation itself, and of far more fatal consequences.' In trenchant and succinct words he described the practical effect of Deism. It weakens, he said, belief in the being and providence of God. 'It utterly takes away freedom in human actions, reduces mankind beneath the brute creation, perfectly excuses the greatest villainies and entirely vacates all retribution hereafter.' He went on to argue that if such beliefs spread, a virtual atheism would result. 'They labour hard to remove a Supreme Being out of the world; or, if they do vouchsafe Him any room in it, it is only that they may find fault with His works, which they think with that blasphemer of old, might have been much better ordered had they themselves stood by and directed the architect.' They try, said

---

[1] Published 1700. Folio of 1,083 lines. Nehemiah Curnock raises an interesting query. Pope was familiar with the Rector's works. Did the initial idea of the *Dunciad* come from reading this satire? He asks, very much more improbably, whether Byron's *English Bards and Scotch Reviewers* may not be a lineal descendant. See *Wesley's Journal* (Standard Edition), Vol. VIII, p. 34 and note.

Wesley, to grapple with omnipotence, and thunder with a voice like God. 'They would like to annihilate hell so that they might be tolerably happy, more quietly rake through the world, and then sink into nothingness.'

This is a second war, declared Samuel Wesley, and it must not be left to generals. Little people also must fire even though it only serves to give the alarm. And they must not quit their post.

Now rightly considered this is a remarkable counterblast. It shows that Samuel Wesley was aware that the philosophers were a greater moral peril than the dramatists. For what you believe about God conditions what you believe about man and the world! He saw that to make God an absentee landlord was not only belittling to God but to man. It robs God of His Fatherhood and man of his sonship. If God is only the supreme architect, infinitely removed from and therefore indifferent to the tragi-comedy of life, there is no ultimate accountability and so no present responsibility. If heaven and hell be removed, you remove likewise the true dimension of life, and contract all things to a smaller scale. If you avoid the prospect of great misery you deny yourself the possession of great happiness, and in Wesley's expressive phrase you quietly 'rake through the world'.

That the dangers which he attacked were sufficiently real can be realized from the most cursory survey of eighteenth-century philosophical thought. Locke had conceived the mind as a *tabula rasa*, upon which as a sheet of white paper, the knowledge we receive is written down. Although Locke agreed that knowledge was made up partly by reflection as well as sensation, it is not easy to see how in his theory he can allow for reflective ideas being supplied to the mind by their own operation. He makes the senses the source of ideas, and reflection can only play the subordinate part of modifying or combining these ideas. This position is closely akin to sensationalism and as such it exercised a profound influence on the school of French materialistic philosophy in the mid-eighteenth century and later. It has close similarities to the 'sensationalist' school in modern Russian philosophy and to the work of the American Behaviourists.

Locke did not follow relentlessly the logic of his own position or else he would have been driven beyond Deism into materialism. Berkeley's attack went to its own extreme. He denied the very existence of matter, for if one abstracts from a concrete object the qualities of which one is aware only in perception, nothing is left.

Esse est percipi. Everything depends for its existence on the percipient mind. Locke had taught that objects, by the impressions made on the senses, produced ideas. This was virtually to reduce spirit to the level of matter. Berkeley argued that only in the ideas of the mind can objects be known. This was virtually to interpret matter in terms of spirit. David Hume had no difficulty later in exposing the ultimate absurdity of this position, but the solid merits of Berkeley he could not so readily appreciate.

A more moderate and effective position was taken by Samuel Clarke who in variance with Locke insisted that in the human mind are ideas which express qualities. But since there can be conceived no quality in pure abstraction, each quality must have its corresponding subject. In this way we can predicate the Being of God to whom certain necessary qualities belong. The argument has an old and respectable ancestry but Clarke restated it in a fresh way. In the universe are certain fixed relations and it is man's wisdom to act in harmony with these. In this way Clarke showed the reasonableness of morals, and restated the dictum that 'it is hard to kick against the pricks'.

Yet the real battleground was not in the struggle of empiricist and idealistic philosophies, but in the long and bitter controversy between the believers in natural and in revealed religion. Behind Locke it was Hobbes who defined most clearly the sensationalist position and he was the true father of those who in the next century attacked the Christian faith. There are two important books which by their very titles show the nature of the controversy. In his book *Christianity Not Mysterious* (1696), John Toland set himself to show that there is nothing in Scripture or Revelation which is not comprehensible by reason. The effect of the book was to discount what seemed above or contrary to reason, and so no room was left for the miraculous and the supernatural.

In 1730 Nicholas Tindal published his book *Christianity as old as the Creation, or The Gospel, a Republication of the Religion of Nature.* Its very title showed that the author had no use for the distinctive and unique features of the Christian faith. There was still no room for miracle, but only for a religion that was natural but not revealed. Between the publication of these books came Anthony Collins's *Discourse on Free-thinking,* 1713. This made reason the supreme guide and so asked for complete religious freedom.

The views of the Deistic writers can easily be summarized.

Since God was removed from the world and existed only as the unmoved Mover, there could be no revelation of His Person. The atoning work, the miracles and resurrection of Jesus were denied. His mediation was shown to be unnecessary. The denial of His divinity carried with it a rejection of the essential features of His teaching. What was not acceptable to reason could be rejected out of hand, for reason was the sole determining guide. This approach to truth left no room for a personal awareness of God nor of prayer to Him as Father. It was an ever-present danger of Calvinism that, stressing the infinite distance between God and His creatures, it might bring men to feel that God was too far removed to care. When Calvinism had lost its early vigour, and the overwhelming greatness of God and His selective choice no longer moved men to deeds of incredible heroism, nothing was left but a religion of morals, in which aided by reason, and otherwise unaided, men gingerly picked their way through the maze of life. If God is lost so that His nature no longer excites awe and reverence, then Christianity is not mysterious, and men have not a creed but a code. The previous century had seen men contending lustily for their faith. There had been wars and persecutions in which religion had played a major part. But now hot passions had cooled. Men's fretted spirits were tired. The wild excesses of the Restoration had been one form of protest against a narrow zeal and an over-scrupulous faith. But even this had exhausted itself. Deism was but the burnt-out fire of a former day when God and His cause had been a rallying call to battle. In such an age when ethics had replaced theology it was natural that a school of moralists should arise discussing the place of benevolence and self-love and their relation to happiness and virtue in an ethical system. It is not within the scope of this book to discuss the writings of Shaftesbury, Hutcheson, and Butler, nor of Hartley, who explained the 'moral sense' in terms of association, and Adam Smith who interpreted it as sympathy.

One line of attack was to use the Deists' own weapons but to use them more effectively. This was done supremely by Butler in his *Sermons* and in his *Analogy*. He gave conscience a new authority; he showed that benevolence and self-love were co-incident, and most of all he sought patiently to show his opponents that if they were to be consistent in their views of God, of nature, and of man, they would be drawn to accept the Christian revelation and therefore the reasonableness of leading a Christian life. But there is none of the unclouded optimism of the Deists, illustrated by Pope's *Essay on Man*. He could not readily believe that

> *All nature is but art, unknown to thee;*
> *All chance, direction, which thou canst not see;*
> *All discord, harmony not understood;*
> *All partial evil, universal good;*
> *And spite of pride, in erring reason's spite*
> *One truth is clear, Whatever is, is right (Epistle I. 284).*

For him, not certainty, but probability was the guide of human life, since all our knowledge is necessarily limited. The argument was well suited to the age. Butler, by an appeal to reason, the one appeal the Deists recognized, exposed the poverty of their views, and made Christianity intellectually respectable.

Now Samuel Wesley was neither equipped nor ready to argue with the Deists. He chose a different method. He made his position clear by vigorously asserting his complete belief in the faith once delivered to the saints. He was especially emphatic in his view of the Sacraments as essential means of grace. To the Deists, since they disregarded the Person of our Lord, Baptism and the Lord's Supper were meaningless rites. They might punctiliously regard the outward forms of worship but they could find no place for them in their philosophy. Samuel Wesley in his *Pious Communicant*[1] was concerned to show that in Baptism we are 'so far regenerate as to be grafted into the body of Christ's Church'. It is not, he declared, that regeneration is completed, but only begun, in Baptism; a 'principle of grace is infused, which we lost by the fall, which shall never wholly be withdrawn, unless we quench God's Holy Spirit by obstinate habits of wickedness. There are babes as well as strong men in Christ'.

The virtual republication of his father's Discourse on Baptism in 1758 meant that, so long after, Wesley still shared completely his father's views. In his sermon on 'The New Birth' John Wesley allowed that a man may be 'born of water' and yet not 'born of the Spirit'. There may be the outward sign but not the inward grace. But he was careful to add that this does not apply to infants. 'It

---

[1] The full title is: *The Pious Communicant Rightly Prepared; or a discourse concerning the Blessed Sacrament wherein the nature of it is described, our obligation to frequent communion enforced, and directions given for due preparation for it, behaviour at and after it, and profiting by it. With prayers and hymns suited to the several parts of that Holy Office.* To which is added '*A Short Discourse of Baptism*'.

is certain that our Church supposes that all who are baptized in their infancy are at the same time born again and it is allowed that the whole Office for the Baptism of Infants proceeds upon this supposition.' The views of Samuel and his son, John, on Baptismal Regeneration were resisted from the first in Methodism and in our present Order of Service for the Baptism of Infants there is an absence of the doctrinal significance that the Wesleys attached to the rite. (This applies also to *Minutes of Conference*, 1936. Memorandum on Infant Baptism.) This has been to our loss, for in avoiding a false theory of baptismal regeneration, we have considerably reduced in strength the rich content of the sacrament. The great Methodist theologians have been wiser. Richard Watson declared: 'To the infant child it is a visible reception into the same covenant and church, a pledge of acceptance through Christ—the bestowment of a title to all the graces of the covenant as circumstances may require, and as the mind of the child may be capable or made capable of receiving it.' William Burt Pope said the blessing God sealed to children was all they were capable of receiving. 'As children of a race under condemnation they are justified freely by His grace through the redemption that is in Christ Jesus. Children of wrath as belonging to the lineage of the first Adam, they are grafted into the Second: their baptism is the seal of their present adoption and the pledge of their regeneration when they are capable of it. Unholy by nature they are sanctified through baptismal consecration to God. . . . The baptism of the children of believing parents is therefore a sign of the washing away of original guilt, and a seal of their adoption into the family of God; a sign of the regeneration which their nature needs, and a seal of its impartation in God's good time.'[1]

Samuel Wesley had an equally profound veneration for the Sacrament of the Lord's Supper. At a time when it was most infrequently administered in the parish churches he urged the obligation to frequent communion. Susanna Wesley in a letter to John (12th July 1731) told of the terrible fall the Rector had from the horse and wagon. But on the Sunday, although he was very ill and in pain, he not only preached twice but 'gave the sacrament which was too much for him to do, but nobody could dissuade

---

[1] W. B. Pope, *Compendium of Modern Theology*, Vol. III, p. 317-18. For a highly illuminating and constructive statement which conserves the essential value of the Wesleys' view of baptism, see Kenneth Grayston's article in *London Quarterly and Holborn Review* (July 1944), pp. 210-18.

him from it'. Even when, in his own words, there was but a step between himself and death, he said to his family: 'Tomorrow I will see you all with me round this table that we may drink once more the cup of blessing before we drink it new in the Kingdom of God. With desire have I desired to eat this passover with you before I die.' The next day he was so extremely weak and in such great pain that only with the utmost difficulty could he receive the elements, but Charles noticed that immediately after he had communicated, he was full of faith and peace.

Even so well disposed a critic as Adam Clarke could find little to praise in the *Pious Communicant* apart from the pious intention. He described it as the most imperfect he had seen of all the literary works of the Rector of Epworth. But at least Samuel distinguished, though crudely, between the Roman and Anglican view of the institution; he did plead for its frequent observance, and he appended paraphrases of six psalms (113-18) which he thought could fittingly be used in connexion with the rite.

There can be no doubt that the high sacramentarian views of the Rector and his example greatly influenced all his sons. It is true that the more immediate influence was that of Daniel Brevint's treatise, *The Christian Sacrament and Sacrifice*, but they were the more easily predisposed to accept Brevint's teaching because of their home training and their father's guidance. They certainly followed his example of frequent communion. Wesley communicated every four or five days and also conducted communion services constantly at which hundreds of Methodist communicants were present; and all this at the time when Bishop Secker was recommending to his clergy the holding of one celebration to break the otherwise long interval between Whitsuntide and Christmas Day.

But it was in his doctrinal position that the Rector differed most sharply from the Deists. He was not blindly but enthusiastically orthodox. He had no place for Socinianism. Even when Socinians made the most extravagant claims for Christ, but allowed a moment's difference between His existence and that of the Father, Samuel Wesley remained unimpressed. They still think, he said, in terms of 'a made God or a subordinate Supreme'. He had, whilst still in a Dissenting Academy, disagreed with the views of Biddle, a prominent English disciple of Socinus. So sharpened, he was able to dissuade Susanna from Unitarian beliefs when first they became engaged. She confessed it was one of life's crowning mercies that 'she was married to a religious orthodox man, and by him was first drawn off from the Socinian heresy'. It was because the dissenting bodies (especially the Presbyterian and many Congregational Churches) were so infected with Arianism in his day that Samuel Wesley rejoiced to have none in his parish. With the strong broom of his zealous Anglican orthodoxy he wanted to sweep his parish clean from all heresy. It was altogether appropriate that when he died, the epitaph on his tomb should read:

AS HE LIV'D, SO HE DIED,
IN THE TRUE CATHOLIC FAITH
OF THE HOLY TRINITY IN UNITY,
AND THAT JESUS CHRIST IS GOD INCARNATE,
AND THE ONLY SAVIOUR OF MANKIND.
Acts iv. 12.

This belief in our Lord's divinity had been the firm foundation of all his preaching.

Consistently with these views, he delighted to speak of the saving work of Christ. The one great hymn that he has left to all the Churches describes the atoning sacrifice made for all men —'Behold the Saviour of Mankind.' For Samuel repudiated the doctrines of election and reprobation. He could not believe that there was an election of a determinate number such as 'puts a force on their natures and irresistibly saves them, or absolutely excludes all the rest of mankind from salvation'. He argued that only those would be condemned who remained impenitent. And he ridiculed the notion that God's prescience overruled a man by saving him whether He willed or no, or by damning him undeservedly. God, he said, has offered the 'pardon of all sin, and the right to life in Christ, to all men without exception, on condition of believing and acceptance'. Saving faith is a steady belief in Jesus as the Saviour of the world, 'and that He will save me, if I depend on Him and obey His commands'.

Once a man is saved he can by the assistance of God's spirit, pray, abstain from sin, and practise duty; and if he continues in these good actions he will have still more aid and go on to perfection.[1]

---

[1] See L. Tyerman, *Life and Times of Samuel Wesley* (pp. 144-6), who after a close study of Samuel Wesley's answers in the volumes of the *Athenian Oracle* and also his *Notes on the Life of Christ*, said that 'no follower of John Wesley holds the doctrine of justification by faith more clearly or firmly than John Wesley's father'.

These views were not only a rejection of Calvinism and Arianism; they denied the whole structure of Deism. He did not choose to argue philosophically. To assent uncompromisingly to the divinity of Christ and His redeeming, mediatorial work, was a far more effective counterblast.

It is significant that at no time were Samuel (junior), John, or Charles Wesley in danger of succumbing to prevailing Deistical opinions. This fashion in thinking was at its height when as young men they were most susceptible to new ideas. They did not waver in their orthodoxy and one strong reason was the teaching and example of a father who rejoiced in his Trinitarian faith. Samuel had builded better than he knew.[1]

[1] John Wesley addressed his arguments principally to Deists in his Sermon on 'The Case of Reason impartially considered' (Wesley's *Works*, Vol. VI, pp. 350ff.); in his 'Earnest Appeal to men of reason and religion' (ibid., Vol. VIII, especially see pp. 3-15); and in his 'Farther Appeal to men of reason and religion' (Part 2) (ibid., Vol. VIII, especially pp. 192-200). The 'Letter to Rev. Dr. Conyers Middleton' also refutes Deistic views in the course of the argument (ibid., Vol. X, pp. 1-79).

Chapter Three

MRS. WESLEY

THROUGHOUT the latter years of the seventeenth century Dr. Annesley was the leading Nonconformist Divine in London and when the young impecunious Samuel won the hand of his youngest daughter he could not have seemed a promising suitor. And yet no marriage has been more momentous in its consequences. Some writers especially of the older school have represented it to be a perfect love match. Others have depicted Susanna as burdened with her husband's tantrums, books, and debts. Strangely, in all this speculation no one has suggested that Samuel was ever burdened with Susanna. She might at times exasperate him by her very calmness, but she never lost her complete hold upon his affections. This is a true reading of the matter. But it is just as true that Samuel having won her love, possessed it to the end. They often quarrelled. What happens when the weight moving with irresistible force encounters the immovable obstacle? It is a nice but abstract question. In human relations, however, when the fiery temper of the husband is met by the quiet unmoving patience and determination of a wife, disagreement amounting at times to a quarrel will certainly result. The proper test of a happy and successful marriage is never an absence of quarrels. Peace can be bought domestically at too great a price. If to preserve harmony the more forceful of the two is ever allowed too easy victory, the possibility of a rich creative relationship is destroyed.

It is true that Susanna bemoaned on one occasion that Samuel and she rarely agreed on a particular matter, but that was because two more than ordinary people, independent in judgement and of strong convictions, were not willing to disguise their proper views just to flatter the other. Their honesty and integrity, lacking all subtlety, might at times breed dissension, but at least there was no sleep of death; no sacrifice of individuality. The children were brought up in a stimulating, quickening atmosphere. Nor were the quarrels mere vulgar brawls. There were no records from the children of ugly scenes that seared their memory, but there was just one account of an open breach and that was a puzzling affair. Samuel must often have uttered the same prayer for the King.

Was it only on this occasion that Susanna refused to say Amen or was it just on that occasion that Samuel chose to notice it? It certainly is undeniable that Susanna would never pray for a cause in which she did not believe. For that reason she would never pray for the success of our arms in the War of the Spanish Succession, and even Marlborough's dazzling victories could not persuade her otherwise.

> Since I am not satisfied of the lawfulness of the war, I cannot beg a blessing on our arms till I can have the opinion of one wiser and a more competent judge than myself on this point—namely whether a private person that had no hand in the beginning of the war but did always disapprove of it, may notwithstanding beg God's blessing on it, and pray for the good success of arms which were taken up, I think, unlawfully. In the meantime, I think it my duty since I cannot join in public worship, to spend the time others take in that, in humbling my soul before God for my own and the nation's sins; and in beseeching Him to spare that guilty land, wherein are many thousands that are, notwithstanding comparatively innocent, and not to slay the righteous with the wicked; but to put a stop to the effusion of Christian blood, and in His own good time to restore to us the blessing of public peace. Since then I do not absent myself from Church out of any contempt for authority or out of any vain presumption of my own goodness as though I needed no solemn humiliation; and since I endeavour according to my poor ability to humble myself before God, and do earnestly desire that He may give this war such an issue as may most effectually conduce to His own glory I hope it will not be charged upon me as a sin; but that it will please Almighty God, by some way or other, to satisfy my scruples and to accept of my honest intentions and to pardon my manifold infirmities.

In any case Samuel must have realized that Susanna had strong Jacobite sympathies and that she accepted *de facto* but not *de jure* the accession of William and Mary.[1] This must have been the climax of a preceding controversy in which the whole question of loyalty was raised. On so vital a principle neither could give way though in effect Samuel left the field to his wife when he took horse for London. It is true he had to attend Convocation but there is little doubt that he left impetuously without any formal farewells, and that the accession of Anne (1702) extricated him from an intolerable position in which his own hot temper had placed him.

---

[1] It is interesting to remember that the mischievous ghost 'Old Jeffrey', who disturbed the Wesley household for a time, seemed also to have the lively Jacobite sympathies of Susanna and some of her children.

On that occasion Susanna might have used the words of her son, John, when his shrewish wife had left him. *Non dimisi non revocabo* (I did not send her away. I shall not call her back.) She did not send Samuel away and she made no move to bring him back. He left and returned of his own accord. This incident apart, we do not know of any quarrel which threatened the very security of the family. Incidentally the return of Samuel did not cause her to modify her views. Many years later (1709) she wrote:

'Whether they did well, in driving a prince from his hereditary throne, I leave to their own consciences to determine; though I cannot tell how to think that a king of England can ever be accountable to his subjects for any maladministrations or abuse of power; but as he derives his power from God, so to Him only he must answer for his using it. But still I make a great difference between those who entered into the confederacy against their prince, and those, who, knowing nothing of the contrivance, and so consequently not consenting to it, only submitted to the present government.'

But we do not depend only on the absence of records. Our knowledge of their Christian characters, the family prayers, and the religious discipline characteristic of them both, makes it hard to imagine violent quarrels in that house of warm and unaffected piety. But the strongest presumptive evidence is in Susanna's equable and tranquil disposition. She would quietly hold her ground but she would do it without fuss or flurry. Samuel might dramatize his grievances but Susanna would never help to make the scene. That is why though they differed so often they did not brawl. With Susanna it was not possible. More real and significant than their apparent disagreements was the love which was ever the solid and enduring basis of their marriage. In Samuel's case this was allied to a deep unstinted admiration for his wife's great qualities. Susanna on the other hand saw him with eyes disconcertingly clear. She knew his faults but she could just as fairly estimate his virtues and his strength. If respect goes, the bloom of love has vanished; but Susanna held him in respect and flew to his defence if any seemed too lightly to regard his worth.

Samuel Wesley four years after his marriage included in his *Life of Christ* a remarkable tribute to Susanna.

> She graced my humble roof, and blest my life,
> Blest me by a far greater name than wife;

Yet still I bore an undisputed sway,
Nor was't her task, but pleasure, to obey;
Scarce thought, much less could act, what I denied,
In our low house there was no room for pride;
Nor need I e'er direct what still was right,
She studied my convenience and delight.
Nor did I for her care ungrateful prove,
But only used my power to show my love.
Whate'er she asked I gave, without reproach or grudge,
For still she reason asked, and I was judge.
All my commands, requests at her fair hands,
And her requests to me were all commands.
To others thresholds rarely she'd incline.
Her house her pleasure was, and she was mine;
Rarely abroad, or never, but with me,
Or when by pity called, or charity.

During his imprisonment in Lincoln Castle (25th June 1705) he wrote to Archbishop Sharpe of his wife's fortitude.

'I thank God, my wife was pretty well recovered and was churched some days before I was taken from her; and I hope she will be able to look after my family, if they do not turn them out of doors as they have often threatened to do. One of my biggest concerns was my being forced to have my poor lambs in the midst of so many wolves. But the great Shepherd is able to provide for them and to preserve them. My wife bears it with that courage which becomes her, and which I expected from her.'

It was during this six months' imprisonment that Susanna in her great distress and poverty was still willing to send her husband such jewellery as she possessed. She even parted with her wedding ring. With equal magnanimity of spirit Samuel returned them to her again. He would not avail himself of a gift given at such great cost.

In one of his letters to his son, Samuel, at Westminster School (September 1706) the Rector wrote at length of the woman to whom he owed so much.

You know what you owe to one of the best of mothers. Perhaps you may have read of one of the Ptolemies, who chose the name of Philometer, as a more glorious title than if he had assumed that of his predecessor, Alexander. And it would be an honest and virtuous ambition in you to attempt to imitate him, for which you have so much reason. Often reflect on the tender and peculiar love which your dear mother has always expressed toward you; the deep affliction of both body and mind which she underwent for you, both before and after your birth; the particular care she took of your education when she struggled with so many pains and infirmities; and, above all, the wholesome and sweet motherly advice and counsel which she has often given you to fear God, to take care of your soul as well as of your learning, and to shun all vicious and bad examples. You will, I verily believe, remember that these obligations of gratitude, love, and obedience, and the expressions of them are not confined to your tender years, but must last to the very close of life, and, even after that, render her memory most dear and precious to you.

You will not forget to evidence this by supporting and comforting her in her age, if it please God that she should ever attain to it (though I doubt she will not), and doing nothing which may justly displease or grieve her, or show you unworthy of such a mother. You will endeavour to repay her prayers for you by doubling yours for her; and, above all things, to live such a virtuous and religious life that she may find that her care and love have not been lost upon you, but that we may all meet in heaven.

In short, reverence and love her as much as you will, which I hope will be as much as you can. For though I should be jealous of any other rival in your heart, yet I will not be jealous of her; the more duty you pay her, and the more frequently and kindly you write to her, the more you will please your affectionate father,

SAMUEL WESLEY.

There is a remarkable letter of Susanna which shows how on her part she regarded Samuel. It has the more value because it was written toward the close of her married life (20th January 1722) when she had a lengthy period of their marriage under review. The Rector had been entrusted by Susanna's brother, Samuel Annesley, with some business transactions with the East India Company. It was obviously a wrong choice and the business was badly handled. From India Annesley wrote an angry letter to Susanna rebuking his brother-in-law in violent terms. Susanna replied in her usual calm and dignified manner, not excusing but explaining her husband's conduct. And first she made plain her loyalty.

'Where he lives, I will live, and where he dies, will I die and there will I be buried. God do so unto me and more also if aught but death part him and me.'

After recounting the unavoidable misfortunes that had overtaken the family, she concluded her letter by answering her brother's charges. It is her very moderation in defence that carries conviction. She will not claim her husband to be other than he is but she will not have him falsely blamed. And since to clear a man from unjust attack is not to set him forth as he is, she will seize the opportunity to speak of his learning, his great preaching ability, and his manifest fitness for a better office.

'My brother has one invincible obstacle to my business, his distance from London.'—Sir, you may please to remember, I put you in mind of this long since.—'Another hindrance, I think he is too zealous for the party he fancies in the right; and has unluckily to do with the opposite faction.'—Whether those you employ are factious or not, I'll not determine; but very sure I am, Mr. Wesley is not so; he is zealous in a good cause, as every one ought to be, but the farthest from being a party man of any man in the world.—'Another remora is, these matters are out of his way.'—That is a remora indeed, and ought to have been considered on both sides before he entered on your business; for I am verily persuaded that that, and that alone, has been the cause of any mistakes or inadvertency he has been guilty of, and the true reason why God has not blessed him with desired success. —'He is apt to rest upon deceitful promises.' But it is a right-hand error, and I hope God will forgive us all.—'He wants Mr. Eaton's thrift'—This I can readily believe.—'He is not fit for worldly business.'—This I likewise assent to, and must own I was mistaken when I did think him fit for it: my own experience hath since convinced me that he is one of those who, our Saviour saith, 'are not so wise in their generation as the children of this world'. And did I not know that Almighty Wisdom hath views and ends, in fixing the bounds of our habitation, which are out of our ken, I should think it a thousand pities that a man of his brightness, and rare endowments of learning and useful knowledge, in relation to the church of God, should be confined to an obscure corner of the country, where his talents are buried, and he determined to a way of life for which he is not so well qualified as I could wish;' . . .

There is here not only love but pride finding forthright expression. Samuel obviously ought to have had high preferment and if the Tories had retained power he doubtless would have done so. But in an age in which Church preferment was so much determined by political loyalties, the long ascendancy of the Whigs was fatal to Samuel's chances. He was so completely at home in town life and so little adapted to the country that he could well have been forgiven had he given way to complaint and repining. Yet he never grumbled as through the long years wore on and he still was called to minister to a difficult clannish people. Here he had come and here he would faithfully work.

It was left to Susanna to express the plain fact that Samuel had uncommon abilities which demanded a wider setting for his work.

The children as they grew were deprived of many things, but at least they grew up against the secure unchanging background of their parent's mutual love.

The Rector of Epworth was a bonny fighter. It might well be said of him that 'in the fell clutch of circumstance he neither winced nor cried aloud'. In equal measure this was true of Susanna. She had to contend in the first half of their married life with an ever-increasing family which had to be supported on totally inadequate resources. To the end of her life the shadow of poverty and debt spread darkly over her path. When the Rector had died and the son had discharged the remaining debts, there was nothing left for Susanna. Her remaining years had to be spent with one or other of her children and she depended upon them for support. She had no social life outside her family and no friendships of those like minded to make some change in the even tenor of her way. She had not the same opportunities as her husband to make occasional journeys to London, until her days at Epworth were over, and she could move about more freely.

But beyond a good-humoured sigh at her husband's manifest inability to be a farmer, she gave herself without complaint to the superintendence of the household and the management of affairs. Nor was there any boredom in her life. No one can be bored who has a full day. The bored are those with much leisure and little occupation. Neither of these conditions could apply to a woman who looked after a husband, many children, a large rectory, and who took an increasing interest in the life of the parish.

Her salient characteristic was her independence of mind and her initiative of spirit. One striking instance both of her ability as a speaker and her power to make quick decisions has come down to us. When the Rector left for the Convocation in 1710 he arranged for a locum tenens who proved to be entirely unsatisfactory. The charge against him was not only that he failed to preach on the great truths of the Christian religion but that he contented himself with a plea for the observance of certain ethical standards. This might have been tolerated if it were not for the references to Samuel. For when it was known that the Rector was heavily in debt and sermon after sermon was concerned with the necessity of paying debts it is not to be wondered that people imagined that an indirect attack was being made on Wesley.

It must have been particularly galling to Mrs. Wesley, always the most loyal of wives, that her children and servants should be obliged to listen to discourses at once unedifying and mischievous.

The locum only held service on Sunday mornings and Susanna began to hold her own services on Sunday evenings outside church hours in the rectory kitchen. The service was intended for the children and servants, but quickly interest grew. A servant asked permission for his parents to come, and soon forty or fifty were assembled for worship each Sunday evening. By the end of January 1711 it was reckoned that two hundred were attending. This, of course, in view of the size of the kitchen, was an over-generous estimate, but certainly the place was so crowded that many stood and others were unable to gain admittance.

Susanna's practice was to lead in the singing of psalms, to read prayers, and then to deliver a short sermon taken usually from the well-stocked library of the Rector. The services must have been the more impressive because she had been spiritually quickened by reading a stirring account of the self-denying labours of two Danish missionaries. It was directly under the inspiration of this book that she took up her private interviews with her children, and so conducted the Sunday evening worship that her loving spirit set others on fire. Families hitherto most irregular in their church attendance came with diligence. But the greatest result was in the new and friendly spirit which everywhere became evident. Susanna was able to say in a letter to her husband that the meeting had 'wonderfully conciliated the minds of this people toward us so that we now live in the greatest amity imaginable'. She said they had reformed their behaviour on the Lord's Day. She added as a further justification for her action that this was the only way open to her of reaching the people and doing them good.

But the Rector was not easy to convince. Shortly after his wife's letter came a furious epistle from the curate, Mr. Inman. He complained not only of the irregularity but of the fact that Mrs. Wesley was having more people at her services than came to the parish church in the morning. There were two or three other people directly influenced by Inman who made similar protests.

The good Rector was perplexed. It was in the first place an

unknown procedure for a service to be taken by a woman. When no precedents can be called, any man might naturally feel uneasy. But the particular aggravation in this instance was that the meeting looked unpleasantly like a Dissenting conventicle which of all things the Rector abhorred. It also seemed to jeopardize the regular worship in the parish church.

Mrs. Wesley had a sufficient answer on both counts.

I shall not inquire how it was possible that you should be prevailed on by the senseless clamour of two or three of the worst of your parish to condemn what you so lately approved. But I shall tell you my thoughts in as few words as possible. I do not hear of more than three or four persons who are against our meeting, of whom Inman is the chief. He and Whiteley, I believe, may call it a conventicle; but we hear no outcry here, nor has any one said a word against it to me. And what does their calling it a conventicle signify? Does it alter the nature of the thing? Or do you think that what they say is a sufficient reason to forbear a thing that has already done much good, and may, by the blessing of God, do much more? If its being called a conventicle, by those who know in their conscience they misrepresent it, did really make it one, what you say would be somewhat to the purpose; but it is plain in fact that this one thing has brought more people to church than ever anything did in so short a time. We used not to have above twenty or twenty-five at evening service; whereas we now have between two and three hundred, which are more than ever came before to hear Inman in the morning.

As to the charge that the Parish Church might suffer, she defended herself by vigorous attack. She showed that the meetings were purely religious and could not possibly be harmful.

If I and my children went a-visiting on Sunday nights, or if we admitted of impertinent visits, as too many do who think themselves good Christians, perhaps it would be thought no scandalous practice, though in truth it would be so. Therefore why any should reflect upon you, let your station be what it will because your wife endeavours to draw people to the Church, and to restrain them by reading and other persuasions from their profanation of God's most holy day, I cannot conceive. But if any should be so mad as to do it, I wish you would not regard it. For my part, I value no censure on this account. I have long since shook hands with the world, and I heartily wish I had never given them more reason to speak against me.

She closed her vindication with a noble appeal to her husband.

Now, I beseech you, weigh all these things in an impartial balance. On the one side, the honour of Almighty God, the doing much good to many souls, and the friendship of the best among whom we live; on the other—if folly, impiety, and vanity may abide in the scale against so ponderous a weight—the senseless objections of a few scandalous persons, laughing at us, and censuring us as precise and hypocritical. And when you have duly considered all things, let me have your positive determination. I need not tell you the consequences if you determine to put an end to our meeting. You may easily perceive what prejudice it may raise in the minds of these people against Inman especially, who has had so little wit as to speak publicly against it. I can now keep them to the church; but if it be laid aside, I doubt they will never go to hear him more, at least those who come from the lower end of the town. But if this be continued till you return, which now will not be long, it may please God that their hearts may be so changed by that time, that they may love and delight in His public worship, so as never to neglect it more. If you do, after all, think fit to dissolve this assembly, do not tell me that you desire me to do it, for that will not satisfy my conscience: but send me your positive command, in such full and express terms, as may absolve me from all guilt and punishment for neglecting this opportunity of doing good, when you and I shall appear before the great and awful tribunal of our Lord Jesus Christ.

And then there was the final objection about her sex to answer. She could hardly be expected to champ and snort at the bare suggestion of this being a hindrance. She belonged to her own century. Nevertheless, her reply was strong and effective even though she felt the objection had some force. 'There is one thing,' she wrote, 'about which I am much dissatisfied; that is, their being present at family prayers. I do not speak of any concern I am under barely because so many are present: for those who have the honour of speaking to the great and holy God, need not be ashamed to speak before the whole world; but because of my sex, I doubt if it would be proper for me to present the prayers of the people to God. Last Sunday I fain would have dismissed them before prayers; but they begged so earnestly to stay I durst not deny them.' The Rector had suggested that perhaps a man could have read the sermon, but Susanna said that no man among them could have done so without spelling a good part of it, and that could not possible edify the rest. She added that her voice was the only one in the family strong enough to be heard by such a number of people!

She refused to discontinue the services except at the express command of the Rector. But he would have been a brave man to issue such an order after the tone and spirit of her letters. He must have heard in reading her letters a very bugle note of defiance. Such a woman was not to be resisted.

Samuel must have appreciated his wife's action more completely when he heard Inman preach from a text the Rector himself had supplied: 'Without faith it is impossible to please God.' 'Friends,' began the curate, 'faith is a most excellent virtue and it produces other virtues also. In particular it enables a man to pay his debts.' And then for fifteen minutes he developed that single theme. Small wonder that, confronted by his curate's incapacity, and the discernible fruit of his wife's devoted work, the Rector could find no single word of blame. On his return the gatherings at the parsonage were discontinued and the full services resumed at the church. But lasting good had been effected. The old strained and bitter relations between the people and the Rector had gone. They were friendly and disposed to greater friendliness. It was these services that marked a new and better spirit in the parish of Epworth. It was indeed the end of a cloudy, rain-swept epoch, and the beginning of a more fruitful and happy relationship between the shepherd and his flock.

Chapter Four

SUSANNA THE MOTHER

WE OWE much to John Wesley's inquisitiveness. Curiosity may have killed the cat but it makes the well-informed man. The Journals are a window opening out on the eighteenth century. They are as interesting to the historian, the sociologist, and the plain man, as they are to the student of Church history. Here is the rapidly changing life of the age unfolding itself before our eyes. Wesley was not only intensely interested in people, in their manners and customs and habits, but in the natural features of the countryside, in the growth of the new industrial towns, and in the arts and letters of the day.

One aspect of this consuming interest in life and men was his inveterate desire to be able to give a reason for everything. It was a trait which his parents noticed with quiet satisfaction and not a little amusement. But John, so far from being the somewhat wild emotional preacher which some foolish persons have imagined him to be, was very much a child of the Age of Reason. He did not like controversy with a bitter personal edge, but he delighted in the cut-and-thrust of argument and discussion: not the *argumentum ad hominem*, but the *argumentum ad rem*. There were indeed few more highly skilled controversialists and none so far from rancour and venom. Even those who deny that he was a great theologian cannot deny that he was a truly great logician. His natural gift of clear logical thinking was incessantly sharpened by study and practice and his sermons and treatises alike show this power of following a thesis through to its seemingly inevitable conclusion.

Now it was precisely this thirst for knowledge that led him repeatedly to beg his mother to send him a detailed account of her method of education. To John's pertinacity we owe the famous letter in which, at last yielding to his request, she set down fully the principles she had followed in educating her children. It is only fair to Susanna that she be allowed to tell her story in her own words. The many summaries that have been given can only partly reflect the spirit of the letter and the attitude of mind which is conveyed in it.

EPWORTH,
July 24, 1732.

DEAR SON,

According to your desire, I have collected the principal rules I observed in educating my family.

The children were always put into a regular method of living, in such things as they were capable of, from their birth; as in dressing and undressing, changing their linen, etc. The first quarter commonly passed in sleep. After that, they were, if possible, laid into their cradle awake, and rocked to sleep; and so they were kept rocking till it was time for them to awake. This was done to bring them to a regular course of sleeping, which at first was three hours in the morning, and three in the afternoon; afterwards two hours, till they needed none at all. When turned a year old (and some before), they were taught to fear the rod, and to cry softly, by which means they escaped abundance of correction which they might otherwise have had; and that most odious noise of the crying of children was rarely heard in the house, but the family usually lived in as much quietness as if there had not been a child among them.

As soon as they were grown pretty strong, they were confined to three meals a day. At dinner their little table and chairs were set by ours, where they could be overlooked; and they were suffered to eat and drink (small beer) as much as they would, but not to call for anything. If they wanted aught, they used to whisper to the maid that attended them, who came and spake to me; and as soon as they could handle a knife and fork, they were set to our table. They were never suffered to choose their meat, but always made to eat such things as were provided for the family. Mornings, they always had spoonmeat; sometimes at nights. But whatever they had, they were never permitted at those meals to eat of more than one thing, and of that sparingly enough. Drinking or eating between meals was never allowed unless in case of sickness, which seldom happened. Nor were they suffered to go into the kitchen to ask anything of the servants, when they were at meat: if it was known they did so, they were certainly beat, and the servants severely reprimanded.

At six, as soon as family prayer was over, they had their supper; at seven, the maid washed them, and, beginning at the youngest, she undressed and got them all to bed by eight; at which time she left them in their several rooms awake, for there was no such thing allowed of, in our house, as sitting by a child till it fell asleep.

They were so constantly used to eat and drink what was given them, that when any of them was ill, there was no difficulty in making them take the most unpleasant medicine, for they durst not refuse it, though some of them would presently throw it up. This I mention to show that a person may be taught to take anything, though it be never so much against his stomach.

In order to form the minds of children, the first thing to be done is to conquer their will, and bring them to an obedient temper. To inform the understanding is a work of time; and must with children proceed by slow degrees, as they are able to bear it; but the subjecting the will is a thing which must be done at once, and the sooner the better; for by neglecting timely correction, they will contract a stubbornness and obstinacy which are hardly ever after conquered, and never without using such severity as would be as painful to me as to the child. In the esteem of the world they pass for kind and indulgent, whom I call cruel parents; who permit their children to get habits which they know must be afterwards broken. Nay, some are so stupidly fond, as in sport to teach their children to do things which in a while after they have severely beaten them for doing. When a child is corrected it must be conquered, and this will be no hard matter to do, if it be not grown headstrong by too much indulgence. And when the will of a child is totally subdued, and it is brought to revere and stand in awe of the parents, then a great many childish follies and inadvertences may be passed by. Some should be overlooked and taken no notice of, and others mildly reproved; but no wilful transgression ought ever to be forgiven children, without chastisement, less or more, as the nature and circumstances of the offence may require. I insist upon conquering the will of children betimes, because this is the only strong and rational foundation of a religious education, without which both precept and example will be ineffectual. But when this is thoroughly done, then a child is capable of being governed by the reason and piety of its parents, till its own understanding comes to maturity, and the principles of religion have taken root in the mind.

I cannot yet dismiss this subject. As self-will is the root of all sin and misery, so whatever cherishes this in children insures their after wretchedness and irreligion; whatever checks and mortifies it promotes their future happiness and piety. This is still more evident if we farther consider that religion is nothing else than the doing the will of God, and not our own; that the one grand impediment to our temporal and eternal happiness being this self-will, no indulgence of it can be trivial, no denial unprofitable. Heaven or hell depends on this alone. So that the parent who studies to subdue it in his child, works together with God in the renewing and saving a soul. The parent who indulges it does devil's work; makes religion impracticable, salvation unattainable, and does all that in him lies to damn his child, soul and body, for ever.

Our children were taught, as soon as they could speak, the Lord's prayer, which they were made to say at rising and bedtime constantly; to which, as they grew bigger, were added a short prayer for their parents, and some collects, a short catechism, and some portion of Scripture, as their memories could bear. They were very early made to distinguish the Sabbath from other days, before they could well speak or go. They were as soon taught to be still at family prayers, and to ask a blessing immediately after, which they used to do by signs, before they could kneel or speak.

They were quickly made to understand they might have nothing they cried for, and instructed to speak handsomely for what they wanted. They were not suffered to ask even the lowest servant for aught, without saying, Pray give me such a thing; and the servant was chid if she ever let them omit that word.

Taking God's name in vain, cursing and swearing, profaneness, obscenity, rude ill-bred names, were never heard among them; nor were they ever permitted to call each other by their proper names without the addition of brother or sister.

There was no such thing as loud talking or playing allowed of; but every one was kept close to business for the six hours of school. And it is almost incredible what a child may be taught in a quarter of a year by a vigorous application, if it have but a tolerable capacity and good health. Kezzy excepted, all could read better in that time than the most of women can do as long as they live. Rising out of their places, or going out of the room, was not permitted, except for good cause; and running into the yard, garden, or street, without leave, was always esteemed a capital offence.

For some years we went on very well. Never were children in better order. Never were children better disposed to piety, or in more subjection to their parents, till that fatal dispersion of them after the fire, into several families. In those they were left at full liberty to converse with servants, which before they had always been restrained from; and to run abroad to play with any children, good or bad. They soon learned to neglect a strict observance of the Sabbath; and got knowledge of several songs and bad things, which before they had no notion of. That civil behaviour which made them admired when they were at home, by all who saw them, was in a great measure lost; and a clownish accent and many rude ways were learnt, which were not reformed without some difficulty.

When the house was rebuilt, and the children all brought home, we entered on a strict reform; and then was begun the custom of singing psalms at beginning and leaving school, morning and evening. Then also that of a general retirement at five o'clock was entered upon, when the oldest took the youngest that could speak, and the second the next, to whom they read the psalms for the day, and a chapter in the New Testament: as in the morning they were directed to read the psalms, and a chapter in the Old; after which they went to their private prayers, before they got their breakfast, or came into the family.

There were several bye-laws observed among us. I mention them here because I think them useful.

1. It had been observed that cowardice and fear of punishment often lead children into lying; till they get a custom of it which they cannot leave. To prevent this, a law was made that whoever was charged with a fault, of which they were guilty, if they would ingenuously confess it, and promise to amend, should not be beaten. This rule prevented a great deal of lying; and would have done more, if one in the family would have observed it. But he could not be prevailed on, and therefore was often imposed upon by false colours and equivocations, which none would have used but one, had they been kindly dealt with; and some in spite of all would always speak truth plainly.

2. That no sinful action, as lying, pilfering[1] at church or on the Lord's-day, disobedience, quarrelling, etc., should ever pass unpunished.

3. That no child should be ever chid or beat twice for the same fault; and that, if they amended, they should never be upbraided with it afterwards.

4. That every signal act of obedience, especially when it crossed upon their own inclinations, should be always commended, and frequently rewarded, according to the merits of the case.

5. That if ever any child performed an act of obedience, or did anything with an intention to please, though the performance was not well, yet the obedience and intention should be kindly accepted, and the child with sweetness directed how to do better for the future.

6. That propriety be inviolably preserved; and none suffered to invade the property of another in the smallest matter, though it were but of the value of a farthing, or a pin; which they might not take from the owner without, much less against, his consent. This rule can never be too much inculcated on the minds of children; and from the want of parents or governors doing it as they ought, proceeds that shameful neglect of justice which we may observe in the world.

7. That promises be strictly observed; and a gift once bestowed, and so the right passed away from the donor be not resumed, but left to the disposal of him to whom it was given; unless it were conditional, and the condition of the obligation not performed.

8. That no girl be taught to work till she can read very well; and then that she be kept to her work with the same application, and for

[1] Pilfering is an unhappy word and is contradicted by rule 6. The original word or the word Susanna intended was probably 'playing'.

the same time, that she was held to in reading. This rule also is much to be observed; for the putting children to learn sewing before they can read perfectly is the very reason why so few women can read fit to be heard, and never to be well understood.

Before any estimate can be made of this teaching, Susanna must be set against her historical background. More than most she has suffered from uncritical adulation. Even the Rector has been made to decrease that she might increase, and his faults have so often been magnified that she might appear the more remarkable. This has provoked its own reaction. Marjorie Bowen has represented her system as that of a stern joyless woman wearied by excessive confinements. A more authoritative historical writer has conceded that Susanna was not a sadist, but startles the reader even by suggesting the idea. She does declare that Susanna seemed harsh and cruel even though she took immense pains over the education of her family. And she adds most unkindly: 'We are not surprised to hear that thirteen of her nineteen children died before they had reached years of discretion.'[1] Dr. Whiteley, writing more moderately, says that Mrs. Wesley's method was far and away harder than the old horn book of the Tudors.

Now judged by any modern standards Susanna Wesley's discipline seems unnecessarily severe. In at least three respects it is at variance with our present educational theories. The teaching was commonly from nine to twelve and two to five, and for children of five that seems overlong. As they grew older it was much less severe: indeed it was light compared with the hours of instruction in many schools of that day. In many Grammar Schools work began at six and continued till eight when there was a half-hour break for breakfast. Then work recommenced until twelve, and in the afternoon from two to five.

Mrs. Wesley's use of the rod has roused the ire of modern critics. She evidently used it before the children could be held morally responsible for their actions. At times she said it was used before they were a year old; and always after one year they were taught to fear the rod. They were not even permitted the luxury of a decent cry. This indeed seems more sinister than anything else. If they were even too frightened to cry except softly their submission must have been abject.

[1] *The English Child in the Eighteenth Century*, Rosamund Bayne-Powell (1939), p. 6. The remark in any case is not accurate.

Closely connected with this wrong use of corporal punishment was her theory, so abhorrent to the twentieth-century mind, that the wills of children must be broken, and the child not only corrected but conquered.

If we had only these three facts upon which to judge Susanna Wesley we might conclude her to be unnaturally harsh. The sober truth is, however, not so highly coloured. She belonged to her own century and not to ours, and viewed in that way the indictment against her loses much of its sting. It was of course a brutal age: the age of Tyburn and Newgate, of floggings and irons and transportation. Some parents spoilt their children by overmuch petting and indulgence. Southey in his childhood sixty years later was rarely allowed out lest he should get wet or dirty or tear his clothes. In some wealthy families every whim of the child was satisfied even to the provision of servants specially to attend on them. Susanna Wesley has caustic references to those parents 'who pass for kind and indulgent, whom I call cruel'. 'Some', she said, 'are so stupidly fond that in sport they will teach their children to do things which later they severely beat them for doing.'

In some cases, however, children were brutally treated. Mary Wollstonecraft's father used regularly to flog his young daughters. And even those who avoided the extremes of softness and brutality, believed in the hardening process for the young. Children who stooped were forced to wear iron collars round the neck with back bands strapped on the shoulders. Flogging was common both in private and in public schools. There were even schools as horrible as Charles Dickens described in Nicholas Nickleby. Conditions were similar both in Dame's Schools and Charity Schools. Both Shenstone and Crabbe in their poetic descriptions of such places vividly describe the active use made of the birch rod. Mrs. Wesley was only using the accepted means of discipline in her use of the rod and she would claim that she was avoiding the extremes of softness and severity. The children were never beaten twice for the same fault, and if they freely confessed to any misdeed they were not punished at all. Whenever they did anything meritorious they were commended and suitably rewarded. The discipline may to us seem severe, but it was enlightened and moderate compared with the ordinary practice of the day.

The more serious charge is that the appeal in her method was to fear and not to love. That was inevitable when her avowed intention was to destroy their self-will and conquer her children. But another century was to elapse before such ideas were generally questioned. The theory of education was not seriously considered in Susanna's day. Dr. Johnson admitted the importance of Milton and Locke but thought that Milton's plan was impracticable and never tried, whilst Locke's plan though often tried was very imperfect.[1] Milton's plan was too academic to have any considerable influence. As Mr. A. H. Body has said in his *John Wesley and Education*, it necessitates a college of Miltons to make it workable. Locke's plan was widely known, but like all innovators he suffered at first by being too far ahead of the march of opinion. He had his followers, but parents and teachers were apt to consider him eccentric and a little odd. His praise of fresh air and sunlight, of outdoor sports including swimming, and his plea for loose clothing must have seemed highly novel and even dangerous to his contemporaries. It is the heresy of one age that often becomes the orthodoxy of the next. He had no respect for the average parent as a suitable mentor for the young, and little more for the teaching given in the schools of the day. That is why he desired, whenever possible, tutors for families. These men were not only to be good scholars, but cultivated men of the world, enlightened and sympathetic and able to impart not only knowledge but an understanding of life. He frowned upon corporal punishment for he argued that children hate the things that are whipped into them. Breaking children's wills would, he thought, produce 'low-spirited morbid creatures who would be useless for the active business of living'.

These exciting ideas only slowly won their way. Rousseau's *Émil* was written long after Mrs. Wesley had died but his almost unrestrained advocacy of the rights of the child would never have appealed to her. Émil grew to twelve years without knowing scarcely the inside of a book. As a matter of fact this idea of the noble savage which lay behind all Rousseau's writings has influenced English political theorists more than educationists. For apart from isolated experimenters it has always been felt in England that a child left to nature would be like a garden without a gardener. By all means accept Rousseau's dictum that a child must be loved and understood and indulged in its sports and pleasures, but this must not be interpreted so generously that there is no firm training

[1] *Treatise on Education*, John Milton. *Essay concerning Education*, John Locke (1694)—an expansion of *Some Thoughts on Education* (1693).

and no reasonable discipline. John Wesley said of *Émil* that the new ideas in it were 'lighter than vanity'. He was influenced by the educational theories of William Law and by the Moravians, but these were not known to his mother.

Susanna cannot then be accused of lagging behind the educational theory of her day. At the time when her children were young she was rather in advance of that theory which was implicit in the contemporary practice of education. She was in any case influenced by theological dogma rather than theories of education. To believe literally and seriously in the fall of man was to believe not in the natural innocence of children but their natural corruption. Wesley nowhere adopts an acceptance of the doctrine of total depravity more fully than in his rigorous views on childhood. In his sermon 'The Education of Children' he did not hesitate to say that children ought to be taught that 'in pride, passion, and revenge they are now like the devil; and that in foolish desires and grovelling appetites they are like the beasts of the field'. Wesley said that by nature man worships himself, and he quoted the dictum of Dryden's hero: 'Myself am King of me.' In accordance with this philosophy Wesley argued that every man is born with pride, love of the world, deviation from truth; neither is any man born just nor merciful.

It was natural that with this grim and forbidding view of the child Wesley should desire the will of the child to be broken in order that it might first be subject to the parent, and then to the will of God. In all this he was only faithfully following his mother's precept and example. If their argument could be expressed in Biblical terms they would doubtless say that the child must be under law before he can be under grace. He must first learn to obey from compulsion that later he may obey from love. It is the farthest extreme from Rousseau's view that the child was naturally good and would only suffer from interference. In our day we lean on neither view but profit from the truth that lies in both.

There is no mention of toys in Susanna's household and it may light up John Wesley's comment that some parents foolishly give their children 'comfits, gingerbread, raisins, and whatever fruit they have a mind to. They feed in them the desire of the eyes by giving them pretty playthings, glittering toys, shining buckles or buttons, fine clothes, red shoes, laced hats, needless ornaments, as ribands, necklaces, and ruffles'. The wise parent, said Wesley (doubtless remembering his mother), will not suffer any other person to give them what she will not give them herself. If anything is offered it will be civilly refused, or else received and laid by. It seems depressing, and arouses sympathy for the children of the Epworth Parsonage, but it is not the complete picture.

The children were definitely not cowed. Susanna may have broken their wills but she did not break their spirits. Indeed, terminology may be misleading. For Susanna, 'breaking' did not mean the crushing of their individuality, but the refusal to let them have their own way, and the rigid insistence that she knew better than they what was in their proper interest. Locke had spoken of parents who 'by humouring and cockering them when little corrupt the principles of nature in their children'. They give him 'what he cries for and do what he pleases'. No wonder, said Locke, that such children grow up 'untoward and perverse'. In Susan Sibbald's words such children became 'perfect pests'. Susanna did at least avoid the possibility of her children becoming spoilt and a general nuisance to society.

It must also be remarked that they never later expressed any distaste of their early schooling. On the contrary, John at least was so impressed that it coloured all his views on education and it remained for him the model of what family training might be. This had its unfortunate effect for it led him to adopt the same principle for his Kingswood School. The boys at an early age left for Public Schools but the girls had no such advantages. And yet we know how high spirited and cultured they were! If they were the products of such a system of teaching, then both in its effect on the mind and character the discipline could not have been so oppressive as it might seem on paper. The tree is known by its fruits and no final judgement on Susanna's method can overlook the results that she obtained.

Educational theory and practice have advanced greatly in the two hundred odd years that separate us from Susanna and her domestic school. There is much to criticize in her views which were so largely those of her age. But is not the final verdict one of complete admiration for a woman who against such odds accomplished so much?

She had a large and ever-increasing family. She was never really well in health. For half of each year, as the Rector said, she was ailing. She had natural as well as man-made calamities with which to contend. She was surrounded by a people ignorant in the main, and ill-disposed. She had a continual and unavailing fight against poverty and a mountain of debts, yet she managed to gather the children round her and to instruct them. They were not only taught to read and write with great ease and skill; they were given a grounding in all the subjects that would give them a well-furnished mind. She had no knowledge of the classics, but the boys for whom alone she thought it would be useful, had the help and instruction of their father; teaching and advice that continued until his death. But Susanna not only taught her children collectively; she set apart a period each week to instruct and assist them individually. It must have been a strengthening and inspiring experience for them all. It was certainly one of the most formative influences on John's life. To the end he remembered what he had heard and received from his mother in those times set apart for him.

Locke, thinking of the brutal methods and the low standard of instruction in contemporary schools, had suggested for rich families the engaging of a tutor with gifts and graces. Samuel in his poverty could not afford such a tutor, and with such a wife he had no need of one. The lovely accomplished and gracious woman was a born teacher who, added to knowledge, had the gift of infinite patience. On one occasion when her husband was an interested spectator in the school he counted the number of times she repeated the same thing to a child. At last he could restrain himself no longer: 'I wonder at your patience; you have told that child twenty times the same thing.' Quick came the reply: 'If I had satisfied myself by mentioning it only nineteen times, I should have lost all my labour. It was the twentieth time that crowned it.'

Her skill and love and patience were repaid by the responsiveness and aptitude of the children. Even more she gained their love and lasting respect. If for a time they felt they were under law they quickly passed to the condition of being under grace. She gave them not only knowledge but a zeal for more; no merely forced obedience could have accomplished that. She survived the acid test of the good teacher that when left to themselves, freed from her control, they still had a great love of sound learning.

In all our history when in any domestic school have there been such pupils and when has there been such a teacher? Wisdom is justified of her children.

As the children grew up they had the nursery, the yard, and

the 'adjoining croft' for their games. Susanna by modern standards was unduly severe in her views on amusement but she was no enemy of innocent fun. She had no time for 'balls, plays, operas, and all such light and vain diversions', and she could not understand how any lover of God could have 'any relish for such vain amusements'. Nevertheless, she roundly turned on à Kempis for his condemnation of all mirth or pleasure as sinful or useless. It seemed to her that the 'honest but weak' man was contradicted by many direct passages of Scripture. We know that she joined with her children in card playing. It was perhaps in the recollection of these games that John Wesley declared in later years with reference to card games that though he could not do it with a clear conscience, he did not feel obliged to pass sentence on those otherwise minded.

As the children grew, their religious development became more and more Susanna's pressing concern. In addition to their attendance at family prayers and to the religious instruction she gave them as an integral part of their education, there were other special ways in which she set herself to help them. Each night of the week she set apart to see her children separately and privately about their principal concerns. 'On Monday', she said, 'I talk with Molly; on Tuesday with Hetty; Wednesday with Nancy; Thursday with Jacky; Friday with Patty; Saturday with Charles; and with Emilia and Sukey together, on Sunday.' These talks must have made a deep impression on the children. In an oft-quoted letter John Wesley referred to those evenings. 'In many things you have interceded for me and prevailed. Who knows but in this too' (renunciation of the world) 'you may be successful? If you can spare me only that little part of Thursday evening which you formally bestowed upon me in another manner, I doubt not it would be as useful now for correcting my heart, as it was then for forming my judgement.'

Another method was to instruct them as they grew older in manuals which she had specially written for their use. The first manual she prepared was destroyed in the rectory fire but she was at pains to rewrite it in 1712. The existence of God was demonstrated by the act of creation, the design and order of the world, and the constitution of man's nature. She argued with great thoroughness against the ideas of chance, or the eternity of matter, or a fortunate coherence of atoms as alternative explanations of the world and its teeming life. Her description of the divine nature and its essential attributes follows an orthodox line but is sustained by many arguments. She discussed the origin of evil and the fall of man with strict reference to the Bible account, and she stressed the necessity of a divine revelation not alone in the written word but in the Word made flesh. In her emphasis on moral virtues and the important place of reason in religion she showed herself a child of her age. Here was the strength of the Deistic position without its weakness! In her theory of innate ideas she would seem to have some knowledge of the philosophers, and almost certainly she knew her Locke. The books in the Rector's study must often have been borrowed!

But this manual was only intended to serve as an introduction to the central truths of the Christian Faith. These she felt could be best understood if she expounded the Apostles' Creed. In a letter of 13th January 1710 to Sukey she used precisely this method in discussing Christian dogma. The Wesley Historical Society's Proceedings (issued in 1898) contains Mrs. Susanna Wesley's conference with her daughter. There was a lengthy introduction dealing with the fact of sin and the need for Christ's atoning work, as well as the nature of faith in Christ as one's Saviour. The Evangelical Revival had not begun and one can hardly expect that faith would mean to Susanna what it meant to the Reformers, or later to her sons. She was content to define it as 'an assent to whatever is recorded of Christ in Holy Scripture; or is said to be delivered by him, either immediately by himself, or mediately by his prophets and apostles; or whatever may, by just inferences or natural consequences be collected from their writings'. It was a far cry from such a definition to the spirited affirmation of John Wesley. Faith 'is not barely a speculative rational thing, a cold lifeless assent, a train of ideas in the head; but also a disposition of the heart'. It was doubtless because Susanna with her neat and tidy mind felt the need for defining more precisely those truths about Christ to be found in Scripture which one must hold by faith, that she seized inevitably on the Apostles' Creed. Step by step, article by article, she worked her way through the Creed. It is only in certain instances that the originality of her mind showed itself. In her remarks on Christ she explained that the word signified anointed. Amongst the Jews, she said, prophets, priests, and kings were all anointed. This led her to discuss how appropriate were those titles when applied to Christ. As a Prophet He fully and clearly reveals the will of

God. As Priest He offers up Himself as sacrifice in our stead and on our behalf. As King He treads down sin and death and all the powers of the kingdom of darkness. In this section she briefly sketches an interesting line of thought concerning our Lord's divinity. No one can dare by any merit of his own to claim God's grace. It must ever be unmerited and free. Our righteousness is filthy rags and our works are nothing worth in the light of all God is and all He has done for us. But though the merits of the noblest and best cannot possibly avail, yet the merits of Christ are all we need to plead. They alone avail with God and by His merits we find favour. Now, argues Susanna, this is what no mere man however exalted can accomplish on our behalf. Jesus must therefore be in her words 'in a state of equality with God'. Speaking of the phrase 'His only son' she says succinctly that Jesus was equal to the Father as touching his Godhead; but inferior to the Father as touching his manhood.

In her commentary on the words 'suffered under Pontius Pilate' her graver eloquence is reminiscent of Cardinal Newman's magnificent and haunting description of all the weight and woes endured when He suffered on our account. In her concluding sentences she said He had a full prospect of all He had yet to undergo.

The conflict was not yet over, the dregs of the bitter cup still remained. He must be forsaken of His Father in the midst of His torments, which made Him thrice so earnestly repeat His petition that if it were possible that cup might pass from him. But the full complement of His sufferings we may suppose to be that He did at that time actually sustain the whole weight of that grief and sorrow which was due to the justice of God for the sins of the whole world. And this we may believe caused that inconceivable agony when His sweat was as great drops of blood falling to the ground.

And though His torments were so inexpressibly great, yet the Son of Man must suffer many things. He must be betrayed by one disciple, denied by another, and forsaken by all. And as He had suffered in His soul by the most intense grief and anguish, so He had to suffer in His body the greatest bitterness of corporeal pains, which the malice and rage of His enemies could inflict upon it. And now the Sovereign Lord and Judge of all men is haled before the tribunal of His sinful creatures: the pure and unspotted Son of God who could do no wrong, neither could guile be found in His mouth, accused by His presumptuous slaves of no less a crime than blasphemy.

In the same high eloquence she described His actual physical sufferings upon the Cross ending with the desolating cry of dereliction.

But though the corporeal pains occasioned by the thorns, the scourging, by the piercing those nervous and most sensible parts of His most sacred body, were wrought up to an inexpressible degree of torture: yet were they infinitely surpassed by the anguish of His soul when there was (but after what manner we cannot conceive) a sensible withdrawing of the comfortable presence of the Deity, which caused that loud and impassioned exclamation: 'My God, my God, why hast thou forsaken me!' And now it is finished and He who could not die but by His own voluntary act of resigning life gave up His pure and spotless life into the hands of His almighty Father.

Her observation on the descent into hell followed the orthodox reasoning of the day. He did not and could not suffer the torments of the damned, 'but He went to triumph over principalities and powers; over the realms of the kingdom of darkness, in their own sad regions of horror and despair'.

The work of the Holy Spirit she finely described as 'sanctifying our natures, illuminating our minds, rectifying our wills and affections; He who co-operateth with the word and the sacraments, and whatever else as a means of conveying grace into the soul'. Adam Clarke pointed out that in this section she anticipated the Methodist teaching on Assurance; e.g. 'It is He that leadeth us into all truth; He helpeth our infirmities, assures us of our adoption, and will be with the Holy Catholic Church to the end of the world' (*Wesley Family*, Vol. II, p. 73). She rightly linked the article on the Holy Ghost with that on the holy Catholic Church for she recognized that only by the Holy Spirit's operation can we be made aware of the fact that believers are one in Christ and that so the Church is one in Him.

When she discussed the communion of saints she made the sound and interesting point that if those guardian spirits are mindful of our preservation in this world, we may suppose them much more concerned for our eternal happiness. 'There is joy among the angels in heaven over one sinner that repenteth.' She strongly affirmed her belief that we are all members of the same mystical body; we all 'partake the same vital influence from the same head and so are united together'. And she concluded 'though their faith is consummated by vision, and their hope by present possession, yet the bond of Christian charity remains; and as we have great joy and complacency in their felicity, so no doubt they also desire and pray for us'.

It is in her treatment of the resurrection of the body, that the gulf between her century and our own yawns most widely. She had no doubt that there would be a 'general rendezvous of every particular atom which composed the several bodies of men that ever lived in the world, and each shall be restored to its proper owner, so as to make the same numerical body, the same flesh and blood, that was dissolved at death'.

She rightly observed that the words 'life everlasting' in the Apostles' Creed do not merely refer to quantity but to quality of life. She said very pertinently that if by everlasting, we only mean that we shall die no more, then the damned are on the same footing as the saints. But she said there was a qualitative difference. They are in intolerable torments. This is of course the authentic language of the orthodox of her day, and one which few in our times could use without explanation or qualification.

But her glowing interpretation of what everlasting life means for the blessed is relevant in every age. It is a solid inexpressible joy for 'eye hath not seen, nor ear heard, neither hath it entered into the heart of man to conceive, what God hath prepared for those that love him'. Since the soul will be perfectly sanctified it will not be possible to sin any more. 'All its faculties will be purified and exalted: the understanding will be filled with the beatific vision of the glorious Trinity; it will be illuminated, enlarged, and eternally employed and satisfied in the contemplation of the sublimest truths.' She said with great shrewdness that even in heaven we cannot hope to know God absolutely as He is, for only God can wholly know God as He is in His uttermost perfection of being. So that only in the divine society of the blessed Trinity is there the fullest reciprocity of love and understanding. 'But our apprehension of His being and perfection shall be clear and just and true. We shall see Him as He is, and we shall never be troubled with misapprehensions or false conceptions of Him more.' She has no doubt that what here seems dark and mysterious and difficult to reconcile with God's justice and goodness, will be explained. We shall see that we have been purified and prepared for our abode with those blessed ones who passed through the same trials before they entered into their eternal reward. Then we shall no longer have the sentiments of earth, but we shall realize that our very afflictions were our choicest mercies. 'And we shall ever adore and praise that infinite power and goodness which safely conducted the soul through the rough waves of this tempestuous ocean to the calm haven of peace and everlasting tranquillity.' 'God who gave us being, preserved us, fed and clothed us in our passage through the world, and what is infinitely more, gave His only Son to die for us, has by His grace purified us and conducted us safe to His glory. Oh blessed grace! mysterious love!'

This letter which she wrote to Sukey and used as a manual for her younger children concluded by stating that the guilt of sin and the defilement of our nature could only be dealt with by the work of conversion or regeneration in the heart by the Holy Spirit. Even then she argued that the conflict of the corrupt nature with divine grace is never finally resolved until the death is swallowed up in victory, and the mortal puts on immortality.

And so there followed a last prayer that 'the Almighty may enlighten your mind, renew and sanctify you by His Holy Spirit that you may be His child by adoption here and an heir of His blessed Kingdom hereafter'.

How far this manual, unless carefully explained by her, would be intelligible to her children is a moot point, but about the merits of the work there can be no doubt. Adam Clarke asserted that the exposition of the Creed was entirely original and both internal and external evidence would seem to justify his assertion. He believed that she erred in stating that inward sin will not be destroyed till death, and claimed that there is not one text in the Bible, fairly and honestly understood, which says we cannot be cleansed from all sin till we come to die. In this contention, however, he is wrong, and Susanna's views were sound.

Whilst by the grace of God the guilt of sin is forgiven, and the power of sin is broken, so that in acceptance of Him as Lord and Saviour we enter into a new relationship whereby in very truth we have become a new creation, dare we claim that Adam's image is now effaced? It is true that after conversion, holiness follows. Being saved, we press on to full salvation. 'Whom He justifies, He also glorifies.' The work of the Holy Spirit in the believer's heart cleans and renews as moment to moment we live in dependence upon Him. But does that imply that the corruption of 'inward sin' as distinct from voluntary transgressions is finally removed? It is a much-observed fact that the closer men get to

God the more they are conscious of their still remaining sinfulness. Paul in all his apostolic labours cried out that he was the chief of sinners. John Wesley in 1753, when he thought himself on the point of death, ordered that to prevent any 'vile panegyric' the following inscription be placed on his tombstone:

> HERE LIETH THE BODY OF JOHN WESLEY
> A BRAND PLUCKED OUT OF THE BURNING;
> WHO DIED OF A CONSUMPTION IN THE FIFTY-FIRST YEAR OF HIS AGE
> NOT LEAVING, AFTER HIS DEBTS ARE PAID,
> TEN POUNDS BEHIND HIM;
> PRAYING,
> GOD BE MERCIFUL TO ME, AN UNPROFITABLE SERVANT.

It was at a much later stage in his ministry that looking back on forty years incessant toil, he said that when he considered what he had been and suffered, he knew it would not bear the light. He could only pray

> *I, the chief of sinners, am,*
> *But Jesus died for me.*

When on one occasion he was at last persuaded to give his testimony he used his brother's hymn: 'O Thou who camest from above.' It was the language of aspiration and not of achievement. But indeed, though he rightly and consistently laid emphasis on the teaching of Christian perfection he recognized that to the last there would not be freedom from ignorance, infirmity, and temptation. He also knew that perfection in his definition of the word would not be reached by the majority of believers until death.

Charles Wesley had in earlier years seemed to suggest an entire ending of sin and a perfecting in holiness as possible to the believer now.

> *O make me all like Thee,*
> *Before I hence remove!*
> *Settle, confirm, and stablish me,*
> *And build me up in love.*
> *Let me Thy witness live,*
> *When sin is all destroyed;*
> *And then my spotless soul receive,*
> *And take me home to God.*

As the years went on, however, Charles tossed and buffeted and knowing better the workings of his heart was increasingly inclined to believe that full perfection could not be wholly achieved until hope was lost in sight. Now in this strict sense of the word Charles was doubtless right. So much John admitted when in a letter to Charles after the latter had published his *Short Hymns on Select Passages of the Holy Scripture* he said: 'I cordially assent that there is no such perfection here as you describe, at least I never met with an instance of it: and I doubt I never shall. Therefore I still think to set perfection so high is effectually to renounce it.' The argument of course was at cross purposes. Charles was thinking of the 'depths of inbred sin'. In dealing with this, faith would have to work itself out in the continual discipline of affliction, trial, and temptation. John was thinking of holiness in more positive terms as the loving God with all one's heart and soul and strength and mind, and one's neighbour as oneself. We are meant with all the saints to prove 'What is the length and breadth and height and depth of perfect love'. Perfection to him was the 'loving God with all the heart, so that every evil temper is destroyed, and every thought and word springs from and is conducted to the end by the pure love of God and our neighbour'. No one can properly deny that when holiness is expressed in these terms, it is a level of life which the individual rightly aspires to receive and progressively to enjoy. For who dare set bounds to God's grace and power?

But Susanna was thinking of perfection not in these inspired and satisfying and glowing terms, but in the later interpretation of Charles. She was thinking of the pride and unbelief that lurks within our human nature even when redeemed, and for entire deliverance from 'inward sin'; for sinlessness without a stain, she rightly declared that we must wait until at last, this corruptible will have put on incorruption.

It is unreasonable to ask that so long before the Evangelical revival she should write as a Methodist, but she wrote nothing that could be denied by her sons. She and her husband had prepared and tilled the ground. Who can marvel at the harvest?

The last treatise she wrote was an exposition of the Ten Commandments, for she said that the two were a summary of the moral law.

Another method which Susanna employed was by letter writing when her children were not gathered around her. One could often wish that the letters which have survived might have contained more gossip of the household and news of the parish. She could not bring herself to believe that the seemingly unimportant happenings of the day-to-day life in Epworth could have interest for those who had left it. There were, however, a few occasions when her letters had a strong domestic interest. Her letter to John (12th July 1731) gave a most vivid description of Samuel's accident in the horse wagon. In any case she was so eager to help advise and instruct them that smaller matters did not seem worth noting. Consequently her letters are disappointing regarded as letters, but interesting when regarded as an extension of her educational method. To the end of her life she had an absorbing interest in the spiritual development of her children.

An important letter to John written on 8th June 1725 defended the character of God against the responsibility of directly causing the misery of any man. Happiness or misery she contended is a choice which a man makes for himself, and true happiness results when a man subjects his animal to his rational nature, and both of them to God. It would seem that at this time John was troubled by certain aspects of Calvinism and sought advice from his mother.[1] In July of that same year she wrote because she found he had some scruples concerning the article on predestination, and she proceeds to maintain that the doctrine as maintained by rigid Calvinists is very shocking and ought to be utterly abhorred. She argued that God foreknew that some would attain to everlasting life, but 'this does not derogate from the glory of God's free grace, nor impair the liberty of man; nor can it with more reason be supposed that the prescience of God is the cause that so many finally perish than that our knowing the sun will rise tomorrow is the cause of its rising'.

There is a very interesting letter in which Susanna made some sane observations on the practice of preaching. She had been attempting with indifferent success to describe what love is in its essential nature, and then she turned to practical advice. You may be curious, she said, to analyse and define the passions and virtues of humankind, but let it always be for your own private satisfaction. Do not give your 'nice distinctions' in public assemblies, for they do not answer the true end of preaching which is to mend men's lives and not to fill their heads with unprofitable speculations. 'After all that can be said every affection of the soul

---

[1] See Letter of John Wesley to Susanna Wesley in *The Letters of John Wesley* (Standard Edition) Vol. I, p. 20.

is better known by experience than any description that can be given of it.' 'In a word,' she continued, 'show what are the effects of zeal rather than waste your precious opportunity in trying to define its essence' (14th May 1727). Other interesting letters of Susanna to John are dated 30th March 1734, 14th February 1735.

A letter written to John early in 1732 was remarkable for the disclosure of her physical infirmity and the sacrifice she had to make in the education of her children. She spoke of 'every member of the body being the seat of pain', and her 'innocent propensities to ease and rest' being crossed 'in every article'. In response to his request for information about her method of education she said that since his birth she had voluntarily lived a retired life in order to employ her time and care in bringing up her children. 'No one can without renouncing the world in the most literal sense observe my method: and there are few, if any, that would entirely devote above twenty years of the prime of life in hope to save the souls of their children, which they think may be saved without so much ado: for that was my principal intention, however unskilfully and unsuccessfully managed.' But even in a letter so strongly personal she moved easily into a discussion of the real presence in the Sacrament. She would not accept any magical change in the elements, but she strongly asserted her belief in Christ being 'eminently present' to impart all the benefits of His Incarnation and Passion. She concluded that no explanation could be wholly satisfactory. It was, to her, full of mystery and the only proper attitude was of wonder and adoration.

In another letter to John she wrote shrewdly on temptation, accepting the view of the heretic Clark, and arguing that one can only rejoice in temptations when they are experienced and already in great measure overcome. Otherwise, in temptations unexperienced we must pray 'Lead us not into temptation', for, said she, 'our nature is frail, our passions strong; our wills biassed, and our security generally speaking consists in avoiding temptations rather than in conquering them'.

In the same letter she warned him against overtaxing his strength and adds laconically: 'unless you take more care than you do, you will put the matter past dispute in a little time' (25th October 1732).

She received from her sons a detailed account of their meetings at Oxford and she wrote in this letter to express her full approval. 'I heartily join with your small society in all their pious and charitable actions which are intended for God's glory; and am glad to hear that Mr. Hall and Mr. Clayton have met with desired success. May you still in such works go on and prosper. Tho' absent in body I am present with you in spirit and daily recommend and commit you all to Divine Providence. You do well to wait on the bishop, because it is a point of prudence and civility; tho' (if he be a good man) I cannot think it in the power of any one to prejudice him against you.'

The extant letters to Charles are not of particular interest, but after he had written about her spiritual condition, she wrote to him what was probably her last letter. She might justifiably have been hurt by a catechism of her state in grace when her whole life provided a sufficient answer, but she actually thanked Charles for his letter believing it was 'dictated by a sincere desire for her eternal good'. She declared that 'there is too much truth in your accusations, nor do I intend to say one word in my own defence, but rather choose to refer all things to Him that knoweth all things'.

Her humility contrasted sharply with the hard dogmatic spirit of Charles Wesley's lines engraved on her tombstone. He asserted that she

> Mourned a long night of grief and fears,
> A legal night of seventy years.

The epitaph suggested that only very shortly before her death did she know an assurance of sins forgiven. It is possible that in the early flush of his evangelical conversion he judged that she did not enjoy the experience of Assurance as he had come to know it. In that sense he might feel justified in drawing the contrast between law and grace. But even on those narrower grounds the contrast is violently and grotesquely overdrawn. Her actions and correspondence alike reveal not only the true Christian, but one dependent on Christ her Saviour and consciously receiving His benefits.

What happened is that at first she could neither understand nor accept the idea of Assurance as it was being taught by her son in the first months of the Revival. So much she admitted in a letter to Samuel (8th March 1739). After all, this whirlwind campaign prosecuted with such reckless zeal must have been a little disturbing to an elderly lady who had been nurtured in a different tradition. (She began making references to her old age when she was fifty-eight years old.) She had received reports which must have perplexed her: hysterical people telling 'silly stories without rebuke'. She confessed that when Mr. George Whitefield had visited her she asked him if her sons were not making some innovations in the Church, which she much feared. Whitefield did his best to calm her, but to the quick ears of the listening woman it seemed as if he also might fall into the same condemnation. When he came to leave she silently prayed that in him 'the wisdom of the serpent might be joined to the innocence of the dove'.

She was not only influenced by exaggerated and misleading reports, but also by the attitude of Samuel, her eldest son, who heartily disliked and distrusted the course his brothers were taking. Throughout this period she had not seen her sons, nor heard their account of the great flame kindled by a spark of grace. When at last they met she was convinced that their doctrine was according to reason and Scripture. In 1739 whilst receiving the sacred elements at the hands of her son-in-law, the Rev. Westley Hall, she confessed to receiving the full assurance that she was indeed the child of God. 'While my son Hall was pronouncing these words in delivering the cup to me, "The blood of our Lord Jesus Christ which was given for thee", the words struck through my heart and I knew God for Christ's sake had forgiven me all my sins.' This explains the reference in Charles Wesley's inscription:

> *The Father then revealed His Son,*
> *Him in the broken bread made known;*
> *She knew and felt her sins forgiven,*
> *And found the earnest of her heaven.*

The change was real and she gladly identified herself with the works of her sons. Samuel was quick to hear and express his grief and astonishment in the language of outraged feelings. In a letter written to her in October 1739 he said:

John and Charles are now become so notorious the world will be curious to know when and how they were born, what schools bred at, what Colleges in Oxford and when matriculated; what degrees they took, and where and when and by whom ordained; what books they have written or published. I wish they may spare so much time as to vouchsafe a little of their story. For my own part I had much rather have them picking straw within the walls, than preaching in the area of Moorfields.

It was with exceeding concern and grief I heard you had countenanced a spreading delusion, so far as to be one of Jack's congregation. Is it not enough that I am bereft of both my brothers, but must my mother follow too? I earnestly beseech the Almighty to preserve you from joining a schism at the close of your life, as you were unfortunately engaged in one at the beginning of it. It will cost you many a protest, should you retain your integrity, as I hope to God you will. They boast of you already as a disciple. . . .

This was one of the last letters Samuel ever wrote. Methodist writers were almost inclined to regard his early death as providential. The chain of reasoning was plain. He was spared the distress of seeing his brothers move ever farther from the old established ways. The man who had complained because Whitefield would not read the Liturgy to his tatterdemalions in the field would have been horrified at the increasing irregularity in the ecclesiastical practices of brother John. The family was spared the strife of tongues, and the cleaving sword of dissension. It meant that Susanna herself was not torn between her great love of Samuel and regard for his views, and her newly found conviction that the work to which John and Charles had been called was of God and was signally blessed by Him. Henceforth with a clear and undivided mind she could devote herself to the life at the Foundery. She had instructed her children at the rectory; she had followed her boys with her letters, and now at the very end of her life she gladly waited on their ministry and gave them the benefit of her guidance and sound advice.

On her husband's death Susanna had stayed first with her daughter Emilia at Gainsborough, then with Samuel at Tiverton (September 1736), and within the year she was happily settled with her daughter and son-in-law, the Westley Halls. The man treated his wife infamously but there is nothing to indicate that Susanna saw any signs of the approaching rift. She wrote to Mrs. Berry (Samuel's mother-in-law) that 'Mr. Hall and his wife are very good to me. He behaves like a gentleman and a Christian, and my daughter with as much duty and tenderness as can be expressed.' After a time, however, she returned to Samuel at Tiverton and stayed with him through the autumn and winter of 1738. It was not an ideal existence for an old lady conscious of continual pain and weakness. They all treated her well, but could offer no haven. John's plan offered her what she most wanted. Windmill Hill was close to Moorfields where the city workers strolled over the green stretches of grass and under the old elms. It was on one side of Windmill Hill that the Government had built a factory for the casting of cannon. But in 1716 a great explosion blew off the roof, damaged the walls and killed many of the workmen. The shock was so great and the alarm so general that the Government decided to have the guns cast at Woolwich, far removed from the masses of population. And so the neglected Foundery stood in ruins until John Wesley saw its possibilities, reconditioned it at a cost of about £800, and made it the headquarters of his work. In addition to the chapel itself and a house for lay preachers, he built a coach-house and stable, and over the band room he fitted apartments for his private use.

It was to this new and last home that Susanna Wesley came. It brought her near to the Halls and near to Hetty in Soho. Anne was at Hatfield, and Kezzy in the family of the friendly Vicar of Bexley. There was every hope that she would meet them all. But more particularly she now had the opportunity of identifying herself more closely with the gallant enterprise in which she had come so wholeheartedly to believe. But when she set out from Samuel's house early in 1739 and made her way by easy stages to London, she could not have dreamt that the son she left in apparently good health was so soon to die (November 1739), and that chapter in her life was to be closed for ever. She learnt much from her sons, but they learnt more from her, and one famous incident reveals how to the very end she remained their mentor.

She sat under the ministry of her sons, but when they were away Thomas Maxfield was selected to take charge of the classes and bands, and to read and expound the Scriptures. It was a short and natural step from this to preach to the ready and attentive congregation. He may have known that had he sought permission it might easily be withheld. There was no precedent for such a step and John was never the man lightly to delegate authority. When he heard of the strange happenings he returned quickly from his journeyings. That anyone should do it was a breach of discipline, but that a layman should do it was unthinkable. It was providential that as he strode into the Foundery it should be his mother whom he met. Even as she asked him what was the matter she must have known. 'Thomas Maxfield has turned preacher I find.' It was a sentence ominous in its curtness. But Susanna had her effective rejoinder. 'John, you know what my sentiments have been. You cannot suspect me of readily favouring anything of this kind. But take care what you do with respect to that young man: for he is as surely called of God to preach as you are. Examine what have been the fruits of his preaching and hear him yourself.'

On any showing it was a remarkable outburst. She had been persuaded as a girl of the truth of the High Church tradition and had followed that way with as much unwavering zeal as her husband. But Susanna was not a slave to any lamp. Those who would know how John came to brave the odium of ecclesiastics, to sit lightly to established custom and embark on irregular practices would do well to misquote the familiar saying and *'cherchez la mère'*. For in both there was the same independence and initiative of spirit; the same willingness to defy convention if the greater good seemed to justify it. The woman who took Sunday services in the absence of her husband and braved his wrath was inevitably the one to range herself alongside Maxfield and justify his action.

To his great credit John Wesley once again took the advice of his mother and listened to Maxfield. It was enough. 'It is the Lord,' said John Wesley, 'let Him do what seemeth Him good. What am I that I should withstand God?' He had already committed himself to field preaching and this was the second revolutionary move. Without lay preaching Methodism could not have become a world Church, and it would have lacked what became its most distinctive element. Susanna argued better than she knew, for on her words great issues hung. It was one last service she rendered her son and her final contribution to the Revival whose beginnings she lived long enough to see.

For even as she participated in the busy life of the Foundery, it was obvious that the 'wheels of weary life' would soon stand still. The only specific cause of death was the inherited complaint of gout, but there had been the aggravation of long years of childbearing and the cares of a large household. And throughout her married life she had never been free from the shadow of burdensome debt. Now with her strength insensibly failing came the news of Kezia's death at Bexley. Did she die of a broken heart because her betrothed had suddenly rejected her in favour of Martha? The explanation seems too romantic for our hard-bitten age. But despite the loving care she had at Bexley, she was only thirty-two when she came to die. In March 1741 Susanna was used to the swift visits of the dark messenger. But Kezzy was her youngest, born just after the ordeal of the rectory fire. It was time for the mother to join her children and await the others.

In the summer of the following year she called her brood around her. Charles was forced through an inexorable sense of duty to go, but as he hurried away, he hoped even with despairing hope that he might return in time. The news of her failing powers reached John in Bristol. He took his services and after preaching to a large congregation on Sunday evening (18th July 1742), he threw his leg over his horse and at once set out for London. On the Tuesday morning when he saw her he wrote in his *Journal*: 'I found my mother on the borders of eternity. But she had no doubt or fear: nor any desire but as soon as God should call, to depart and be with Christ.' On the Friday he records in his *Journal* that he sat by his mother's bedside. 'She was in her last conflict; unable to speak but, I believe, quite sensible. Her look was calm and serene, and her eyes fixed upward, while we commended her soul to God. From three to four the silver cord was loosing and the wheel breaking at the cistern; and then without any struggle, or sigh or groan, the soul was set at liberty. We stood round the bed, and fulfilled her last request uttered a little before she lost her speech: 'Children, as soon as I am released, sing a psalm of praise to God.' (He supplemented this account in a letter written to Charles on 31st July 1742. In this he described his mother's condition, the commendatory prayer he offered, and the requiem which he and his sisters sang. But he says her death occurred the day before, i.e. 30th July. This agrees with the reference to his mother in a letter to Howell Harris, 6th August 1742, and also his account in the *Arminian Magazine* (1781), p. 312.)

Charles not only heard from brother John but also from Sister Anne (Mrs. Lambert), who spoke of how Susanna was released from her sufferings twelve hours before her actual death. Those around caught words of rejoicing and heard her whisper: 'My dear Saviour! are you come to help me in my extremity at last?' Until she lapsed into unconsciousness her remaining hours were spent in praise. The Wesleys knew how to die in triumph! How many children devoted to their parents have exclaimed in sudden outburst that they desired to die before them. John must have been thinking with especial tenderness of his mother when with access of feeling he wrote in 1727 expressing the wish that he might predecease her and declaring how happy she who had so signally served God would be in her closing hours.

She replied with her usual sanity, telling him to correct his fond desire of dying before her 'since you do not know what work God may have for you to do ere you leave the world'. She went on to declare that she surely ought to have the pre-eminence in point of time and go first to her rest. She then asked that were it possible she would not desire a display of grief at her death, but if it could benefit the children spiritually she would like them with her at the end. This comment led her by revulsion of feeling into self-reproach. Her essential humility of spirit led her to ask how she could ever hope to be of service by her manner of dying. 'But as I have been an unprofitable servant during the course of a long life, I have no reason to hope for so great an honour, so high a favour as to be employed in doing our Lord any service in the article of death. It were well if you spake prophetically and that joy and hope might have the ascendant over the other passions of my soul in that important hour. Yet I dare not presume, nor do I despair, but rather leave it to our Almighty Saviour to do with me both in life and death just what He pleases, for I have no choice' (26th July 1727).

She did not presume but she had her heart's desire. Her children were with her when she came to die; she was both joyous and hopeful; and her radiant spirit enabled them to rejoice and not to weep as her life flickered fitfully toward its close. In death as in life she was able to serve her Lord. None of those around the bedside could forget in after years the manner of her going. 'On Friday last', John Wesley wrote to Howell Harris, 'my mother went home with the voice of praise and thanksgiving.' And so every wish in her letter to John fifteen years before was amply fulfilled. She met death as she had hoped and found it had no sting. Her children were with her and did not embarrass her with their grief. She was joyful and they could sing. Many times in his life John Wesley turned back to that small room in which an old woman in extreme weakness was stronger than the strong. It was not alone her relationship to John that drew 'the innumerable company of people' together for the burial service. The women who came to the Foundery classes must have learned to love her, and to all the Methodist society she must have been a mother in God. After her body had been committed to the ground John Wesley spoke from the words: 'I saw a great white throne and

Him that sat on it, from whose face the earth and heavens fled away and there was found no place for them. And I saw the dead, small and great, stand before God: and the books were opened: and the dead were judged out of those things which were written in the books, according to their works.' Wesley wrote in his *Journal* that it was one of the most solemn assemblies he ever saw, or expected to see. So greatly passed a truly great woman. It was fitting she should be laid to rest in Bunhill Fields, City Road, near to the graves of John Bunyan and of Isaac Watts, and only a stone's throw from the site where Wesley's Chapel was soon to be built.

It is perhaps not generous to over-emphasize the uninspired memorial lines of Charles and their seeming reflection on her earlier Christian Faith. He wanted to set in strong relief the shining evangelical experience into which she consciously entered in the first dawn of the Revival, and he set it against a far too sombre background. His insight was temporarily obscured by a theological pedantry. In order to emphasize an important phase in her religious experience he was trapped into unwise and misleading exaggeration.

But the real Charles uttering his more considered judgement is to be found in the funeral hymn which he wrote shortly after her death. It has been rightly taken as an unnamed tribute to his incomparable mother and father.

> *What are these arrayed in white,*
> *Brighter than the noonday sun,*
> *Foremost of the sons of light,*
> *Nearest the eternal throne?*
> *These are they that bore the cross,*
> *Nobly for their Master stood,*
> *Sufferers in His righteous cause,*
> *Followers of the dying God.*
>
> *Out of great distress they came,*
> *Washed their robes by faith below,*
> *In the blood of yonder Lamb,*
> *Blood that washes white as snow.*
> *Therefore are they next the throne,*
> *Serve their Maker day and night;*
> *God resides among His own,*
> *God doth in His saints delight.*

More than conquerors at last,
Here they find their trials o'er,
They have all their sufferings past,
Hunger now and thirst no more;
No excessive heat they feel
From the sun's directer ray,
In a milder clime they dwell,
Region of eternal day.

He that on the throne doth reign,
Them the Lamb shall always feed,
With the tree of life sustain,
To the living fountains lead:
He shall all their sorrows chase,
All their wants at once remove,
Wipe the tears from every face,
Fill up every soul with love.

This is not only an inspired paraphrase of the famous passage in the seventh chapter of Revelation but the filial tribute of one to whom much was given. But her true memorial was in her children and in their work. And yet if she is judged apart from her children she still remains one of the most remarkable women in history. It is altogether proper that she should have her place in the window of great women at Liverpool Cathedral. Like all the saints she was supremely great in what she was, rather than in what she did. And again in the manner of the saints, although she wears an eighteenth-century dress and speaks with an eighteenth-century accent, her personality has a timeless appeal. She is still a contemporary. And still she teaches for those who are willing to learn.

Chapter Five

THE FAMILY GHOST

IS IT POSSIBLE to regard a ghost as a member of a family? Everything depends upon the ghost. The Epworth ghost was certainly very real to the members of the household and no serious writer about the family has had the temerity to disregard him. In that sense he is one of the ghosts who live. And yet to attempt to ask who he was is a certain invitation to trouble. It is much more profitable to ask what were the consequences of his visits and in particular how did he affect the life and thought of John Wesley? In a sense the ghost is like the problem of evil. In both cases, the origin may not be known, but the consequences certainly are.

One reason why it is not unnatural timidity to avoid an explanation is that the material at our disposal is so confusing and in part contradictory. Yet no ghost has been better authenticated. There is a wealth of circumstantial evidence.[1] Nor does it come from one particular quarter. Samuel, the eldest son, was of course teaching at Westminster and the separate members of the family wrote to him their independent accounts. The news naturally excited him and he was persistent in wanting answers to his questions. In this way he heard from his father and mother and from his sisters Emily and Susanna. Indeed, his curiosity was so insatiable that his mother almost impatiently wrote: 'I cannot imagine how you should be so curious about our unwelcome guest. For my part I am quite tired with hearing or speaking of it: but if you come among us, you will find enough to satisfy all your scruples, and perhaps may hear it or see it for yourself.' In her letter Susanna said that Hetty was also going to write. It is very

[1] John Wesley, returning home in 1720 preparatory to going to Oxford, collected all the available evidence and it was published in the *Arminian Magazine* in 1784. The Rev. Samuel Badcock became the possessor of many Wesley MSS. through Mrs. Earle, the daughter of Samuel Wesley, junior. The MS. relating to the ghost he gave to his friend, Dr. Priestley, who incorporated it in 1791 under the title *Original Letters, by Rev. John Wesley and his Friends*. This account was fully summarized by Tyerman in his *Life and Times of Samuel Wesley*, Chapter 17, pp. 348–64. Perhaps the fullest account is in Adam Clarke's *Wesley Family*, Vol. I, pp. 247–91, and also in Southeys *Life of Wesley*. Adam Clarke used not only the *Arminian Magazine*, but Priestley's papers, and after giving all the facts criticized Priestley's conclusion with shrewdness and then made his own observations. No later writer has added any material facts but each has made his deductions according to his own bias.

probable that she did and in that case her account was either lost or deliberately suppressed. Nothing could be more unfortunate, for whilst no natural explanation will cover all the factors, Hetty was the human agent most involved; the *point d'appui* of the disturbances. The mystery deepens when it is remembered that although John Wesley with his customary thoroughness undertook a complete sifting of the evidence in 1726 there was an important lacuna in his account. He had a full report from his father and mother and also from Emily, Molly, Sukey (Susanna), and Nancy. To these memoranda he added an account from the Rev. Mr. Hoole, a neighbouring clergyman, who had stayed a night and heard many paranormal noises and knockings. Then John Wesley received a vivid report from Robin Brown, the manservant, who repeated also the experience of Betty Mussy, the maid. Finally he wrote a summary of the main facts as they had been presented. All this was transcribed in the Rector's journal (1716). Finally in three issues of the *Arminian Magazine* (October, November, and December 1784), John Wesley wrote his considered review of the whole affair. The gap in this thorough piece of research is that he never gave an account of what he had received from his sister Hetty. It is beyond belief that he would get a report from his other sisters, but not a word from the sister who seemed most affected. Did she refuse to speak, or was her report suppressed? We shall never know. All that has come down to us from John is the report of how one night Hetty was waiting to take her father's candle when she heard someone coming down the garret stairs walking slowly by her, then going down the best stairs, then up the back stairs, and lastly up the garret stairs. At each step the house shook from top to bottom. The next morning she told her elder sister, who said: 'Pray let me take away the candle tonight and I will find out the trick.' She took Hetty's place and also heard noises and knockings and the added experience of an open door being thrust violently against her. But more significant things happened to Hetty of which John Wesley himself gives no account. It would be most interesting to know the reason.

What precisely did happen in the Wesley household between December 1715 and January 1716? The ghost was seen by Sukey, by Hetty, by Susanna (Mrs. Wesley) and by Robin Brown, but all their accounts differed. To Sukey and Hetty it appeared like a man in a long nightgown, but to Susanna Wesley it seemed more like a badger with no discernible head and to Robin Brown like a white rabbit. The daughter's accounts are similar, and those of Robin and Susanna are in rough agreement but the phenomena observed by the girls and the adults differ completely. Either the younger were mistaken, or the older, or both. The only other conclusion is that both were right but were observing different entities. On the whole it seems probable that all four, being in an excited and nervous state, were the victims of hallucination. Their evidence is slight and conflicting. In each case it rested on a single appearance. They each had no more than a fleeting impression of something in rapid flight. If the story of 'Old Jeffrey' (the name given to the ghost by Emily and accepted by the rest of the family) was of such flimsy fabric it could never have survived two centuries of handling.

But it is the auditory and not the visual phenomena that are baffling and not lightly to be explained. Every member of the family, the servants, and the clergyman guest during that period heard unaccountable noises, and often the sounds were heard when the whole family was together. On 1st December the maid heard dismal groaning, but was laughed out of her fears. A few nights later several members of the family heard strange knockings in different places. There was a succession of four knocks and then a pause before the next four knocks began. It continued day and night either in the garret, nursery, or the green chamber. At last the Rector was told but remained stoutly incredulous, yet the following night he heard it nine times by his bedside. This was too much even for a disbelieving clergyman. He got up and searched in vain, but afterwards he heard the knockings with the rest of the family. One night when the noise was especially violent, the good Rector and his wife rose and lit a candle to see if the children were disturbed. At that moment it seemed as if someone had thrown a bag of money which emptied at her feet. Meanwhile there was the noise of bottles being dashed to a thousand pieces, coming from under the stairs. In the Hall the mastiff met them whining and striving in his fear to find some security by wedging between them.

It was after this that Mr. Hoole, the Rector of the nearby parish of Haxey, was persuaded to stay the night. Often the noise had been like the winding of a jack, but on this particular night it was like a carpenter planing deals: but more commonly it was an intermittent series of three knocks, repeated for many hours. Hoole and Samuel went down into the kitchen and then heard sounds from the room they had left. When they returned up the narrow stairs, they heard a noise like the 'slaring' of feet, and the trailing of a loose nightgown.

Samuel never lacked either physical and moral courage, and now, firmly convinced he was dealing with the powers of evil, he resolved to challenge it. He went to the place from whence the sounds seemed to come and in his loudest voice he cried: 'Thou deaf and dumb devil, why dost thou frighten the children that cannot answer thee? Come to me in my study that am a man.' Instantly the particular knock he used on his own door was employed with loud reverberation. Next evening as he tried to open the study door, it was thrust back on him and he almost fell. Knockings sounded on each side of the door, but though Samuel adjured the spirit to speak there was silence. Then because evil spirits love the dark, Samuel blew out the candle. The Rector turned to Anne who was with him and said: 'Two Christians are an over match for a devil; go downstairs, and it may be, when I am left alone, it will have courage to speak.' But despite his insistence there was no speaking, and even the knocks came to an end.

But that was not the only game Old Jeffrey played with the Rector. Seemingly it had Jacobite sympathies, for at morning and evening prayers there were always knocks when the prayers for the King were said. When Samuel began, 'For our most gracious Sovereign Lord', etc., the din was so great that he declared he would say three and not two prayers for the King. On 27th January 1716 two faint knocks were heard at the King's name, and afterwards no further disturbance was made.

So much for Samuel, but the daughters had their own tale to tell. Emily one night heard a noise like an enormous piece of coal splintering in the kitchen. Later she heard a noise like a great stone flung among many bottles under the stairs. Susanna caused a horn to be blown for half a day to frighten Jeffrey, and Emily was convinced that this accounted for his behaviour becoming suddenly worse. The little man, she thought, was in a temper. For after that time there was no quiet after a quarter to ten at night. At first the noise seemed to suggest the quick winding of a jack. Then came the loud and hollow knocking such as none of the sisters could imitate. Emily speaking for her sister Hetty said that she had the worse experience of hearing knocking under her feet, and when she moved, the underneath knocking followed her. Such an experience, wrote Emily, 'would terrify a stouter person'.

Molly had other details to add. She and Sukey frightened by noises had jumped into bed one night, when the warming pan by the bedside jarred and rung as did the latch of the door. A great chain outside the door seemed to fall and the house shook from top to bottom. Sukey spoke of the way latches on doors would rise and fall of their own accord, as well as noises like falling chains, and heavy strokes on Hetty's bed. Anne, commonly called Nancy, had the unpleasant experience of being followed from room to room in the day-time, and when she made any sort of noise, the sound was repeated behind her. The bed on which she sat one night was lifted up and down several times and as it reached a 'considerable height' she quite understandably would not sit there any more.

Robin's account was in some ways the strangest of all. Old Jeffrey frequently used to visit him in bed, walking up the garret stairs like a man in jack boots with a nightgown trailing after him. When he entered the room he made a noise like the gobbling of a turkey cock, and then stumbled over the boots by the bedside. One night Robin took the dog with him, but as soon as the latch began to jar, the dog crept into bed and made a howling that alarmed the rest of the house. Once the handle of his mill was turned with great speed and Robin was vexed rather than alarmed, because there was no corn in it to be ground.

And lastly there was the dog. When the disturbances first began, the dog would bark and leap and snap on one side and another, and often it would do so before any person in the room had heard any sound at all. But as the days went on he only trembled and crept away. The family knew by these signs that the noises were about to begin, and the dog was never wrong.

Hetty's story was never told by herself. At least if it was told, it has never been repeated. But from the evidence of others, especially her mother, we know that she was the object of particular attention. 'Your father and I observed that Hetty trembled exceedingly in her sleep, as she always did before the noise awaked her. It commonly was nearer her than the rest which she took notice of, and was much frightened, because she thought it had a particular spite at her.' And then came a cryptic and most exasperating remark. 'I could multiply particular instances but I forbear.' What was this mystery surrounding Hetty?

Let it be said at once that Old Jeffrey was not an alias for Hetty Wesley. Ever since the happenings took place writers have been trying to find some human agency as the explanation of the happenings. The most far-fetched explanation is that of W. B. Stonehouse (*History and Topography of the Isle of Axholme*) who supposed that some practical joker had installed a piece of machinery in the large garret under the roof of the house. How it could have been put there without one of the family knowing, how it could be started up, how it could account for the many kinds of noises, the author does not stop to explain.

Scarcely more credible is the explanation of the famous Dr. Joseph Priestley into whose hands the papers came. He thought the whole affair was a trick played jointly by the servants and neighbours. But so many disturbances occurred when neither servants nor neighbours could have been present. They were not highly intelligent and if they had been capable of one decent hoax, they certainly could not have sustained an extraordinary variety of sounds and effects day and night for over a month. We are dealing with a greatly gifted family, each member of which had character and intelligence. However clever servants and neighbours might be they could not impose on such a family for so long without detection.

This brings us to the family itself. All the available evidence shows that they had no doubt whatever of the supernatural nature of the disturbances. Indeed they had no hesitation in attributing them to diabolic agency. Emily said frankly in a letter to her brother Samuel that far from being superstitious, she was too much inclined to infidelity; she therefore heartily rejoiced at such an opportunity to convince herself beyond any doubt or scruple, that beings exist apart from those we see.

But though all professed to believe in its supernatural origin, was one of the family playing a part? And was that person Hetty Wesley? Some have thought so but the idea is plainly untenable. She was often asleep when the noises occurred, and often when phenomena were located in a particular place she was absent. In any case when noises of different kinds occurred at different times in different places, she lacked the competence and ubiquity and motive that were necessary. This spirit was not playful. It was mischievous, destructive, malevolent. If Hetty possessed both the means and the ability to play such tricks, she would not be morally capable of such behaviour.

If one had to describe a being capable of the Epworth phenomena one would conceive a sprite of low intelligence but of a certain cunning. It would have a perverted sense of humour, a delight in mischief, a love of loud noises, and a desire to terrify. In short, it would be a very inferior devil, rather like a nasty minded, stupid child who happens not to be human.

This brings one very near to a definition of the poltergeist. In psychical research the poltergeist is 'a secondary personality, intelligence, spirit imp or familiar with unpleasant characteristics'. The two words thus joined are German and literally mean a noisy or blustering ghost. But of course a poltergeist must be distinguished from the ghost as we understand that term. 'A ghost that once was man', wrote Tennyson; but a poltergeist is not human. Consequently whilst ghost stories are regular features of Christmas annuals, and every truly respectable Manor House is proud of its family ghost, no one has ever felt gratified because the house he occupied suffered from the attention of poltergeists. A ghost is usually harmless and quiet and is as easily disturbed as any timid fawn. In most instances it is benevolently disposed to the family whose house it haunts. If a ghost is said to haunt, the poltergeist is said to infest a house. For he is neither kindly nor quiet nor easily affrighted. He desires to plague the occupants and to that end will play mischievous tricks involving a maximum of noise. He is not to be daunted nor even exorcized. He will answer threats with increased fury of performance and he will operate as easily by day as by night.

The poltergeist phenomena have been recorded for many centuries. In the days of witchcraft trials the caprices of unholy sprites appeared largely in the reports of the trials. Since those days of recorded observation the disturbances of poltergeists[1] have been the same in all places and at all times. The kind of noise and manner of disturbance have been subject to minor variations but the character of the phenomena has remained the same.

Out of a wealth of documentary evidence certain conclusions emerge.[2] Despite slight evidence to the contrary poltergeists cannot be seen nor can they be touched. And whilst they make such an infernal noise, they cannot speak. They have the telekinetic power of displacing or propelling objects. They can push

---

[1] Strictly the plural of poltergeist is poltergeister, but in English usage the plural is -s.
[2] A selected but comprehensive bibliography will be found at the end of the late Mr. Harry Price's important book, *Poltergeist over England*. He had given a lifetime to psychical research and was perhaps our best-known investigator. Every student of poltergeist phenomena is under great debt to him.

or pull vigorously. When Samuel one evening tried to open the study door he met with a violent but invisible resistance, whilst Emily one night had an open door thrust strongly against her.

There are other conclusions which seem almost as well established. Mr. Harry Price, working on the available evidence, estimated that poltergeists prefer girls to boys in the ratio of ninety-five per cent. to five per cent. He also was persuaded that the mysteries of sexual energy especially around the age of puberty have much to do with the paranormal happenings. If this were true it would throw a strong light on the case of Hetty Wesley. She obviously was not the conscious nor direct agent in the disturbances at the Epworth Rectory. And yet just as surely she was the one human being with the closest links to 'Old Jeffrey'.

Samuel, writing to his sister Emily from Westminster said: 'I wish you would let me have a letter from you as from every one of my sisters. I cannot think any of you very superstitious, unless you are much changed since I saw you. My sister Hetty, I find, was particularly troubled. Let me know all. Did anything appear to her?' Evidently the keen-witted Samuel from the letters he received had concluded that Hetty was principally concerned.

It was to Hetty's bed the poltergeist would come and knock whilst Hetty would flush and tremble and turn uneasily in her sleep before she waked. It was Hetty alone who found on occasion the noises followed her as though under her very feet. When Canon W. J. Phythian-Adams, a well-known contemporary Anglican scholar, studied the Borley Rectory poltergeists he said: 'Whatever the explanation may be it seems certain that the energy which plays the pranks is drawn mainly if not exclusively from living persons (often young ones) who thus become its unconscious "accomplices".' Mr. Sacheverell Sitwell in his book on poltergeists expresses the view that in the dozing of the psyche before it awakens into adult life there is a favourite playground for the poltergeist. In the impressive number of well-documented poltergeist cases which Mr. Harry Price had collected he showed how so frequently a young girl is the *point d'appui* of the disturbances. It is a remarkable fact that in witchcraft trials it was commonly a 'young girl' who was the victim, and who suffered from 'possession' by hurtful powers.

The modern theory in psychical research would be that there

is a transfer of energy from the medium to the poltergeist.[1] On this supposition it was Hetty Wesley who all unknowingly gave the poltergeist its kinetic energy. Is it possible that energy radiating from her could be 'picked up' and used? *Omnia exeunt in mysterium.* The facts we know; the explanation eludes us. One thing is certain. No case is better documented. By strange good fortune the household consisted of many members all far above the average in intelligence and character. Certain members of the family wrote their own separate accounts of the disturbances to Samuel the eldest son. John and Charles were away at school but later, when John was of maturer years (17 years old), he made his own inquiries. We have therefore the letters of the family, the journal of the Rector, the report of John Wesley, and the final account in the *Arminian Magazine* written toward the end of Wesley's life. Frank Podmore in a series of books expressed his disbelief in any supernatural explanations of psychical phenomena. Mr. Harry Price indeed called him that arch-sceptic, and yet it was Podmore who described the Epworth happenings as 'the most fully documented case in the history of the subject'. Mr. Price had taken a particular interest in the astonishing disturbances spread over a century at Borley Rectory. This he would probably regard as the most fully authenticated case. He himself had been enabled to conduct experiments there which were entirely successful. Even so, he calls the Epworth poltergeist 'a classic, perhaps the classic of the early cases—amongst the best authenticated ghost stories'.

I do not know of any natural explanation that fits the facts. Nothing is explained, when it is explained away. These are apocalyptic days in which we are not so ready, as once we were, to dismiss the hosts of darkness as a figure of speech. Recently two books by reputable scholars have rehabilitated the Devil as a live Being of quite Satanic importance.[2] How is it possible to go through two world wars and still speak negligently of the Devil? And once the mind admits the possibility of evil

---

[1] Mr. A. J. B. Robertson, the Cambridge scientist, suggests as an alternative explanation that 'the apparent entities are equally explicable as being secondary personalities of the medium' (*Poltergeist over England*, p. 379). This explanation seems as hard to believe as the other.

[2] *Talk of the Devil*, by Denis de Rougemont; *Satan: a Portrait*, by Edward Langton; and the remarkable series of novels of the late Charles Williams dealing with the occult, though written by a fervent Anglican, are pointers in this direction. In theology, Karl Heim and Paul Tillich are foremost thinkers among many who accept the idea of demonic forces.

spirits—can it logically stop short at the idea of the poltergeist? In any inquiry into the Epworth mystery the poltergeist explanation would seem to answer more questions and cover the facts more completely than any other approach to the problem. But even if this be granted, we are still in great darkness. We do not know what they are, how they come, nor why they go. In effect all we do is to reject the natural and admit the possibility of a supernatural explanation.

In his *Life of Wesley* Southey said a sufficient end would be achieved, if 'sometimes one of those unhappy persons who, looking through the dim glass of infidelity, see nothing beyond this life, should, from the well-established truth of one such story, be led to a conclusion that there are more things in heaven and earth than are dreamt of in their philosophy'. Certainly this was the effect on John Wesley. He was never tempted to disbelieve, but Old Jeffrey had a profound effect on all his later thinking about the unseen world. All the family shared his belief that it was a proof of supernatural agencies. Emily thought it was due to witchcraft. 'About a year since', she said, 'there was a disturbance at a town near us that was undoubtedly occasioned by witches; and if so near, why may they not reach us? Then my father had, for several Sundays before Old Jeffrey came, preached warmly against consulting those that are called cunning men, which our people are given to; and it had a particular spite against my father.' The Rector when advised to leave the Rectory had replied: 'No, let the devil flee from me: I will never flee from him.' Despite his belief in it as an evil spirit, he thought the whole circumstances would make 'a glorious penny book for Jack Dunton' (his brother-in-law, and the publisher of his early books). Susanna felt it might be a spirit, premonitory of death. When she knew her three boys were safe, she supposed it was a warning that her brother, Samuel Annesley in India, had died. With her robust common sense she wrote to John (November 1724): 'If they could instruct us how to avoid any danger, or put us in the way of being wiser or better—there would be sense in it, but to appear for no end that we know of unless to frighten people almost out of their wits, seems altogether unreasonable.'

John Wesley had no doubt that there was a reason. The disturbances were full of significance to him. It is fashionable to suppose that this was because of his great credulity. Southey is the first of many biographers who have laughed at his childish notions. 'He invalidated his own authority', said Southey, 'by listening to the most absurd tales with implicit credulity, and recording them as authenticated facts.' But a distinguished modern biographer shows far more insight when he declared that such beliefs were outstanding proofs of Wesley's independence and judgement and boldness of mind. 'To hold such belief, at a time when the English forms of righteous complacency on the one hand and of arrogant cynicism on the other were never more fully and more precisely developed, was a striking proof of original character especially in one whose clear mind repelled with contempt any sort of vagueness or mystery, and to whom the methods of keen logic and close argument were always congenial.'[1]

People ceased in the late seventeenth century to persecute witches and except in isolated country parts abandoned all belief in the practice itself. The eighteenth century rejoiced in its freedom from all superstitions. It was the century of illumination: of Deism and the rule of reason. To believe in witches was to make oneself an eccentric or a barbarian. If, beyond a vague belief in God as the great Architect, people scouted the idea of the supernatural, then obviously they laughed at abnormal happenings as mere hocus-pocus; the vestigial remains of a superstitious age. John Wesley was very willing to accept a natural explanation of the seeming occult if it did no violence to his reason or the plain evidence of the facts. But he would never approach any problem with a predetermined bias rejecting certain conclusions in advance. He brought the trained mind of the scholar, the patience of the investigator, and the devotion of the Christian believer to bear upon all life and certainly upon its darker places. Those who do not accept the Christian revelation may easily feel that he was over credulous. And certainly for him life was a battleground of good and evil in which each side had the help of unseen Hosts. He was quite sure that God's writ ran through his world and though he did not doubt the demonic forces and their power to harm he could gleefully cry with Martin Luther:

> *And let the Prince of Ill look grim as e'er he will;*
> *He harms us not a whit,*
> *For why? His doom is writ,*
> *A word shall quickly slay him.*

[1] C. E. Vulliamy, *John Wesley*, 1931.

Those who believe too little may complain that he believed too much in the providence and active help of God. Certainly his beliefs sounded strange in the ears of his fashionable contemporaries. But Wesley went serenely on, not doubting the powers of good or evil, and only finding his vindication in our own apocalyptic age when all neat and cosy ideas have been shrivelled up and men walk in the presence of ghostly Powers on the thin edge of a dark precipice.

The whole family records of Old Jeffrey left him in no doubt that the disturbances went far beyond ordinary explanation. From henceforward he could not doubt the reality of paranormal sights and sounds. 'With my latest breath will I bear witness against giving up to infidels one great proof of the invisible world, I mean that of witchcraft and apparitions, confirmed by the testimony of all ages.' In his journeyings (July 1770) he came across a case of a young woman who said of her illness that in former times it would be said she was bewitched. Wesley roundly commented: 'And why should they not call it so now? Because the infidels have hooted witchcraft out of the world; and the complaisant Christians in large numbers have joined them in the cry. I do not wonder so much at this—that many of these should herein talk like infidels. But I have sometimes been inclined to wonder at the pert, saucy indecent manner wherein some of those who trample upon men far wiser than themselves; at their speaking so dogmatically against what not only the whole world, heathen and Christian, believed in past ages, but thousands learned as well as unlearned, firmly believe at this day. I instance in Dr. Smollett and Mr. Guthrie whose manner of speaking concerning witchcraft must be extremely offensive to every sensible man who cannot give up his Bible.'

It was some years later (22nd May 1776) that he read Pennant's *Journey through Scotland*, and qualified his approval by saying that he would not give up to all the Deists in Great Britain the existence of witchcraft 'till I give up the credit of all history, sacred and profane. And at this present time, I have not only as strong, but stronger proofs of this, from eye and ear witnesses, than I have of murder, so that I cannot naturally doubt of one any more than the other.'

The strong interest Wesley always took in abnormal happenings did not mean that he flew at once to a supernatural solution. It will suffice to recall the fact that when he came to Bristol in 1762 he found the city agog with excitement over the mysterious scratchings on the windows and walls and other unaccountable sounds at a tavern called 'The Lamb'. Wesley asked in his *Journal* how the disturbances were to be accounted, 'by natural or supernatural agency?' He was satisfied but inclined to be suspicious over the whole affair. Were the landlady's daughters really bewitched? It was only when those two redoubtable girls, Molly and Dolly Giles, had been birched that the story came out. Their mother had greatly desired to buy 'The Lamb' and wished to depreciate its value by frightening people away from property so manifestly haunted. Unlike Shakespeare's Glendower, the spirits she conjured from the 'vasty deep' were too substantial, and the two daughters were the cause of all the strange disturbances. Bristol was amused and annoyed. Wesley was calmly satisfied. He had an answer which accounted for all the facts.

The great reason why Old Jeffrey and every other unearthly disturbance mattered so much to John Wesley was that he believed they provided one line of irrefutable argument against the sophistries of Deism. He said that 'if but one account of the intercourse of men with spirits be admitted, their whole castle in the air . . . falls to the ground'. He did not therefore desire that 'this weapon' should be wrested out of men's hands. For he argued that whilst there are numerous arguments beside this, yet neither reason nor religion required that we be 'hooted out' of one of our positions. We dare not advance beyond the position of recognizing phenomena not easily to be explained. John Wesley had no doubt of supernatural agencies at work. It served to confirm him in his conviction of the unseen world. Old Jeffrey had his uses after all.

Chapter Six

DEAR SAMMY

SAMUEL WAS the first-born and always had the first place in Susanna's heart. She had an extra maternal solicitude because it seemed as though he would never learn to speak. Her relief was overwhelming when one day, searching anxiously for him, she heard his voice from under the table: 'Here I am, mother.' He was then nearly five years of age and they were the first distinct words she had heard him speak. It may have been because of this circumstance that she never took up her children's education till they had reached the age of five. Samuel was the only child to receive not only his mother's instruction but for a year to have as tutor, Mr. John Holland, who kept a small private school at Epworth. It was this good scholar of irregular and eccentric habits of whom the Rector said in one of his letters to Samuel (20th December 1707): 'your worthy schoolmaster, John Holland, whose kindness you wear on your knuckles . . . now lies in Lincoln gaol.'

In 1704, when Samuel was fourteen years of age, his parents secured him an entrance to Westminster School and to their great joy he became a King's Scholar there in 1707. The school enjoyed at that period a very high reputation for sound education. The famous Dr. Busby had become headmaster in 1640 and continued in charge for fifty-five years. It was said of him that he despaired of no scholar, however dull, but chose the appropriate means to develop his mind. He wrote many of the elementary books used by the school and paid special attention to the classics. Samuel entered the school on the classical side and quickly showed outstanding ability. Epworth was too distant and the family resources too straitened for him to return home at vacations and consequently exciting happenings at Epworth such as the Rectory fire and the abnormal disturbances, he could only know by letter. But homes in London were open to him. He visited his father's mother, the gallant high-hearted widow of the Rev. John Wesley, and also Matthew and Timothy Wesley, the brothers of his father. The Rector's sister, Mrs. Elizabeth Dyer, was also in

London, and it is very likely that he was welcomed there as well. In the year 1711, perhaps owing to the influence of Francis Atterbury, at that time Dean of Westminster, he entered Christ Church, Oxford. In a remarkably short time he had completed his degree and returned as an Usher to Westminster.

He was now in a position to help his family, and he cheerfully took up a burden which he was never able to lay down until death released him. When Charles was only eight years old, brother Samuel asked for him to be sent to Westminster (1716). He not only defrayed the cost of Charles's education but watched over the course of his studies to such good effect that Charles became a King's Scholar in 1721 and his expenses were thereafter borne by the Foundation.

His liberality extended to the whole family. The old Rector in a letter written toward the end of his life (28th February 1733) spoke the plain truth when he said to Samuel: 'You have been a father to your brothers and sisters, especially to the former, who have cost you great sums in their education, both before and since they went to the University. Neither have you stopped here, but have showed your pity to your mother and me in a very liberal manner, wherein your wife joined with you, when you did not overmuch abound yourselves, and have even done noble charities to my children's children.' This helps to support Badcock's statement that he divided his income with his parents and family but prohibited any mention of the fact while he lived.[1]

When her husband died it was to Samuel's house at Tiverton that Susanna inevitably turned. First there had been a short stay with Emily whilst Kezia the youngest went to Samuel, and then Susanna took her daughter's place. Whilst during her widowhood Susanna travelled more than she had done in her previous life, it was Samuel's home she regarded as particularly her own. And only when Samuel had died did she settle at the Foundery, Moorfields, and allow John to take his brother's place.

The attachment of Susanna to her first-born was stronger than a continued sense of indebtedness. Her love and pride were strongly evident in all her correspondence with him. In a letter written in 1709, after he had decided to take Holy Orders, she impressed on him the solemn nature of his calling. In a century in which William Cowper was to say of clerical place seekers that they were willing

[1] cf. Stevenson's *Memorials of the Wesley Family*, p. 253.

> *To make the symbols of atoning grace*
> *An office key, a pick lock to a place,*

it is refreshing to read her insistence on exemplary virtue and devotion. She declared that 'low common degrees of piety are not sufficient for the sacred function'. Remembering the many hard drinking, soft living, all-too-tolerant parsons, Susanna's words come like a stinging slap on the face. 'I cannot see how clergymen can reprove sinners or exhort men to lead a good life, when they themselves indulge their corrupt inclinations, and by their practice contradict their doctrine. If the Holy Jesus be indeed their Master and they are really his ambassadors, surely it becomes them to live like his disciples, and if they do not, what a sad account must they give of their stewardship.'

She revealed her own tidy mind and love of order when she counselled him to apportion his time for private devotion, study, and recreation. She argued that so many drift along like straws on a river, but he must act on principle, and conduct his business with method. It is not altogether a matter of chance that in later years her other sons and their friends at the Holy Club were known as Methodists.

She wrote a remarkable letter to him at the end of the following year (28th December 1710) in which she answers fully his complaint that he feels himself to be 'unstable and inconstant in the ways of virtue'. Her advice on the culture of the spiritual life must have strengthened him greatly. One of her sentences deserves to be remembered for its salty truth. 'How many persons on a deathbed have bitterly bewailed the sins of their past life and made large promises of amendment if it would please God to spare them; but none that ever lived or died repented of piety and virtue.'

It is in this letter that she threw off momentarily her usual reserve and thanked him for dropping the title of madam. She told him there was more love and tenderness in the name of mother than in all the complimentary titles in the world, and she said that she 'loved him as her own soul'. Nowhere else in all her letters does Susanna write with such depth of feeling. It was in this year that she sent him her own interpretation of the Apostles' Creed and asked him not only to read it but copy it out. She told him that she knew of the abundance of good works on such subjects but since she was his mother, she hoped her writing 'tho' mean' would have its own appeal. She asked him that as she had employed her youth and vigour in his service so he would not despise the little she could do in her declining years.

In all her letters Susanna shows herself the devoted mother as well as the faithful and shrewd adviser. Other interesting letters from Susanna to Samuel her son are dated 4th August 1704; 22nd May 1706; 7th May, 30th August, 27th November 1707; 14th February 1709; and 25th January 1717. And as she gave, so she received. In all the great disturbances and sorrows at Epworth Rectory she turned to her eldest son. He comforted her when the Rector was in Lincoln Jail. Five days after the disastrous fire she wrote to 'Sammy' giving him a remarkably plain and unemotional account of the fire, desiring obviously to set his mind at rest. She herself had only just received food, warmth, and some sort of shelter, but she concluded her letter by saying that in God's great mercy they had all escaped, and that Samuel was in no wise to be discouraged. When Old Jeffrey commenced his unpleasant disturbances, Susanna wrote at once to Samuel and followed it with a second more circumstantial letter. And when there came the greatest trial of all the widow instinctively turned once more to her first-born son.

Samuel was just as happy in his relations with his father who must have been of great help to Samuel the son in his classical studies before the fourteen-year-old boy set out for Westminster School. In one of his early letters (17th September 1706) the Rector paid a tribute to Susanna which is worthy to rank with Steele's great encomium of his wife. He begged Samuel to be willing to support and comfort his mother in her old age and not in any respect to show himself unworthy of such a parent.

Sometimes the letters were a pleasing mixture of parental advice and the details of local happenings. In one such letter (29th December 1707) he expressed his gratification that Samuel had confided in him and begged his son to regard him not only as a father but a friend. It is a good thing to have someone to whom one can confide one's weaknesses and private thoughts, but ordinarily, wrote the Rector, a father is not chosen for such secrets. 'However,' he went on, 'you seem disposed to trust me and I will betray no secret.' And then, surprisingly, the Rector made a handsome offer. 'If you want to tell me something in complete secrecy write to me in Latin.' But on other occasions the father wrote in the role of mentor and guide. 'Read the histories of

Joseph, Daniel, and Lot, and, if you please, the thirteenth satire of Juvenal' (October 1707). Advice, such as this, comprising almost a whole letter and in itself so meaningless, can only be understood as the answer to some particular question the son had raised. This in turn suggests that the Rector kept himself tolerably informed about his son's studies. This correspondence of tutor and pupil soon became that of fellow students. The old Rector sought continual advice from Samuel about the projected work on Job. When at last the *Dissertations* were completed and Samuel senior had sent them to Samuel junior, the father still sought the son's advice about the proper order.

1. As to the placing the Dissertations. As you say the prolegomena are something aguish; though that and all the rest I leave (as often before) to your judgement, for my memory is near gone; neither have I the papers in any order by me.
2. The '*Poetica Descriptio Monstri*' I think would come in most naturally after all the Dissertations of the Behemoth and Leviathan; but you, having the whole before you, will be the most proper judge.
3. Do with the '*De Carmine Pastoritio*' as you please.
4. '*Periplus Rubri Maris*' comes with the geography when Mr. Hoole has finished it.
5. I remember no extracts, but that from the '*Catena*' which is 616 folio pages; but I think I got the main of it into thirty quartos, which I finished yesterday, though there is no haste in sending it, for I design it for the appendix.

As for the *Testimonia Arianorum* περί του Λογου it happens well that I have a pretty good copy, though not so perfect as that which is lost, and will get Mr. Horberry to transcribe it as soon as he returns from Oxford though I think it will not come in till toward the latter end of the work, as must your collation at the very end only before the appendix; and I shall begin to revise it tomorrow. (18th June 1731.)

It would appear not only that the son gave advice and a certain amount of help, but that the Rector expected him to complete the work. The collation duly appeared in the finished work but for some reason the *Testimonia* and the very necessary appendix were not published.

One last token of the Rector's confidence in Samuel was manifest in his strong request for the son to succeed him at Epworth. He frankly set before him the reasons why he wanted his son. Apart from his ability and undoubted fitness for the living, there was the circumstance that once the Rector died Susanna would need to have the Rectory. It was only when Samuel declined the offer that the Rector turned to John, to find once more that the offer did not seem so attractive to the sons as he had hoped. John's refusal seemed to sting the old man more than Sammy's refusal had done. In a long letter he confided his disappointment and mortification to his eldest son and begged him to take up the cudgels. (4th December 1734.)

The very next day Samuel sharpened the weapons from his father's armoury and sought to persuade his brother that the simple tasks at Epworth were to be preferred to the academic seclusion of Oxford. But John was not to be drawn so easily. The argument was sustained until March 1735, two months before the Rector died. John still was adamant. No man could move him once he had decided on the course to take. In this case the almost tearful entreaties of the father reinforced by the strong expostulations and reproaches of his elder brother could not weaken his determination. The correspondence sends a strong shaft of light on that iron resolve which made John Wesley inevitably a leader of men: the first and only Pope in Methodism.

But Samuel at least had tried to help his father, and had loyally and with sustained effort carried out the Rector's last emphatic wish. In care and understanding, in readiness to advise and in swiftness to help, Samuel was the model son. Indeed if he had not accepted burdens so readily and carried them on such broad shoulders, one might have felt that he was asked to carry too much. In one of his letters (28th February 1733) the Rector assumes without question that when he dies his son, Samuel, will take Susanna into his own house immediately, 'where your wife and you will nourish her, till we meet again in heaven'. Having thus safely disposed of his wife in the case of his prior decease, the Rector proceeds to say with just as much ease and assurance, that Samuel will be 'a guide and stay to the rest of the family'. Although Samuel's relations with his brothers are better known he was kind and generous to his sisters and even to their children. He took Hetty's part when such support was sore needed and he urged John to stand as godfather for one of her children. 'Your reasons for not standing for Hetty's child are good and yet were they as good again there is one against them that will make them good for nothing, viz. the child will not be christened at all unless you and I stand *E malis minimum*' (21st June 1733).

In the father's letter there is no request and certainly no demand. The Rector just states as a matter of plain fact that his eldest son will look after the widow and be a stay to all the family. It is all unconsciously a magnificent tribute to 'dear Sammy'. For behind the old man's calm statement that his son will undertake such immense responsibility, there lies the experience of Samuel's nature and of his kindnesses over the long years. It was because of all he had done in the past that the Rector knew he could depend on him in the uncertain future. His son 'could not deny himself'. In a remarkable family Samuel has his own particular claim to be remembered.

When Samuel's name is mentioned the customary reaction is to recall his disagreement with his famous brothers. In discussing the merits of that famous controversy the admirers of John and Charles unhesitatingly line up behind them. Indeed, many in excess of enthusiasm, go farther, and round fiercely upon the elder brother. This is less than fair to Samuel, and that for many reasons.

In the first place such a condemnatory attitude ignores the real relationship which existed between the three. If Samuel was all that a son could be to his parents, he was certainly a magnificent brother. Charles was under a special debt of gratitude, for Samuel not only secured his entrance to Westminster, and supported him financially whilst he was there, but watched over his studies and made it possible for him to go to Oxford. Charles became Captain of the School and won a scholarship of £100 per annum which was tenable till marriage. With it he entered Christ Church, Oxford, in 1726.

John did not benefit from Samuel's oversight in study but he constantly sought his advice and was often given it without seeking. When made a Fellow of Lincoln he still sent sermons to his eldest brother for comment. And sometimes the criticism was not palatable. It is interesting in the correspondence to see how John gradually adopted a different attitude writing not as one who learns but as one who teaches. In the letters about the succession to the Epworth Rectory, John deals with Samuel as an equal in the cut and thrust of argument. But from Savannah (23rd November 1736) John is giving his brother counsel. At the time therefore when the battle of wits over the Revival was joined the antagonists were equally matched. When therefore we judge the issue it is never fair to do it with any personal bias. The brothers certainly wrote without rancour, and without any loosening of the strong ties of affection which bound them so closely.

Another and equally weighty reason for refusing to condemn Samuel is that he occupied a perfectly reasonable position. The Revival in its earliest days led to emotional excesses which disturbed even John and Charles, and might justifiably have perplexed anyone who at a distance could know of the strange happenings without being able to measure the larger good. Samuel was at a threefold disadvantage. He was by temperament, training, and conviction a High Churchman. He was far removed from the actual scene, and his information came largely from a woman who was deeply prejudiced against the whole course of events. If he was in error at all, it was that he accepted too lightly the evidence of a witness so manifestly biased.

On their return from Georgia, Charles Wesley, and afterwards John Wesley, had lodged with a well meaning but temperamental family friend, Mrs. Hutton. She it was who wrote in great alarm to Samuel protesting that John had turned into a wild enthusiast and fanatic and was influencing her two sons to follow in his strange courses. John, on Sunday 28th May, four days after his conversion, had declared that prior to 24th May he was not a proper Christian at all. This seemed a wild utterance both to Mr. and Mrs. Hutton and she wrote urging Samuel to put a stop to such madness. Samuel did not wait to hear his brother's account but replied at once and expressed his entire sympathy with her point of view. He said that if she was concerned for her two sons, he was equally troubled for two 'whom I may in some sense call mine'. It was not to be expected that one who believed that Christian discipline, worship, and Sacraments were the necessary conditions of acceptance with God should understand John's new emphasis on saving faith. He could only ask God to stop the progress of the lunacy.

Thus encouraged, Mrs. Hutton returned to the attack with further broadsides. She protested that the converts were directed to get an assurance of forgiveness. They were all expected to give the day and hour of their conversion and her son no less than others had been able to particularize about his spiritual rebirth. She said in words that had prophetic significance that John Wesley had become her son's 'pope'. For how many others did he in later years occupy precisely that position? Samuel felt it was high time to write to his brother to ascertain the facts and

John replied in a reasoned and temperate letter (30th October 1738). But Samuel was not to be mollified so easily. He wrote with equal freedom from rancour but still convinced that the new doctrines were delusive and dangerous. But in a prayer borrowed from the Litany he concluded by saying that they both could invoke God 'to strengthen such as do stand, to comfort and help the weak hearted; to raise up those that fall; and finally to beat down Satan under our feet.'

Samuel was not convinced by John's reply and hardened his tone. He could neither understand nor accept John Wesley's teaching on the witness of the Spirit. And so the correspondence continued, each assuring the other of his affection, but each standing his own ground. In the last letter of the series, written just two months before his death, he congratulated John on the building of a Charity School, and the near completion of a second, and he fervently wished that a Church could also be erected for the colliers. He went on to express his dismay at Whitefield's ecclesiastical irregularities and feared that John might follow him. He did not fear, he continued, with the small discipline existing, that the Church would excommunicate John but John might excommunicate the Church. He was still perturbed about the ecstasies and agonies of hysterical listeners but his tone was milder and rather that of a puzzled inquirer than a frowning judge. He concluded with expressions of love and assured John that he was mending in spite of foul weather. (3rd September 1739.)

On 14th November, Charles Wesley had a letter from a mutual friend to say his brother was dead. At once he and John set out for Tiverton in order to comfort their widowed sister-in-law. John recorded his impressions in the *Journal*: 'On Wednesday 21st November 1739 in the afternoon we came to Tiverton. My poor sister was sorrowing almost as one without hope. Yet we could not but rejoice at hearing from one who had attended my brother in all his weakness, that several days before he went hence God had given him a calm and full assurance of his interest in Christ. O may every one who opposes it be thus convinced that this doctrine is of God.'

Now some would try to show that the Rector and Susanna, together with Samuel, all died in the full assurance of salvation as understood by John and Charles. Susanna most certainly accepted the Methodist emphasis some years before she died.

Since the old Rector died before the Revival dawned, it is only possible to claim him on the grounds of intelligent anticipation. Just as he foresaw a religious awakening, so say the special pleaders, he seized in his Christian experience on the distinctive element in the Methodist contribution. But in actual fact all that can be claimed is that in the tradition of Christians in all communions and in all ages he died well.

It is in that same sense that we can speak of his schoolmaster son. In his last letter his attitude had noticeably changed but he had by no means expressed himself satisfied with the answers of John. He still had questions to ask and criticisms to make. The old touch of asperity had gone; the new mellowness was apparent. But how much farther could one safely go? When he came to die he had neither seen his brothers nor witnessed the work of the Revival at first hand. The utmost therefore that one may affirm is that in the growing weakness of those last weeks, and with his eyes on distant hills, Samuel saw the Revival and its teaching in a new perspective. But an assurance of his interest in Christ was not the witness of the Spirit in the Methodist sense of the phrase. It was rather that commitment to God and acceptance of His will which banishes all doubts and fears, and enables the Christian to know in Richard Baxter's imagery, that one may have to pass through dark rooms, but they are the way into God's Kingdom.

There is no need to try and force the Samuel of those last weeks into a Methodist mould. He was none the less a sincere Christian because he remained unwaveringly a devoted High Churchman. As any intelligent Methodist would repudiate the exclusive claims of the Roman Catholic Church so he would never ask that other Christians should tread his particular path and speak with his particular accent. In the Conference of 1747 the following questions and answers were given.

Q. Must there not be numberless accidental variations in the government of the various Churches?

A. There must in the nature of things. As God disperses His gifts of native providence and grace, both the officers and the offices in each ought to be varied from time to time.

Q. Why is it that there is no determinate plan of Church Government appointed in Scripture?

A. Without doubt because the wisdom of God had a regard to the necessary variety.

If the truth were fully known it is probable that the hand of Samuel lay more heavily on John and Charles than theirs had ever laid on him. His thirteen years seniority to John, and the schoolmaster element in his make-up, made him *in loco parentis* to his brothers. Even John with all his great independence of mind and with the almost irresistible pressure of his people's needs bearing upon him, clung desperately to his mother Church and in all his innovations sought an orthodox justification. If he was restrained partly by his own convictions, he was held back also by the memory of his parents, and by the formidable ghost of Samuel.

With Charles, the influence of Samuel was greater still. In all the formative years of his life from young boyhood to manhood he had seen his parents at infrequent intervals, but Samuel had been with him always. His elder brother was a man in a responsible position when Charles was but a child. It was Samuel who guided his studies and watched his religious growth.

To go to Oxford and on to Georgia and to return to London was to swim constantly in the ken of brother John. For a time—for a long time—the hold of Samuel was weakened. Then came the liberating experience of an evangelical conversion, the intoxication of sharing the leadership in a great crusade. But middle age crept on and the daring ardour of youth ceased to flame so brightly. There were the growing responsibilities of married life. The Revival was sweeping into unchartered channels. There was the constant disapprobation of the Bishops and the hostility of so many clergy. The growing importance of Wesley's preachers and the new prerogatives they were desiring to assume, weighed increasingly upon him. Above all there was a haunting fear. What would John do next? Samuel had done his work well. Old habits of thought reasserted themselves. His eldest brother had been an uncompromising High Churchman sacrificing worldly prospects because he clung so tenaciously to his views. The unfriendly would call him bigoted and even intolerant. He only knew that he loved his Church and would consider any departure from its ways as a rank betrayal. And it was Samuel, who being dead, yet spoke to Charles in those latter years. When John fought for his brother he fought with a ghost and the ghost had the stronger power. Charles could not and would not undo his Methodist past, but neither could he shake off the earlier days with Samuel. And so he stood still whilst John moved forward.

He was still a Methodist but one who stayed resolutely within the Anglican fold. It was Samuel *redivivus*. The brother who had died first, still had the final word.

It is rather hard on Samuel if he is remembered only because he was the eldest son and brother in a famous family. He is interesting in his own right. All the brothers were classical scholars of outstanding quality, but whereas John and Charles widened the range of their activities, and John very markedly the range of his reading, Samuel was able to pursue his classical studies to the end. (During Samuel's twenty years at Westminster he is credited with being mainly responsible through indefatigable labours for the erection of an Infirmary at Westminster in 1719. It is now St. George's Hospital, Hyde Park Corner.) Whilst still a scholar at Westminster he was taken by Dr. Thomas Sprat, Bishop of Rochester, to read to him in the evenings. Samuel resented this interruption to his studies and forcibly expressed himself in one of his letters written in Latin to his father. 'He (the Bishop) will always be exceedingly troublesome to me in sacred and profane learning; for he obliges me to interrupt those studies to which I had applied myself with all my might. Spending my last year in this college, where being a senior, I do not need the hospitality of friends, he has taken me away both from my studies and from school, not only without benefit, but without even the appearance of utility or pleasure. Today he is from home, else I should not have time to write this letter. He chose me from all the scholars: me who am both hoarse and shortsighted to read books to him at night.' (August 1710. The translation is that of Adam Clarke, who said of his later Latin compositions in prose and verse that they showed how much he relished the beauty of the Latin tongue.)

The good Bishop evidently made Samuel feel very cross and yet it was no small compliment to be asked by one of the foremost scholars and literary men in England to share evenings in the company of the learned dead. In a rather neat phrase Samuel referred to Bishop Sprat as his *inimicus amicus* (his unfriendly friend).

At Christ Church, Oxford, he enjoyed a reputation for classical scholarship and had his own place among the wits. Back at Westminster as an Usher, he was very friendly with Vincent (Vinny) Bourne, a fellow Usher, who not only composed some excellent Latin verse but committed himself to the thankless task of translating English poetry into Latin. Amongst Samuel's poetic works there is a neat translation of one of Vinny's poems entitled *Melissa*. In the Poems of Samuel Wesley Junr., edited by James Nichols, the Latin of Bourne and the English translation of Samuel are set side by side. The first eight lines of the poem will give some impression of Samuel's happy facility in translation.

> *If, friend, a wife you mean to wed,*
> *Worthy of your board and bed,*
> *That she be virtuous, be your care,*
> *Not too rich, and not too fair:*
> *One who nor labours to display*
> *New complexions every day,*
> *Nor, studying artificial grace,*
> *Out of boxes culls a face.*

In another joint literary undertaking the roles were reversed, for after Samuel had given his poetic English version of the *Song of the Three Children* (from the Greek fragment in the Apocrypha), Vincent Bourne made an excellent Latin translation of his friend's poem, and died with the labour of love still unfinished.[1]

Vinny Bourne taught William Cowper when he came up to Westminster, and the poet said of him: 'I love the memory of Vinny Bourne. I think him a better Latin poet than Tibullus Propertius, Ansonius, or any of the writers in his way except Ovid, and not at all inferior to him. I love him too with a love of partiality because he was usher of the fifth form at Westminster when I passed through it. . . . It is not common to meet with an author who can make you smile, and yet at nobody's expense: who is always entertaining and yet always harmless: and who though always elegant and classical to a degree not always found in the classics themselves, charms more by the simplicity and playfulness of his ideas than by the neatness and purity of his verse.'

Such a man must not only have stimulated Samuel's love and learning but must have been a source of comfort and satisfaction during those difficult years at Westminster in which Samuel had to tread his own particular wine-press.

Samuel's great learning never received adequate recognition because of his unpopular political opinions, but as a sop to losing the Under-Mastership of Westminster, he did have the

---

[1] Both the English and Latin versions of the Song are to be found in *Collected Poems*, edited J. Nichols (London 1862), p. 382.

consolation of securing the Headmastership of Tiverton Grammar School in 1732. He had always been a good teacher as well as a first-rate scholar, but in the seven years that remained to him, he showed that he had his own share of the Wesley endowment of leadership. He was a great headmaster and in a few short years accomplished a remarkable work. In the very first year of his residence, forty fresh boys were added to that country school, and numbers continued to increase as parents from far and near learnt of this man of exact scholarship but sprightly in manner, and good humoured and kindly in disposition. In one or two of his poems we know how the place appealed to him. He wrote in a poem, *To Mr. Davy:*

> *How happy glides my life away,*
> *I almost am afraid to say,*
> *Lest overstrain'd it seem to be,*
> *And too poetic poetry. . . .*
> *My fortune moderate I confess:*
> *I well could like it, were it less.*
> *Contented with it, as it lies,*
> *I don't expect to fall or rise.*
> *No anxious thoughts my mind engross*
> *With hope of gain or fear of loss;*
> *Nor would I spend an hour to aim*
> *At gaining that child's rattle, fame.*
> *Plenty and peace my household bless,*
> *And constant, cheerful cleanliness.*
> *Here kings and lords and knights may see*
> *True conjugal felicity.*
> *No jars or jealousies are spread;*
> *No rivalship divides the bed;*
> *Nor time nor sickness can remove*
> *The rooted friendship of our love.*
> *My palace, built in Stuart's reign,*
> *Ere Jekyl's Statute of Mortmain,*
> *Pleasure affords without expense,*
> *Retirement with magnificence.*
> *Without, are beauteous prospects seen,*
> *Gardens and river, hills and green.*
> *Within, my books at will supply*
> *Delightful, useful company.*

He goes on to say that he has raised the fees to twenty pounds and this has caused consternation to many since the two previous Headmasters were willing to lose money rather than ask for it. Samuel declared that doubtless half the shire would acclaim his worth if he would

> *Spend on my gentry every groat*
> *Obliged prodigiously for nought.*

His policy in refusing to be intimidated by public opinion was justified by results. Not only were the internal conditions improved, but the whole tone of the school was raised and Samuel gained not public rancour but goodwill. Meanwhile as the lines to Mr. Davy show, Samuel himself was perfectly happy in a most congenial sphere. Have there been many schools, like Tiverton in Samuel's day, in which at the time of examinations public entertainments were arranged?

When he died at so untimely an age, the whole town and countryside mourned his loss. The epitaph on his tombstone says, without any of the customary eighteenth-century exaggeration, that, for the benevolence of his temper and the simplicity of his manners, he was deservedly beloved and esteemed by all. In the long and honoured record of that famous school no name shines with more lustre than that of the Usher at Westminster, whose bitter disappointment led him to his greatest piece of work.

Chapter Seven

CHURCHMAN AND POET

SAMUEL WAS the Jacobite in the family, and those who would assess his place in the eighteenth-century gallery of portraits, must remember not only his learning, but his devotion to a lost cause. All the Wesleys were, in the current acceptation of the term, High Churchmen, but only Samuel went farther and identified himself with the Stuart cause in his political creed. His mother shared his sympathies, but with the accession of Anne all hopes of a Stuart restoration vanished and she accepted the situation with her customary philosophic calm.

Samuel in this respect followed the logic of heart and not of mind. If Samuel had reason to bemoan his connexion with Dr. Sprat, he had infinitely greater reason to bemoan his meeting with Francis Atterbury, who succeeded Sprat as Bishop of Rochester in 1713. The man became his evil genius and yet Samuel remained unswervingly loyal to him. Probably it was through Atterbury's influence that he returned from Oxford to become usher at Westminster and by his advice entered soon afterwards into Holy Orders. The Bishop was not so much the high-spirited Irishman spoiling for a fight as the restless schemer who was finally apprehended and removed to the Tower in 1722 as one concerned directly in a plot to bring back the Pretender. Atterbury pleaded his own cause before the House of Lords in a masterly speech in which he attempted to show the falsity and improbability of the accusation. It would seem, however, that the sentence of perpetual banishment was not severe, for after his death correspondence came to light which established his treasonable intentions. In 1717 in a letter to the Pretender he said: 'My daily prayer is that you may have success. May I live to see that day: and live no longer than I do what is in my power to forward it.' It ought, however, to be remembered in his defence that once on the Continent he made no attempt to communicate with the Pretender and seemed actually to evade the attempts of the Pretender to get in touch with him.

Samuel, despite all the evidence, refused to believe a word against his friend and patron. It was a gallant attitude to maintain because nothing would have been easier than to drop an inconvenient friendship once the friend was securely across the water. Or if that course seemed too drastic, he could at least have been content to follow the slow meandering course of a quiet correspondence. But to champion Atterbury's cause in public, to defend his honour on every possible occasion, to direct fierce lampoons against those in power and most of all to attack the great Sir Robert Walpole himself, was to slam the door against all possible preferment. Samuel was wholly aware of the fact and the inscription on his tombstone only did him common justice when it declared that he was

> *Of such scrupulous integrity,*
> *That he declined occasions of advancement in the world*
> *Through fear of being involved in dangerous compliances;*
> *And avoided the usual ways to preferment*
> *As studiously as many others seek them.*

Samuel would regard any compliance as dangerous that seemed a betrayal of friendship. Even he, however, was not wholly proof against the disappointment of not succeeding to the undermastership of Westminster after nearly twenty years of distinguished service. The *Verses Written under Severe Disappointment* provided a safety valve for his wounded feelings:

> *Oppress'd, O Lord, in Thee I trust,*
>   *To Thee, insulted flee:*
> *Howe'er in mortals 'tis unjust,*
>   *'Tis righteousness in Thee.*

> *To God why should the thankless call*
>   *His blessings to repeat?*
> *Why should the unthankful-for-the-small*
>   *Be trusted with the great?*

> *To Thee my soul for mercy flies,*
>   *And pardon seeks on high;*
> *For earth,—its mercy I despise,*
>   *Its justice I defy.*

> *Grant me, O Lord, with holier care,*
>   *And worthier Thee, to live!*
> *Forgive my foes, and let them dare*
>   *The injured to forgive.*

> *Thy grace, in death's decisive hour,*
> *Though undeserved, bestow!*
> *O, then on me Thy mercies shower!*
> *And welcome, judgment, now!*

There are indications that Atterbury appreciated the friendship maintained by Wesley at such cost. His daughter, Mrs. Morice, was so overborne by a sense of her father's misfortunes that she quickly sank into an illness from which she never recovered. When she realized she was dying she begged to be allowed to see her father, and with the required permission, she sought out her father with 'great spirit and courage'. The two had twenty hours together and in her last words she thanked God who had allowed them to meet once more before parting for ever. It may well have been that the loss of so devoted a daughter hastened his own death. Samuel Wesley wrote an *Elegy* in which he described the daughter's grief on her father's banishment and how it hastened a consumption which she lacked the will to fight. He described her journey to her father and the long tedious days before they finally met. The poem reached its finest flight in the description of the meeting and the father's attempt to hide his sorrow and concern from his daughter. The elegy ended with a description of the bereaved father's grief and the hope that his course well ended, he might find at last 'the loser's conquest, and the exile's home'. Atterbury was much affected by this fresh demonstration of love and sympathy. '24th April 1730. I have received a poem from Mr. Morice which I must be insensible not to thank you for, your *Elegy* upon the death of Mrs. Morice. It is what I cannot help an impulse upon me to tell you, under my own hand—the satisfaction I feel, the approbation I give, the envy I bear you, for this good deed and good work; as a poet and as a man, I thank you, I esteem you.'

A month later (Paris, 27th May 1730) he expressed his gratitude again: 'I am obliged to W. for what he has written on my dear child: and take it the more kindly because he could not hope for my being ever in a condition to reward him—though if ever I am, I will: for he has shown an invariable regard for me all along in all circumstances; and much more than some of his acquaintances, who had ten times greater obligations.'

The next month (30th June) he returned to the theme and thanked Samuel for the verses which 'touched' him 'very nearly'.

He said he was as grateful for the Latin lines preceding as for the English which followed. 'There are a great many good lines in them; and they are written with as much affection as poetry. They came from the heart of the author, and he has a share of mine in return; and if ever I come back to my country, with honour, he shall find it.' Such praise coming from one he admired so greatly and defended so passionately must have sounded sweet in Samuel's ears.

The whole story of his relationship with Atterbury throws a strong light on his own heroic qualities of spirit. He was loyal in friendship and many waters could not quench his love. In his long *Elegy* he dared to write

> *When pyramids, unfaithful to their trust,*
> *Crumble to atoms, with their founders' dust;*
> *When solid marble, mouldering, wastes away,*
> *And lies desert the monumented clay;*
> *Thou still shalt live, to deathless fame consign'd;*
> *Live like the best and bravest of mankind.*

He had shown a devotion that had survived the vicissitudes of fortune.

The greatness of Samuel lay in his fidelity to principle even though it meant the blighting of hopes and the forfeiture of prospects. Few are willing in the service of truth and honour, to sit so lightly to things that many hold so dear. For an exiled Bishop, Samuel turned his back on any prospects of fame and fortune. If this be chivalry then he was in truth 'a very parfit gentil Knight'.

Samuel is to be remembered not only as scholar and teacher; High Churchman and Jacobite; but as poet and satirist. Even apart from the magic of his surname he might still be remembered by the few as a minor poet in the Augustan age. He showed a surprising initiative and freedom from convention at a time when, under the absolute dominance of Pope and Dryden, literary canons had a certain inflexibility. Incidentally the chief literary influence on his poetry was not Pope, but Prior. He was not bound by the closed couplet which chafed so many and which only Pope could outsoar with ease. Like his brother Charles he was continually experimenting with metre and unlike Charles he essayed many forms of literary expression. He wrote songs, hymns, epigrams, satires, odes, elegies, epitaphs, paraphrases, translations, prologues, and epilogues. Yet strangely in all this versification he did not write a sonnet. If his powers had been equal to his technical versatility he would have been a considerable poet, with the added interest of one who would not always march in step.

He had a wider range of subjects than so many Augustan poets whose whole interest was bounded by the life of the town and the chatter of the Coffee Houses. Even so there were whole areas of life which he left untouched. In common with all his age he had no interest in the natural beauty of the countryside. The nearest approach is in his *Lines on a Blackbird* but even here language and thought are both conventional. And for him as for his fellows the lot of the ordinary man was no fit subject for poetry. The poor were still the great unknown.

He did, however, avoid the worst excesses of the Augustan school. He did not, like so many, employ his Muse in the apostrophizing of abstractions. He was not capable of sinking so low as the unhappy Bard who sang 'Inoculation! heavenly maid'. He did not continually personify virtues and vices, and in the contemporary fashion write of them in the feminine gender. And he did not speak in the stilted unreal tones into which the classical style of poetry so easily degenerated. There was genuine feeling in so many of his poems especially when he was dealing with his favourite subjects of death, or marriage, or his own family life. Fourteen of his poems are concerned with marriage, usually of some particular person. Twelve poems are on the subject of death. Always when he wrote about his friends and heroes, or when he defended his own views, he wrote with sincerity and candour.

There are three particular features of his poetry which ought not lightly to be forgotten. First of all he had a pretty wit and his satiric verses had more venom than any gadfly sting. In an Epigram, an elaborate analogy between the unjust steward of the Gospel story and Sir Robert Walpole, he asks:

> *In merit which should we prefer,*
> *The steward or the treasurer?*
> *Neither for justice cared a fig;*
> *Too proud to beg, too old to dig;*
> *Both bountiful themselves have shown*
> *In things that never were their own.*

> *But here a difference we must grant:—*
> *One robbed the rich to keep off want;*
> *T'other, vast treasures to secure,*
> *Stole from the public and the poor.*

In another verse epigram he bitterly praises Walpole for his clemency in banishing Atterbury and concludes:

> *Thou never justly recompensed canst be*
> *Till banished Francis do the same for thee.*

In a still more bitter vein he speaks of the heavy taxation under Walpole's administration and finds his own grim consolation:

> *Four shillings in the pound we see,*
> *And well may rest contented,*
> *Since war—Bob swore't should never be—*
> *Is happily prevented.*
>
> *But he, now absolute become,*
> *May plunder every penny;*
> *Then blame him not for taking some,*
> *But thank for leaving any.*

His nine-verse Litany with its refrain, 'May we be delivered', was a savage attack on the Whig oligarchy. There are twenty-four poems extant directed against Walpole and his administration.

But Samuel could be neater and more devastating in satire when his passions were not so fully engaged. His lines on the erection of a monument to Butler in Westminster Abbey are a perfect example of his mordant wit.

> *While Butler, needy wretch! was yet alive,*
> *No generous patron would a dinner give:*
> *See him, when starved to death, and turn'd to dust,*
> *Presented with a monumental bust!*
> *The poet's fate is here in emblem shown—*
> *He ask'd for bread, and he received a stone.*

There is a crushing attack on those flowing and falsely flattering eulogies inscribed with such delight on eighteenth-century tombstones. It is fitting he should head the poem *The Monument, Post funera virtus.*

CHURCHMAN AND POET

> *If on his specious marble we rely,*
> *Pity a worth like his should ever die!*
> *If credit to his real life we give,*
> *Pity a wretch like him should ever live!*

He speaks in an ageless accent when he deals with the menace that 'in-laws' can be to any marriage:

> *Rather than give the dear one cause to grieve,*
> *A friend, a brother, nay, a parent, leave.*
> *'Tis well if two for lifetime can agree:*
> *None e'er should marry to a family.*

On the Preacher's theme, *Vanitas: omnia vanitas*, he has his own wise comment most pithily expressed:

> *No, not for those of women born*
> *Not so unlike the die is cast;*
> *For after all our vaunt and scorn,*
> *How very small the odds at last!*
>
> *Him raised to fortune's utmost top*
> *With him beneath her feet compare;*
> *And one has nothing more to hope*
> *And one has nothing more to fear.*

Another comment on false values is in his *Epitaph on an Infant*, with its concluding lines:

> *What crowds will wish their lives below*
> *Had been as short as thine!*

With a lightness of touch worthy of the Cavalier poets he praises a lovely lady:

> *No colours laid by pencil on*
> *Can match her eye, her skin, her hair;*
> *Who paints the splendour of the sun,*
> *May paint the splendour of the fair.*

A second feature of Samuel's poetry is that he shared the family gift of hymn writing. If his hymns are compared with those of Charles when at the highest flight of his creative genius they may seem of no great worth. But if one can forget the hymns of Charles and of Isaac Watts and the single great hymn of Dryden, and if one can then remember the doggerel of Nahum Tate and of even lesser poetasters his work can be more properly assessed. Since Samuel's day the output of hymns has grown prodigiously, but the great hymn writers remain pitifully few. Samuel then must not be overshadowed by his brothers' glory. He had a real talent and one can only bewail his scanty output. It is remarkable that at a time when any show of feeling in religion was abhorrent we should have lines so finely written and so instinct with deep emotion as his hymn on the Passion of our Saviour.

> *See streaming from the accursed tree*
> *His all-atoning blood!*
> *Is this the Infinite? 'Tis He!*
> *My Saviour and my God!*
>
> *For me these pangs His soul assail,*
> *For me the death is borne;*
> *My sins gave sharpness to the nail,*
> *And pointed every thorn.*
>
> *Let sin no more my soul enslave;*
> *Break, Lord, the tyrant's chain;*
> *O, save me whom Thou cam'st to save,*
> *Nor bleed nor die in vain!*

The implied truth in the negro Spiritual that we were all there when they crucified the Lord and all had our share in the awful deed, has never been more finely expressed than in those two most moving lines:

> *My sins gave sharpness to the nail,*
> *And pointed every thorn.*

His hymn on the Sabbath Day is still well known and its last verse often quoted.

> *The Lord of Sabbath let us praise,*
> *In concert with the blest.*
>
> . . . .
>
> *He rises, who mankind has bought*
> *With grief and pains extreme;*
> *'Twas great to speak the world from nought,*
> *'Twas greater to redeem.*

His hymn to God the Father speaks in that restrained manner that the fastidious John Wesley of impeccable poetic taste could employ so well.

Hail, Father! whose creating call
Unnumbered worlds attend.

The two further hymns to the Son and to the Holy Spirit are not of equal inspiration, but in his Hymn to the Trinity he again rises in his invocation to the height of his theme. 'Hail Holy holy holy Lord'. Perhaps the best-known hymn of Samuel was his 'Verses on Isaiah 40$^{6-8}$ occasioned by the death of a young lady'. 'All flesh is grass, and all the goodliness thereof is as the flower of the field. The grass withereth, the flower fadeth, but the word of our God shall stand for ever.' They are no longer included in our hymnbook and the sentiments seem strange to modern ears, but the poem is a splendid commentary on the verses and moves with mounting force to its inevitable climax:

The morning flowers display their sweets,
And, gay, their silken leaves unfold;
As careless of the noon-day heats,
And fearless of the evening cold.

Nipp'd by the wind's unkindly blast,
Parch'd by the sun's directer ray,
The momentary glories waste,
The short-lived beauties die away.

So blooms the human face divine,
When youth its pride of beauty shows;
Fairer than Spring the colours shine,
And sweeter than the virgin-rose.

Or worn by slowly rolling years,
Or broke by sickness in a day;
The fading glory disappears,
The short-lived beauties die away.

Yet these, new rising from the tomb,
With lustre brighter far shall shine,
Revive with ever-during bloom,
Safe from diseases and decline.

> *Let sickness blast, and death devour,*
> *If heaven must recompense our pains;*
> *Perish the grass, and fade the flower,*
> *If firm the word of God remains.*

The poem does not lapse in thought or expression but proceeds strongly to the last two memorable lines. It cannot be said that any of Samuel's hymns will live as long as the English language, but he had a spark of that divine fire which blazed so gloriously in brother Charles.

The third characteristic of Samuel's poetry is the strongly personal element running through it. He pilloried his enemies and praised his friends. One of his most witty poems was written about that notorious bookseller, Edmund Curll, who sold pirated editions of books and amongst other sins that belong to an unscrupulous bookseller

> *Didst thou not the Oration print,*
> *Imperfect, with false Latin in't?*

Samuel didn't like the man and described with verve and in high glee how he steered his hasty, hapless course to Westminster only to receive exemplary punishment.

> *Lo! wide-extended by the crowd,*
> *The blanket, dreadful as a shroud,*
> *Yawns terrible, for thee, poor Mun,*
> *To stretch, but not to sleep upon.*

After the blanket-tossing described in witty detail Samuel described in mock sympathy the hapless victim led to the table and spread across it, whilst

> *The rest around, a threatening band,*
> *With each his fasces in his hand,*
> *Dreadful as Roman lictors stand.*

They did not allow the man's breeches to obstruct them in their self-imposed task.

> *And with a lash, as is their fashion,*
> *Finish'd each smart expostulation.*

Wesley concluded philosophically:

> *Though all that can by man be said*
> *Can ne'er beat sense into thy head,*
> *Yet sure this method cannot fail*
> *Quick to convey it to thy tail.*

He reserved his final jibe for his closing lines:

> *For ever this shall grate thine ear,*
> *—Which is the way to Westminster?*[1]

Samuel's political invective might seem surprisingly daring and splenetic to our more tender feelings. In his own day he was but one of a large number who as they brandished their weapons gave and asked no quarter. And naturally there was a numerous reading public eager to enjoy this form of political controversy. But there was no sly venom and subtle innuendo in Samuel's verses; only hard hitting in scorn of consequence. In any case many of his political poems were written as a young man,[2] and whilst he always kept his rod in pickle, asperity increasingly gave way to a certain dry and almost genial humour.[3] He showed his freedom from malice in his own suggested Epitaph:

> *Here Wesley lies in quiet rest,*
> *Hated in earnest for his jest.*
> *Here he his worldly bustle ends,*
> *Safe from his foes and from his friends.*

And always his pen flowed more freely in the service of his friends. He never wrote about his hero Francis Atterbury without an active mingling of love and sympathy, and the *Elegy* was at once a fervent panegyric and a last diatribe against his foes. After Atterbury it was Harley, Earl of Oxford, who drew his unstinted praise. Six poems were addressed to him or his daughter, the Lady Margaret Harley. It is commonly supposed that Samuel secured the headmastership of Tiverton owing to the Earl of Oxford's good offices on his behalf. In one of his poems Alexander Pope speaks of the friendship between Samuel Wesley and his two patrons, Atterbury and Oxford. He concludes the poem:

---

[1] *Neck or Nothing.* Consolatory letter from Mr. Dunton to Mr. Curll on his being tossed in a blanket in year 1716. Samuel pretends it is Dunton who writes because Dunton, another publisher and bookseller, did similar malpractices.
[2] See Nichols's comments in *Collected Poems*, p. 610.
[3] See his lines on Dr. Middleton, 'pertly dogmatic against dogmatizing', and on Dr. Swift.

> *That both were good must be confess'd,*
> *And much to both he owes;*
> *But which to him will be the best,*
> *The Lord of Oxford knows.*

His verses upon his father pass beyond the mere tribute of filial piety. He showed not mere affection but a deep respect and admiration for the Rector's poetry, for his learning and for his many virtues. Although his poem, *The Epitaph*, has no particular designation, it is the Rector he must have had in mind and the simple eloquent lines are all unknowing a vindication of his father's character against the attacks of would-be detractors:

> *A clergyman his labours ends,*
> *And weary sleeps at rest below;*
> *Who, though his fortune found not friends,*
> *In person hardly knew a foe.*
>
> *Minding no business but his own,*
> *For party never loud to strive;*
> *His flock not only mourn him gone,*
> *But even loved him when alive.*
>
> *A conscience clean his forehead cheer'd,*
> *Unsour'd by poverty was he;*
> *And always praised, though not preferr'd,*
> *By every prelate in the see.*
>
> *But good men view with small regard*
> *The treatment here on earth they find;*
> *Secure in heaven to meet reward*
> *From the great Bishop of mankind.*

Samuel also wrote a long poem extolling the strong yet kindly virtues of his father-in-law, the Rev. John Berry, A.M., Vicar of Watton in Norfolk. It was called *The Parish Priest*. Berry died in 1730 and the poem was published in 1731. A second edition was called for in 1732.

Samuel wrote so many poems to his friends on the occasion of their marriages because his own was so happy. Writing to his sister, Anne, when she became Mrs. Lambert he could not desire more for her than a union as happy as his own.

> *The greatest earthly pleasure try*
> *Allow'd by Providence Divine:*
> *Be he a husband blest as I,*
> *And thou a wife as good as mine!*

Even when he does not directly mention his wife, as in his poems to Mr. Juson and Mr. Pierce on their marriage, his own marriage is always the background against which he proffers his sage advice.[1]

It was his pleasant habit on occasion to write a poem for his wife on her birthday. One was even composed to be sung to the tune of a popular song of the day, 'The Sun was Sunk Beneath the Hill'. It went off to a merry start:

> *Let various seasons boast their pride,—*
> *The spring with flowers the earth adorn,*
> *While cloudless days the summer glide,*
> *And autumn show her fruits and corn;*
> *These may demand a vulgar lay;*
> *I sing of a December's day.*

But were the eight verses ever sung, and if so who sang? Did the worthy couple lift up their voice in unison? How embarrassing for his wife. It must not be supposed that Samuel Wesley's love was blind. He scorned those who love by impulse and feeling alone. 'For how can pleasure solid be, where thought is out of season.' He confessed she is not 'a belle, a beauty, or a wit', and consoled himself for her lack of glittering attractions by stressing that he had the one pearl of greatest price.

> *To their idols let them fall;*
> *Love is mine, and love is all.*

Actually he has given us a picture of her in another of his poems, *A Character*:

> *Her hair and skin are as the Berry brown;*[2]
> *Soft is her smile, and graceful is her frown;*
> *Her stature low, 'tis something less than mine;*
> *Her shape, though good, not exquisitely fine;*
> *Though round her hazel eye some sadness lies,*
> *Their sprightly glances can sometimes surprise.*

[1] See also Samuel's lines to Mr. Forrester, Mr. Lloyd, and Mr. Jewell on their marriages.
[2] Mrs. Samuel Wesley was Miss Berry before marriage.

> But greater beauties to her mind belong;
> Well can she speak, and wisely hold her tongue.
> In her, plain sense and humble sweetness meet;
> Though gay, religious, and though young, discreet.
> Such is the maid, If I can judge aright,
> If love or favour hinder not my sight.
> Perhaps you'll ask me how so well I know;
> I've studied her, and I confess it too.
> I've sought each inmost failing to explore,
> Though still the more I sought, I liked the more.

His happiest poems to his wife are his so-called Anacreontics:

I

> O, to see my Nutty smiling,
> Time with amorous talk beguiling,
> Love her every action gracing,
> Arms still open for embracing,
> Looks to mutual bliss inviting,
> Eyes delighted and delighting,
> Spotless innocence preventing
> After-grief and sad repenting;
> Neither doubting, both believing,
> Transport causing and receiving;
> Both with equal ardour moving,
> Dearly loved and truly loving!
> Long may both enjoy the pleasure
> Without guilt and without measure!

II—1715

> Ere I found you fair and good;
> Ere the nut-brown maid I view'd;
> Sunny walks and spreading trees,
> Sports and theatres, could please.
> Soon as e'er my Love was known,
> All I left for her alone.
> Golden hours glide smiling on,
> Golden all without the sun;
> Since I, happy all the while,
> Hear you talk, and see you smile.

Sunny meads and living trees,
Sports and theatres, displease;
Learning's self and friends, adieu!
Joys are centred now in you.
Yet by learning shall I prove
Partly worthy of your love.
Hope so glorious will despise
Aching head and watering eyes:
Hope so glorious will allay
Midnight watch and toil of day.
Books for you aside were thrown,
Now resumed for you alone.

III

Meanest rhymer that I am,
Scoff'd and branded for the name;
Still I write, if you approve;
Glory shall submit to love.
Were I fill'd with poet's fire,
Sweet as gay Anacreon's lyre,
Verse if you should disapprove,
Glory should submit to love.
Truth you read without disguise;
Stranger I to sugar'd lies,
Faithless fawning flatteries!
Love like mine will still compose
Verse as faithful as my prose.
Fabling poetry shall ne'er
Paint you lovelier than you are.
Talk of goddesses who will,
Still you're dear, but woman still.
Be but what you're now, I'll ne'er
Wish you lovelier than you are.

IV

Dear, and ever dear, whom I
Wooed and won without a lie,
Let my growing passion prove
Still more pleasing to my Love.

Verses smiling have you view'd,
Graced alone with gratitude:
Still they're grateful: may they prove
Still more pleasing to my Love!
Here no witty falsehood shines;
Here no tinsel gilds the lines.
This suffices, if they prove
Full of truth and full of love!
Truth can never need a lie:
Truth is sense and poetry.
Truth alone could Nutty move:
Truth is happiness and love.
May our age be as our youth,
Full of love, and full of truth!
One the other never grieving,
Undeceived and undeceiving;
Happy thou, transported I;
Faithful, blest, without a lie!

The poetic quality of these poems is mediocre indeed though the lines run smoothly. But they throw a strong light on his completely happy married life. It was well that their love was strong, because apart from the financial burden of supporting others, and apart from the material set-backs in his career, they were called upon to suffer many bereavements. Although they had a large family only two (a boy and a girl) seem to have survived infancy. It was a shattering blow to Samuel when his little son died in 1731. The moving and eloquent lines, *For a sick child*, based on John 4[46-53], may, though without actual proof, have been written during his boy's illness. One verse will suffice to show the torment of the father,

O save the father in the son
Restore him Lord to me!
My heart the miracle shall own
And give him back to Thee.

He also wrote movingly on the *Death of a Daughter*. The one child who lived married a Dr. Earle in Barnstaple, but though she had several children no record of their later lives has survived.[1]

---

[1] There is a tradition which I have not been able to substantiate that Samuel's grand-daughter married Marshal Ney, the famous General who stood by Napoleon. See Stevenson's *Memorials of the Wesley Family*, p. 256.

There is other evidence lighting up his devotion to his wife and home. He said in a letter to John (18th November 1727) that he wished to God his father and mother were as easy in one another and as little uneasy in their fortunes as his wife and himself. He declared in that sense, it was a case of *Tydides melior patris*. This absence of quarrelling was not solely due to Samuel's amiability. He had definite ideas of the husband's authority and expressed them in his marriage poems, but like many other wives Mrs. Samuel Wesley knew how to keep a real measure of power whilst being, in Samuel's words, 'joyful to obey'. He asked his friend 'to choose the Lord to be; rather than to appear', but in his own case the line would seem to refer more aptly to the wife than to the husband. Mrs. Hall (Martha Wesley) knew her sister-in-law well and said that a couplet in one of Samuel's poems, *The Pig*, summed her up completely,

> She made her little wisdom go
> Farther than wiser women do.

If she was in no sense a remarkable woman she made her husband remarkably happy. Amongst many unhappy marriages of the Wesley family, those of Samuel and of Charles Wesley stand out in their deep tranquillity and joy.

Samuel lacked both the distinguished appearance of his brothers and their power of leadership. He had talents in many fields but genius in none. Unlike his brothers he left behind no rich enduring legacy. But he lived life fully and he lived it well. He hurt none and helped many. He lived a good, and in spite of many sorrows, a happy life. In an age of rationalism he remained a convinced Christian and a faithful son of the Church. In an age of sycophancy and easy honour he held his course unmoved by threat or by dangling promise. In a rich combination of qualities of mind and heart he rose far above the generality of his fellows. He does not need the reflected glory of John and Charles. They were the greater luminaries. But he also was a burning and a shining light. There are not two brothers to be remembered. There are three.

Chapter Eight

THE WESLEY SISTERS

THE LOT of the Wesley sisters is a matter for tears. With the possible exception of Hetty they lacked the genius of the Bronte sisters but they moved against a similar background. Epworth was almost as remote from the life of the Metropolis as Haworth, and the girls were doubly isolated because they could not have social intercourse with the people around them nor had they access to the circles of the gentry. They were therefore confined overmuch within Parsonage walls and lived within the chill shadow of fathers who had high intentions but lack of understanding. It would almost seem as if they were doomed to play their parts in high tragedy. Since their lives were relatively uneventful the drama lay in the play of spirit rather than outward circumstance. But the parallel cannot further be forced. For whereas the Brontë sisters were dogged by ill-health, the Wesley sisters were dogged by ill-fortune. It might well be argued that though, apart from Mary, they lived longer, they were more actively unhappy than the girls on the Haworth moors.

Their misfortunes are focused in the story of Hetty (Mehetabel), most lovely, most spritely, most talented, and most unhappy of them all. Quiller-Couch wrote one of his finest novels about Hetty and said that of all his books it was the one which he could regard with most satisfaction. No one will deny the essential truth of his narrative nor his faithful and sympathetic portrayal of his luckless heroine. But he oversimplifies the cause of her misfortune and belabours too severely the 'laborious Tyerman' and all those critics who 'do not face the facts because they do not dare'. By this outburst he means all those who will not share his unmitigated condemnation of the Rector as the chief author of her wrongs. Even the faithless lover and the drunken husband do not show up so badly as the tyrant of Epworth.

It is this picture which colours the minds of those who champion Hetty and her sisters, and pour out their wrath on the father. But one can dare to face the facts—all the facts—and still resist stoutly the conclusion that one has 'an uneducated habit of mind' because one differs from Quiller-Couch. If one is to criticize his work, not as a brilliant piece of fiction, but as serious historical research, it must be said that he finds his devil too easily. His main conclusions ought to be accepted but they must certainly be modified. There are certain factors, not stressed by Quiller-Couch nor his school, which deserve the courtesy of mention. Both Samuel and Susanna desired to give their three sons the best available education. And this by dint of heroic effort and sacrifice they accomplished. It was an incomparable gift not only to the sons but to the world. Would John without it have founded the Methodist societies? We do not know, but most certainly had it been attempted, he could not have brought to the task the same full and rich equipment. Could Charles have written his hymns? Of course! But would they have been the same in quality? The answer is not so certain.

But it may be argued that Samuel could have provided for his sons, and still not neglected his daughters. Such reasoning ignores the material facts. It was a case of either/or, but not a case of both. The Rector's unavailing fight against debt made it impossible to see his sons through school and university and still to make similar provision for his daughters.

In twentieth-century days it might be maintained that he need not have made the accident of sex a fatal handicap to the girls. Why not give the chance of a good education to those (whether sons or daughters) who could take it? But in the eighteenth century, careers for women was a phrase without meaning. All trades and professions were open to the boys, but apart from teaching, scarcely any livelihood was open to women. It was against this unfair tilting of the balance that Lady Mary Wortley Montague, Mary Godwin, and Mary Wollstonecraft raised their voices as the century wore on. Apart from the education received at home, where could the Wesley girls have gone except to a fashionable boarding-school? The fees at such schools seemed to be in inverse ratio to the learning given. John Wesley's strictures on them are familiar to all the readers of his *Journal*. He said in a famous passage that they were places of pride, vanity, and affectation, and that if parents wanted to send their children headlong to hell the best way would be to send them to a fashionable boarding-school. Another shrewd critic described such schooling as a 'dedication to the pomps and vanities of the Devil, in complete defiance of baptismal vows'.[1]

[1] Mrs. Montague—see *Wesley's England*, J. H. Whiteley, p. 322.

It would seem that since a girl was predestined whether as wife or spinster for home life the subjects were selected with that end constantly in view. They were taught to sing and to play the harpsichord and guitar; they were instructed in reading, the art of good penmanship, the casting of accounts, and embroidery. We know how close was the contact with French life and thought in the eighteenth century and how the French language had finally superseded Latin as the *lingua franca*. It is probable not only that French was taught in most girls' schools, but taught well. At Miss Pinkerton's School the curriculum advertised that 'Young Ladies are Compleately Finish'd in Ev'ry Polite as well as Usefull Branch of Education, viz. French, Musick, Dauncing, Deportment, Writing, Fine Work, Plain Work, Childe-bed Linnen'. In that list, deportment is perhaps the all-important word. The young ladies were instructed how to hold themselves, how to sit and rise gracefully, how to enter and alight from a carriage, and how to behave decorously in any company. Miss Bayne Powell (*The English Child in the Eighteenth Century*) speaks of the tyranny of curtsies and conventions in the life of such children.

The greater number of girls in the upper classes did not go to school at all. It was considered unnecessary when a governess could teach them for £20 a year all that it was deemed necessary to know. They accepted the dictum of Shelburne, the first Marquis of Lansdowne and a statesman of merit, that a little spinning and some moral training was all that was required for women of his class. 'Women', he said, 'are domestic animals and should never be taught to go from home.'

In the light of contemporary theory and practice, the Rector and Susanna did all that could be expected in the education of their daughters. Susanna's instruction was supplemented on occasion by the Rector. Hetty herself was so ready and promising a pupil that he gave her some grounding in the classics. After the disastrous fire Susanna (Sukey) and Hetty had the further advantage of being sent for many months to the hospitable home of the urbane and cultivated Matthew Wesley. No one knows what education the girls received at Epworth but if a tree can be known by its fruits, then their training offered fair comparison with any in their day. Only girls of considerable culture could receive and appreciate the letters their mother sent to them; much of the correspondence was an unwitting extension of their education in Christian doctrine and moral theology. Their own letters reveal their quick and lively minds and in writing to their brothers, a vicarious interest in the greater world outside. Was Adam Clarke right in surmising that their parents educated them to be governesses? Emily at least had no difficulty in securing a post as teacher (1730) at the boarding-school of a Mrs. Taylor in Lincoln. She had so much to do and was so ill paid that she took the brave step of leaving and setting up a school of her own at Gainsborough. She was still there when the old Rector died (1735) and only abandoned the school when she married Mr. Harper. Her general learning was such that the fastidious John Wesley pronounced her 'the best reader of Milton that he ever heard'.

Kezia and John corresponded frequently and he sought to guide her reading, forgetting that the *res angusti domi* prevented her following so ambitious a programme. In one pathetic outburst she says that she realizes that the pursuit of knowledge and virtue will most improve the mind but that she can neither buy nor borrow the books she wants, and at that precise moment had only Nelson's *Method of Devotion* and the *Whole Duty of Man* as her reading matter.

Martha (known as Patty) Wesley sustained her cultural interests to such good effect that after a long and unhappy married life with its great vicissitudes she was still able in old age to delight the famous Dr. Johnson with her company, and to be a most frequent and welcome visitor to his house. Indeed he begged her to come and stay and her only reason for refusal was that she feared she might stir to further jealousy Mrs. Williams and Mrs. Du Moulin who already resided there. But she talked with him constantly on matters of theology and philosophy without suffering the verbal castigation that was so often the lot of others.

But it is Hetty who is the supreme vindication of the early training given to the daughters. Her natural gifts were developed and her conversation, her letters, her poetry, and the testimony of others, are several tributes to her independent mind and ready scholarship. Her reading was wide and balanced. She knew Latin and some Greek, but English she could write like a master. It was part of her unhappiness that she who 'would have been an honour to the first man in the land' should have married one who intellectually was so greatly her inferior.

Whatever charge is laid against Samuel the Rector he must be acquitted of such complete immersion in the prospects of his sons that he neglected to provide an education for his daughters.

K

There is, however, a second charge which is much more serious and is sustained with such deadly effect by Quiller-Couch. Did he really understand his girls? Was he overmuch concerned with their future? Did he use his authority disastrously when their suitors appeared? In the England between the wars a play and a novel were each concerned with the relation of a father to his children and each had its own wide popularity. Rudolf Besier's play, *The Barretts of Wimpole Street*, showed a Victorian father ruling his family like an autocrat. When he entered a room his sons stood up rigidly, clicked their heels, and said, 'Sir'. To incur his displeasure by opposing his commands was to invite the thunderbolts of Jove. Doubtless Mr. Barrett was more than ordinarily severe, but in his exercise of authority and the unquestioning obedience he expected, he was only typical of his times. To go from Barrett to Sorrell is to make a journey of less than a hundred years and yet to enter into a different world. Warwick Deeping's novel, *Sorrell and Son*, is the picture of any modern parent who secures his child's obedience through love and not through power. He seeks to understand him and to win his affection so that his response is willing and unforced. At its worst this attitude leads to a stupid disregard of the difference between the generations. Such parents allow an unrestricted freedom to their children, delight in the language of slangy heartiness and ask for nothing better than that their children should treat them as 'pals'. *Optimi corruptio pessima*. Whatever may be the excesses, we believe our modern approach is right, and are therefore more prone to deal severely with the mistaken ideas of parental authority in ages before our own. And so inevitably Samuel Wesley comes under the lash. But if he is to be judged, common fairness demands that he be treated as a child of his age and not of our own. He lived more than a century before the redoubtable Mr. Barrett and certainly therefore at a time when the father's authority was unquestioned. He believed it was his duty to rule and guide and help his children and he set himself conscientiously to do it. In accordance with those principles he secured for them all, and especially the boys since they needed it most, as liberal an education as he could afford. He found for his girls what openings he could. Emily secured a post as a teacher, and when temporarily she returned home to Wroot, it was at the urgent request of her mother and not her father. She wrote in a letter to John: 'My Mother was earnest for my return' (7th April 1725). She soon came back to her teaching. Susanna (Sukey) stayed in London first with her uncle Matthew Wesley and afterwards with a maternal uncle, Samuel Annesley, and then precipitately married so that the need of a suitable occupation did not arise. Mary was a cripple and so the question of leaving home did not arise. Hetty was sent to Kelston and as governess to the two small children of Mrs. Grantham she had an easy happy post in the comfortable home of a wealthy and well-disposed lady who treated her with great kindness. When she decided to return home it was so much her own decision that Mr. and Mrs. Grantham were dumbfounded at the suddenness of it all. She left because her unhappy love affair had become general knowledge and she elected to meet the family on their own ground. Martha (Patty) also went to Mrs. Grantham during the time that Hetty was teaching there and although she had the light if somewhat ambiguous post of 'companion', her ease of mind was destroyed because she felt banished from her loved one. It was this failure to settle down which caused her to return to Wroot within the year (1725). After a few years at home she came in 1729 to stay with her Uncle Matthew in London and this second visit lasted six years. She left her uncle only when she married the ineffable Westley Hall. Kezia (Kezzy) the youngest child became a pupil teacher in Lincoln and both gave and received instruction for her board alone without an allowance even for clothes. Her letters (26th January, 12th July 1729; 20th January 1731) to John Wesley reveal her preoccupation with her poverty and ill-health. When she returned to Epworth, however, it was not solely because of the intolerable spartan conditions at Lincoln, but because her father was becoming increasingly feeble, her sisters apart from Mary had left home, and her mother had great need of her help in the management of the Rectory. When Mary married John Whitelamb in 1734, Kezzy alone remained of the nineteen children to care for the house and her ageing parents.

This record of the daughters' occupations has not been so brief that one fact does not stand out like a jagged rock. Samuel (and Susanna) made what provision they could for their daughters to make a start in life.

The different conceptions of the father's authority in the eighteenth century and our own day is nowhere more strikingly shown than in the question of marriage. We may seek to influence our children but we are loth to interfere with their choice. Samuel

Wesley was entirely in consonance with his age when he sought to arrange the marriages of his children. Virginia Woolf in her spirited defence of the proper status of women[1] has shown for those who did not know it already, how little a woman in that day could follow the promptings of her own heart, and how much she was subject in her mating to the will of her parents. It was not necessarily a disastrous state of affairs. The over-romanticized ideas of 'falling in love', and marrying even against the parent's advice may lead to great unhappiness. In France, where marriages are still largely arranged, there is no evidence that such unions are notoriously more unhappy and short-lived than in our contemporary England. We may have surfeited excessively on Hollywood glamour and the glorification of sex. The ideal conditions are fulfilled when children are sensitive to the judgement and advice of wise parents and their own ultimate choice carries parental approval. Doubtless the interference of father and mother may be foolish and hurtful and this may be aggravated when they desire a union from mercenary or coldly calculating motives of self interest. But given wise parents who love and understand their children and seek only their greatest good, a case may still be made out for their judicious and persuasive intervention. If parents heavily overstressed their responsibility in the eighteenth century, they can sometimes undervalue their proper role in our enlightened age.

Samuel, like other fathers in his social class, took his duties seriously. He wanted nothing for himself. He was not ambitious in a worldly sense for his daughters. He desired only to save them from the wrong man and to ensure them a reasonable prospect of married happiness. Quiller-Couch pushed his special pleading ridiculously far when he suggested that the Rector hated 'that anyone should offer love to his daughters'. He had far too little initial sympathy with the Rector to form an unbiased judgement.

Emilia (Emily) the eldest daughter met an Oxford student named Leybourne whilst she was staying in London with her Uncle Matthew. She was lonely and lacked both money and employment. In a letter to John she said that Leybourne had the 'highest understanding and the sweetest temper in England'. Emily nestled in his sympathy and comfort for three long years. In the full tide of her love for him, any reflection on his integrity seemed both monstrous and malicious. She darkly attacked a

[1] *A Room of One's Own* (1929; Penguin edition 1945), p. 37.

'near relation' as 'the groundwork of all her misery'.[1] But although the affair was broken off she did not so much as mention her father, but imputed it to her mother's command and her own indiscretion. Poor Emily suffered badly. For over half a year she declared that she could not sleep at night and resolved in her misery that she would never marry. She cried out in a letter to John:

> Let Emma's hapless case be told
> By the rash young or the ill-natured old.

Four years later (1729) she is still talking of Leybourne and begging John not to withdraw his friendship but to assist him in his distress. For herself she spoke of death as 'a consummation devoutly to be wished'.

Gradually, however, she came to realize that her mother and brother Samuel were right and that she had been deceived. She said in a letter to John on 7th February 1733 that 'when I loved L. he loved not me, though he was rogue enough to persuade me he did. Well so much for that!' So much for that indeed, but her love affairs were by no means over. When she was over forty years of age she found a man whom she could describe as a faithful friend, a delightful companion, and a most passionate lover. He was a Quaker and a physician. One might well have thought that Emily had found safe anchorage. But once again there was family interference and this time from her beloved brother John. His objection seemed mainly to have been based on the fact that the worthy Doctor was a Quaker! Emily half playfully and half sadly complained that her own brother for whom she had the tenderest regard and whom she had never wilfully grieved or disobeyed should press on her as a strict duty the necessity of parting for ever from her companion. She asked in despair what was there now left in life worth valuing. She felt she could no longer strive against the stream, but her tone was not one of bitterness or reproach and she ended the letter in her accustomed affectionate way.[2]

Perhaps she was not so sorely stricken! In that same letter she told John that she was more opposed to her lover's Whig principles

[1] Although in one letter she speaks of R. Wes., it is most probable that Samuel her brother, who was in London of course, and knew and keenly disapproved of Leybourne, was the one to whom she referred. If not Samuel, it was Mrs. Samuel Wesley.

[2] 7th February 1733. It is a melancholy fact that so much of the unhappiness of the Wesley family was caused by their interference in each other's love affairs. The sisters let each other alone. But the Rector and his three sons all interfered with marriages on occasion and not always wisely.

than his Quaker faith. She had a violent argument lasting two hours on the question of politics and was upset at being so strongly contradicted. She told John that she had an avowed doctrine that an unmarried woman could never be in the wrong in any conversation with a bachelor. The Doctor finally lost his chance when he found Emily talking to another man. His proprietary airs stung Emily to assert that until a man had proposed marriage and been accepted he had no reason to complain if a woman spoke to other men and enjoyed their friendship. She left the medical man to drink that unpalatable physic, and said almost gaily in her letter, 'So farewell George Fox, and all thy tribe, for Rockwood and Ringwood and Towler and Tray'.

Just before John Wesley sailed to Georgia he married Emily to Robert Harper, an apothecary of Epworth. It was not a romantic affair. Both were in middle life and Emily had suffered too much to be capable of *'une grande passion'*. In any case he was not the man to evoke it. He was a complete failure in business and whilst he took a large part of her school profits 'he thought himself very kind if once in six months he gave her ten shillings'. She wrote a broken-hearted letter to John in which she said that she had sold many of her clothes for bread, and lacked the common necessaries of life. 'I have yet a bed to lie on but Christmas will soon be here, and if Bob Harper will do nothing to raise a half-year's rent I cannot get it myself, though I could somewhat toward it: and 'tis a cold time of year to be turned out of doors.' Hetty had written a poem full of graceful compliments to her sister on the occasion of her marriage, but alas! all that could be said of that unhappy event was that it soon ended. When Emily came to the Foundery in 1740 she came alone. It is not altogether certain that Harper had died. The only positive information to be derived from her letters is that he had died before 1750. At first she stayed with her mother and threw herself into the busy life at the Foundery, but later when West Street Chapel was taken, John maintained her in the chapel house. Here she lacked nothing and entered at last into her happiest days. Before the Deaconess Order was thought of she fulfilled that ministry. Her sole concern was for the services of the Chapel, the welfare of the Society and the care of the people.

> 'Twixt the mount and multitude
> Doing or receiving good.

When she died at her chapel apartments she had in very truth only to pass from one room in God's house to another.

Susanna, the next daughter, chose to go her own way in her love making, and she found that possible because she was staying with her uncle in London. Quite possibly both the Rector and his wife would have objected and on highly sufficient grounds, but they could not undo an irrevocable act. Mrs. Samuel Wesley described Richard Ellison, her son-in-law, as a 'gentleman of good family, but a coarse, vulgar, immoral man', and the Rector roundly declared that Dick Ellison's company was not more pleasant to him than all his physic. Indeed, Dick Ellison's profligacy was one matter on which all the members of the Wesley family were agreed. Martha (Patty) said that he wanted 'all but riches', whilst Samuel junr. thought that Dick Ellison prided himself on having neither religion, good nature, nor manners. Even his 'riches' did not remain. There was first of all the fire which destroyed their house and was inexplicably the immediate cause of their separation. The underlying cause doubtless was his 'harsh despotic and coarse' nature and his profligate manner of life. 'Under his unkindness she well-nigh sank into the grave.' When he was already without wife and children and property, his land (owing to the Commissioner of Sewers' neglect) was left under water for two years, and all his cows died. In these desperate circumstances he came to London and sought help from his brother-in-law. John, who was never deaf to the cry of the miserable, persuaded Ebenezer Blackwell, the banker, to let Dick Ellison benefit from the charity of a Mr. Butterfield.

His wife and their four children were safely hidden from him in London and despite all his entreaties and stratagems they never returned to him. One oft-quoted story says that he advertised his death, and she returned for the obsequies, but finding it a trick returned to London at once. The generous action of John may have 'stabbed his spirit broad awake' because he remained in London and for the last few years of his life he attended the Foundery services and died in peace. Charles Wesley writing to his wife, said: 'Yesterday evening I buried my brother Ellison. Sister Macdonald, whom he was always very fond of, prayed with him in his last moments. He told her he was not afraid to die, and believed God, for Christ's sake, had forgiven him. I felt a most solemn awe overwhelming me while I committed his body to the earth. He is gone to increase my father's joy in Paradise, who often said that every one of his children would be saved, for God had given them all to him in answer to prayer. God grant I may not be the single exception.'[1]

Mary (Molly) never allowed her deformity to warp her nature. All the family speak of her with love and in tender pride. Her mind was as lovely as her face and Hetty spoke of her as 'one of the most exalted of human characters'. She had no option but to be the household drudge and she transcended her lot by accepting it. In two letters which have come down from her she spoke of gloves. Writing to Charles (20th January 1726) she said he had no need to thank her because she was rewarded by his acceptance of them. Writing to John on the same day she said in merry vein: 'Please get Miss Betsy to buy some silk to knit you another pair of gloves, and I don't doubt you will doubly like the colour for the buyer's sake.' If in the only evidence we have the needles are clicking busily, point is given to her own remark to Charles that she 'would be glad if she could spend her whole life doing good to fellow creatures'.

She was devoted to her father and certainly she had a special place in his affections, and yet it is a true instinct which caused Quiller-Couch to portray her as the vehement champion of Hetty in the family quarrel. There was not only a strong bond uniting the sisters, but Mary, though in Charles' words 'a patient Grizzle', was no dumb ox. She was as high-mettled and courageous as her sisters.

She did not expect a man to cross her path, and yet strangely her love story was the sweetest and most satisfying of all the sisters before it terminated so quickly in her death. 'Poor starveling Johnny', when he came to reside at the Epworth Rectory, was very much the tall gaunt scarecrow Mrs. Wesley's words suggested. As a poor boy in the neighbouring village of Wroot he did not receive more than a limited education in the endowed school of the village. John Romley at that time was in charge, and doubtless spoke of John Whitelamb to the Rector.

A queer but deep-grounded friendship sprang up between Samuel and the young man, and it was based upon the debt each owed the other. John acted as the Rector's amanuensis and drew the execrable illustrations for the *Dissertations on Job*. But a man may be a good scholar and a most indifferent artist. Certainly John Whitelamb eagerly absorbed all the Rector had to teach

[1] London, Seven Dials. 11th April 1760. Susanna (Sukey) his wife died December 1764 at the age of 69 years. See *Letters* (Standard Edition), Vol. 4, p. 276.

him. It was wholly due to the generosity of the Wesley family that he was able to go to Oxford. There at Lincoln College, with John Wesley providing free tutorship, he gave himself wholeheartedly to his studies. John Wesley said in a letter to his father (June 1731): 'John Whitelamb reads one English, one Latin, and one Greek book alternately, and never meddles with a new one till he has ended the old one. If he goes on as he has begun, I dare to take upon me to say that by the time he has been here four or five years there will not be such a one of his standing in Lincoln College, perhaps not in the University of Oxford.'

After his ordination, he returned to Epworth in 1733 and served as curate in the parish. It was now possible to lift his eyes a little higher! During those years in the Rectory what unequalled opportunity there was of knowing the worth and attractive goodness of Mary. But in those days despite her friendliness, she was as serene and unapproachable as any star. Now as a priest in orders the prize incredibly had come within reach. Heaven stooped to earth and one poor man pushed his way among the stars when Mary confessed her love for him. What would the Rector say? Nothing except to give his blessing!

Indeed, he was so pleased at the match that forthwith he wrote to the Lord Chancellor and declared his willingness to surrender the living at Wroot to Whitelamb if the Lord Chancellor, in whose gift it was, would likewise give his consent.[1] He also said that he would gladly give him a little glebe land at Wroot where 'they will not want springs of water'. Then followed a kindly portrait of his son-in-law. 'He is indeed a valuable person, of uncommon brightness, learning, piety, and indefatigable industry; always loyal to the King, zealous for the Church, and friendly to our Dissenting brethren, and for the truth of this character I will be answerable to God and man.' (14th January 1734.)

The Lord Chancellor acceded to the request and the happy couple moved into a place they loved. It was like a fairy story for one of the Wesley sisters when she actually loved and married the man she wanted and shared with him the work closest to her heart. But they did not live together happily ever after. In one short year she had died in childbirth and her dead child was buried with her. There is a simple entry in the Parish Register at Wroot which hides a mountain of sorrow,

[1] The gift actually was the King's, but the Lord Chancellor's influence would be considerable.

'1734, November 1st. Mrs. Whitelamb, wife of Mr. Whitelamb', and then the signature, 'John Whitelamb, rector'. Poor Johnny had lost all at one fell stroke. In the abyss of his grief he tried to go to Georgia, but he could not gain permission. No other way opened to him and so he remained the broken-hearted rector in this same village for another thirty years. But under such a blow even the fires of the Revival could not warm his cold heart. The unfriendly speak of his drifting into a religion not far removed from Deism. A letter to Mrs. Hall in 1755 would suggest that in his later life he was attracted to the Roman Church. 'I cannot see', he said, 'how Christianity can possibly support itself much longer in the world without recurring to, and sheltering itself under the wing of Mother Church.' Whilst he faithfully preached and untiringly laboured among his people he was 'a stricken deer'.

There is one picture which seems fittingly to symbolize his condition after Mary's death. When John Wesley returned to Epworth to preach and stood on his father's tomb surrounded by the great and gaping crowd, John Whitelamb stood alone and at a distance. Wesley spoke of a rapture he could not feel and an assurance he did not possess. He listened quietly and as quietly he stole away.

All the family lamented Mary's sudden death and two of Hetty's poems were written in her memory. She said that her sister had lived and died without a foe.

> *How should I mourn or how commend*
> *My tenderest, dearest, fairest friend?*

Her long poem *To the Memory of Mrs. Mary Whitelamb* was a sustained eulogy in which her sincerity made itself felt in the elegant classical eighteenth-century verse. In her concluding lines she summed up her sister's many virtues.

> *To soundest prudence (life's unerring guide),*
> *To love sincere, religion without pride;*
> *To friendship perfect in a female mind,*
> *Which I nor hope nor wish on earth to find;*
> *To mirth (the balm of care) from lightness free,*
> *Unblemished faith, unwearied industry;*
> *To every charm and grace combined in you,*
> *Sister and friend—a long and last adieu!*

Mary must have been very lovely to inspire such admiration and such love.

Mehetabel (Hetty) was the next daughter but hers is a special case and must be treated by itself. After Hetty came Anne (Nancy) and less is known of her than any of her sisters. 'Happy the nation that has no history', and happy a Wesley daughter with no biography. She alone seems to have had a suitable and happy married life. John Lambert, whom she married about 1725, was a land surveyor, highly intelligent and greatly respected. The Rector and Susanna regarded him with favour and Samuel, Anne's brother, was so well pleased that he wrote a poem, *To Sister Lambert on her Marriage*, to celebrate the auspicious occasion. From Charles Wesley's *Journal* we learn that intemperance was Lambert's besetting weakness and Hetty's husband, William Wright, did not help him in that regard. The entry in his *Journal* for July 1738 suggests that when he visited his brother and sister Lambert, they accepted his 'gospel of forgiveness'. Had there been a cloudy sunset doubtless some whisper of it would have survived them. It seems possible that in this one instance a happy choice was fulfilled in a happy married life.

John Wesley's references to his sister are happy in tone and suggest that he looked on her home as a resting place in which from time to time he could look round at loving faces and be at ease.[1] When he dined there in December 1726 he acted as her son's godfather and after dinner as he was about to leave he ran into fresh company and stayed through the evening. He wrote to her from Georgia and when he returned he called on her variously in the early morning or the afternoon or in the evening for dinner. The last entry about her in his *Journal* is the most striking.

Toward the end of December 1741 John had felt unwell. In the afternoon of 31st December he knew he was in a fever but he had promised to conduct a burial and a high temperature was not sufficient to deter him from his task. So many had gathered around the grave that Wesley could not resist the desire to use the occasion to tell them about the good woman who had been interred and to urge them so to live that their last end might be like hers. After 'the almost innumerable multitude' had departed John thought there might be a chance of lying down. But at that

---

[1] *Letters* (Standard Edition), Vol. I, p. 37; *Journal*, Vol. I, p. 185; Vol. II, pp. 520, 272, 388–9, 413.

moment Sir John Ganson[1] came to see him and after that interview it was time to go into the pulpit.[2] After the Service there was a Society Class in which many were deeply moved. It was not until 10 p.m. that he was able to commit himself into God's hands to do what seemed good.

He slept quietly, but on the following morning (1st January 1742) he was in a high fever and 'consented' to keep his bed. But he laid down one condition. All were to see him who desired to do so. He recorded that fifty or sixty came to speak with him and after he had helped them all he sent for the Bands,[3] meeting in the Foundery, that they might magnify God together. John afterwards turned to Sister Anne who was present and asked if she was not offended. 'Offended!' she said. 'I wish I could always be with you. I thought I was in heaven.' Anne must have had close contact with the Foundery because she had the double magnet of John and of her mother, who was living there. It was indeed the following July that her mother died and Anne was present to cheer the gallant spirit over and to lay the tired body quietly to rest.

The absence of further references in the *Journal* suggest that she may not long have survived her mother. But if we do not know the number of her children, or the date of her death, we know the all-important fact. She was happy! That alone gives her a distinctive place among the Wesley sisters.

Martha (Patty)[4] was the next daughter and might by contrast be called the unhappiest of them all! It seems ironic because the omens at first were so propitious. She was a particular favourite of her mother, or so the rest of the family thought. Martha had her own answer to their charge. 'What my sisters call partiality was what they might have all enjoyed had they wished it, which was permission to sit in my mother's chamber when disengaged, to listen to her conversation with others, and to her remarks on things and books out of school hours.' The story about Martha which no one omits to tell is how when the children were all frolicking in the nursery their mother said: 'You will all be more serious one day.' Then Martha piped up: 'Shall I be

---

[1] A Middlesex magistrate and landowner whom John Wesley later commended (8th December 1764) for his firmness in dealing with anti-Methodist violence.
[2] At the Foundery.
[3] The Bands were an early institution in Methodism similar to the Classes. John Wesley was of course living in the Foundery.
[4] Although to avoid confusion we shall call her Martha she was known to the whole family as Pat or Patty.

more serious, Mamma?' 'No!' said Susanna with great finality. At fourteen she went to stay in London with her uncle Matthew, and although she missed the family circle and the religious observances of Epworth, she was free to attend any Church of her fancy and went often to St. Dunstan's or to St. Paul's Cathedral. The three years in London enlarged her whole appreciation of life and when she returned to Epworth it must have seemed dull indeed.

Picture a beautiful and cultivated girl ripening into womanhood and back from the sights and sounds of London finding at Wroot a young schoolmaster who throws her ardent glances! He was one of the very few eligible suitors in the whole countryside and Martha may have fallen in love with him. Despite the general impression, and despite particular accusations, Samuel Wesley did not interfere with the love affairs of his daughters more than conscientious parenthood demanded at that period. So much we have already seen! But are there two exceptions? Were Hetty and Martha both crossed in their love-making by the Rector and did they bitterly resent it? What are the facts? In Hetty's case the Rector discovered something about Romley, the schoolmaster, which he did not like. He not only broke off the correspondence but sent Hetty off to Mrs. Grantham where she found ample time to bemoan her unhappy fate. When she returned home she carried her misery with her.[1]

The Rector was right in his judgement of Romley.[2] This was the very man who as priest-in-charge at Epworth refused John Wesley permission to preach in his father's Church and led John in sheer extremity to address the huge crowd from his father's tombstone in the Churchyard. When John returned to Epworth in 1744 he heard Romley preach two sermons 'exquisitely bitter and totally false'. In the following May Romley's sermon 'from beginning to end was another railing accusation'.

His singing voice on which he had so greatly prided himself was lost because of his heavy drinking and dissolute habits and the parishioners complained that they could not hear him.[3] If report

[1] It is probable that the Rector did not oppose Martha at all, because strong evidence indicates that the real love affair was between Romley and Hetty. Stevenson (*Memorials*, p. 358) is misleading.
[2] Despite his misgivings Romley was for a short time his curate and even assisted him in some small degree as an amanuensis for the *Dissertations on the Book of Job*.
[3] Messiter, in his *Notes of Epworth Parish Life* (pp. 62-72), gave a rather more favourable view of Romley and said that a throat affection caused his parishioners to ply him with liquor as the best cure for his complaint. This aggravated his drinking habits.

is to be trusted his reason left him in 1751 and shortly after being confined he passed out of his ravings into an unregretted death.[1]

But however unsuitable Romley would have been as son-in-law and whatever evidence the Rector had against him it was the blunder of a heavy handed father to separate the two so forcibly. If it was done in the eighteenth-century manner so much the worse for that manner. The Rector never understood Hetty.

Martha might be pardoned for returning with ardour the advances of the Rev. Westley Hall. At that stage in his life he might have deceived the elect. She was once again in London and Westley Hall came to know her because he was a friend and a fellow student of both her brothers at Oxford. Despite Hall's unscrupulous wooing of Kezzy when he visited Epworth, the family accepted him when he returned to Martha and claimed her hand. There is no reference to any objection made by the Rector, and Susanna openly gave her consent assuring her that if she had obtained the consent of her uncle there was no obstacle. Uncle Matthew was certainly not unwilling—because he gave her a handsome wedding present and made further provision for her in his will.

They were married in 1735 and for the first few years Westley Hall retained the good opinions of the Wesley family. Mrs. Wesley stayed with the Halls after her husband's death and wrote in a letter that 'he behaved like a gentleman and a Christian with as much duty and tenderness as could be expected'.

But there was a seam of vicious weakness in the character of Hall which soon became apparent. He became in turn a Moravian, a Quietist, and a Deist. Like John Dryden's picture of Buckingham, 'he was everything by starts and nothing long'.[2] His conduct seemed to deteriorate with his views. Despite the fact that at Salisbury his wife bore him ten children of whom nine died in infancy, he made many irregular associations and actually seduced a seamstress whom Martha had all unsuspectingly taken into the house. When this girl was in child pangs the servants, knowing the father, refused to help and disclosed their reason to Martha. She at once sought out a midwife and after the child was safely born, she paid a neighbour to look after the house whilst she went

---

[1] Quiller-Couch, in *Hetty Wesley*, presented a portrait of Romley even when a young curate, as vain, unstable, and insincere.
[2] *Absalom and Achitophel.*

to London, found and forgave her husband and persuaded him to return. When Charles Wesley asked her how she could so help 'her husband's concubine' she said: 'Pity is due to the wicked: the good claim esteem. Besides I did not act as a woman but as a Christian.' It was because of his ungovernable temper and shocking infidelity that the Wesley brothers took the one surviving child and had him educated away from home. It seemed, in all his bright promise, that he might be a source of consolation and strength to his mother, but when he was fourteen years old he sickened with smallpox. The mother rushed to his bedside but he was already dead when she arrived.

Meanwhile Westley Hall both preached and practised polygamy. He would leave his wife for months at a time and finally chose to go with a woman to the West Indies. When his mistress died he returned to England and Henry Moore says that 'his injured and incomparable wife showed him Christian attention until his death'. These words spoken by Moore to Adam Clarke were not only recorded in his *Wesley Family*, but copied by subsequent biographers. Then John Dove told the affecting story of how when he came to die Westley Hall exclaimed: 'I have injured an angel! an angel that never reproached me.'[1] That is no doubt what he ought to have said and the words are symbolically true. They provide an effective fall of the curtain. Other writers have copied them and in her life of Susanna Wesley, Eliza Clarke made her own imaginative comment on the speech. 'These words made up to Mrs. Hall for all the sorrow he had caused her.'

Yet it is possible that she never saw Hall after he returned to England. One must choose between Moore's unsupported testimony against the testimony of the members of the Wesley family, and the absence of other references. The death-bed story is certainly apocryphal. There seems evidence, however, that before he died (2nd January 1776) he had professed penitence for his sins. During his long absences Martha had become very friendly with Charles Wesley's wife and took an almost maternal interest in her niece and nephews. When Sally grew up she became Mrs. Hall's most intimate and beloved companion. During these latter years Martha knew a great measure of joy and tranquillity. As she refused always to say a hard or unkind word about her husband, so with that same equable temper she seemed able to make the best of people and of circumstances. When

[1] *Wesley Family* (London 1840).

Charles and his wife moved to London she had their constant society as well as the busy life of the Methodist societies in London. She also became friendly with Dr. Johnson. On the very day (9th April 1761) that John Wesley was in danger of death as he made an unsuccessful attempt to cross to Ireland in a violent storm, Martha Hall was dining with Dr. Johnson and discussing resurrections, apparitions, and voices of the dead. Boswell recorded that she resembled her famous brother both in figure and manner, 'lean, lank, preaching Mrs. Hall was exquisite'.

But it was John who filled the circle of her days, and when he died the world had no recompense to offer. She died because she was old and had no further will to live. When Sally[1] asked if she might be near in her last moments she replied: 'Yes, if you are able to bear it, but I charge you not to grieve for me more than half an hour.' As her weakness increased and the end drew near she told Sally that she must leave her by night, 'for if you should not sleep—then your anxiety would create mine'. It was entirely characteristic that in the very shadow of death, she should think of others. Just before she died she beckoned Sally and gently whispered: 'I have now a sensation that convinces me my departure is near: the heart's strings seem gently but entirely loosened.' When Sally asked if she was in pain she said, 'No, but a new feeling', and then as the Dark Messenger approached, she pressed Sally's hand and said: 'I have the assurance which I have long prayed for. Shout!' The Wesleys knew how to die. She who could not even whisper, wanted another to shout. It was a word brother Charles loved to use. Christians were to shout as they travelled the wilderness through. But she would shout not alone on the journey, but even at journey's end!

For four months she had survived her brother, the last remaining member of the Epworth children, and when she died it was altogether fitting that she should be buried in the same vault as John. He was eighty-seven years and she was eighty-five years old when death released them. But that of course is a calendar reckoning. 'Age shall not weary them nor the years condemn.' To us who follow after they were gay and gallant adventurers who, having lived triumphantly, triumphed also in death.

The story of Kezia (Kezzy), the youngest, can be quickly told since so much is already known. It will be remembered that when she left Epworth to take a post at Lincoln as pupil teacher,

---

[1] Charles Wesley's daughter. The two had a very great affection for each other.

she was forced shortly to return home because she simply could not exist on the terms of her employment. It was when she was at home looking after her ailing and ageing parents that the shadow of the wretched Westley Hall darkened her path. At that time Hall was a friend and fellow student of John and Charles, standing high in their regard, and when he came with John to Epworth the whole family received him warmly. He did not choose to tell them that he was already betrothed to Martha and John was evidently unaware of the fact. For a girl of her century, Martha had moved with initiative and speed. Kezzy was young and attractive and the other fair charmer was away. Always with Hall, out of sight meant out of mind, and he proceeded to woo Kezzy with ardour. He met with no resistance either from Kezzy or her parents. None of the three had any notion that his word had been already pledged. Kezzy stood in a strange and wonderful world committed to a man who seemed the epitome of all the virtues, and happy in the approval of her father, mother, and of brother John.

Westley Hall returned to Oxford and later went on to London and renewed his attentions to Martha who seems not to have heard of the Epworth episode. This can be accounted for by supposing that with his plausible tongue he put his own ingenious construction on the Epworth affair and deceived Martha as he had deceived her sister. Early the following year (1735) Martha was married and at once incurred the family wrath. Samual Wesley addressed to her a poem of sixty-seven blistering lines in which he relieved his hot anger. It ended in a climax which must have been terrifying to poor Martha:

> *Sooner shall light in league with darkness join,*
> *Virtue and Vice, and heaven and hell, combine,*
> *Than her pure soul consent to mix with thine;*
> *To share thy sin, adopt thy perjury,*
> *And damn herself to be revenged on thee;*
> *To load her conscience with a sister's blood,*
> *The guilt of incest, and the curse of God!*

John Wesley was at the time of the marriage preparing to go to Georgia. When he had returned and six years after Kezzy's death he wrote a strongly worded letter to Westley Hall in which he accused him of 'having stolen Kezia's heart from the God of her youth;

that in consequence she refused to be comforted, and fell into a lingering illness which terminated in her death; and that her blood still cried unto God from the earth against him.'

Both the brothers were misinformed. Though John did at least attack Westley Hall and not his sister. Martha's defence proceeded along three main lines. Before Hall met Kezzy he was engaged to her, and if she had openly stated this fact there could not have been the general misunderstanding. She had, however, precipitately committed herself without her parents' consent, and could not therefore disclose the true position. She might be blamed for marrying Westley Hall after she had proof of his inconstancy,[1] but at least she had a prior claim upon him.

The second fact is that when she wrote to her widowed mother giving all the facts, Mrs. Wesley did not withhold her consent, nor did Martha's uncle, Matthew Wesley.

But Kezia herself is the principal witness. She was so satisfied with her sister's conduct that she freely went to live with the Halls for a number of years after her father's death. This incidentally not only suggested that she bore no grudge against Martha but that she had no live affection for Hall. She could scarcely have stayed under his roof in those first years of his marriage had she loved him. That contention would appear to be sustained by a letter she wrote to John (June 1734) in which even before her sister's marriage she said that she was as indifferent as it is lawful for any person to be, whether she changed her state or not. She declared she thought a single life was the more excellent and would give several reasons for that conviction. It is a nice point whether that letter represents her true mind or whether it was written in the aftermath of disappointment and pique.

Owing to the generous financial provision of John Wesley she was able to spend her later years in the household of Henry Piers, Vicar of Bexley. Here she was happy not only because of their exceptional kindness but because she became very friendly with the Gambolds at Stanton Harcourt and paid them long visits. In these days Charles frequently called upon his favourite sister, and there is one *Journal* reference to a happy day with John. Whilst Charles 'shamefully unwilling' went to Newgate on his

---

[1] But how easy it is for a woman in love to accept an explanation even against her better judgement. John Dove (*Wesley Family*, p. 256) quotes Henry Moore, a close friend of Martha, as saying that Martha felt her brothers to have been right to the extent that after Hall had behaved so badly it would have been better for both Kezzy and herself to have refused him.

ministry of mercy among the prisoners, John and a number of friends went down the river to Greenwich, 'reading and singing' as they sailed. At Blendon they were joined by Kezzy. After dining, John had a talk with Kezzy. At four they set out singing with William Delamotte as companion and they sustained it for an hour and a half. Then it was time for Wesley to get back to his society meeting and the happy party broke up. It is in such sudden shafts of light that the joyous relationship of the brothers and their sisters is revealed.

Kezzy was never robust and was only thirty years of age when she died. We know from the reliable testimony of Martha that Kezzy had formed a true love attachment in these last months of her life, but this time it was Death who stood between her and her hopes. It would seem that Charles may have been present at her death for he wrote: 'March 10th, 1741. Yesterday morning Sister Kezzy died in the Lord Jesus. He finished his work and cut it short in mercy. Full of thankfulness, resignation, and love, without pain or trouble, she commended her spirit into the hands of Jesus and fell asleep.'

Chapter Nine

HETTY

HETTY (Mehetabel) Wesley has been taken out of this chronological record of the sisters because in so striking a circle she still stands alone. It was the Wesley poltergeist who depended upon her energy so that she became the main centre of disturbance. That was ever to be her unenviable lot. None of the sisters seem so uneasy in their eighteenth-century frame. She had all the desire for freedom of movement and self-expression without the means of fulfilling it. It was because she was born out of due time that she presented such a problem to her father. Quiller-Couch and all the later critics of the Rector seize quite rightly upon his treatment of Hetty. Their complaint against his dealings with the other daughters can be fairly and fully answered; but with Hetty the Rector showed an unreasonable severity. This, however, does not warrant the defamation of his character. It was more a failure of sympathy and understanding than the heavy hand of the tyrannical parent. There was, in the legal phrase, an incompatibility of temperament. Samuel had given her extra attention in her studies because he recognized the early signs of mental power, but of what use were brains and beauty when they could not be turned to proper account? Hetty suffered from frustration of purpose. The others, whilst in various degrees unsettled, did not as deeply rebel against a woman's inevitable lot. Hetty was born to be unhappy because she could not deny her own nature. She had initiative and independence of mind but could only survey her world from the window of a country Rectory. True, the countryside possessed its young men and there was diversion in love-making. But they were either unsuitable in her parents' eyes or her own, and her affections were not seriously engaged until she was twenty-seven years old.[1] At such an age a woman may rightly be judged to know her own mind, and submit to no impediments in her desire for marriage.

Both she and her father were forthright in their judgements and determined in their course of action. That this created mutual misunderstanding can be guessed by the ending to a little poem Hetty wrote for her mother:

[1] The love affair with Romley was the most important, but it was not long-lived.

Pray speak a word in time of need,
And with my sour-looked father plead
For your distressed daughter.

She was ardently wooed by an unnamed lawyer. In this instance there was a head-on collision of temperament. Samuel disliked lawyers in general, and this suitor of Hetty, in particular. Later events would seem to justify his impression of the young man's flightiness and insincerity of purpose. But the years were slipping on, and this time, Hetty was not to be baulked. Forbidden to meet him openly, she made clandestine appointments. The young man, denied access to the house and knowing it was impossible to gain the Rector's favour, urged Hetty to elope with him. Quiller-Couch's imaginative reconstruction of events was doubtless right in substance. Hetty consented to go with him believing that he intended marriage. The next day she was sadly undeceived and despite his entreaties, she resolved to return home and face the consequences of her folly.

It argued great courage to return to a home in which she could only be sure of Mary's unwavering love and loyalty. The others including her mother would be shocked and grievously hurt, whilst the Rector would show no glimmer of understanding. It was in such a mood that she vowed to accept the first proposal of marriage made to her. Mary, fearful of the consequences of so rash a promise, sought desperately to dissuade her from such a folly. Hetty, however, could only peer into the thick gloom of a meaningless future. In the rebound from her faithless lover she sought escape from an intolerable situation in the sanctuary of marriage.[1]

In this resolve, she was at one with the Rector. If he regarded her misadventure with horror, it was because such a sin seemed heinous in an age that lacked our easier judgements and our larger tolerance. There were two circumstances which in the Rector's eyes aggravated the enormity of the offence. He was a clergyman and her shame was his own. How could he instruct others and offer his people an example in godly living when his own daughter had behaved so wantonly. It seemed to prejudice his work so faithfully performed over the long years. There was

---

[1] Some historians think that the lawyer still desired marriage but that the Rector would have none of it. cf. Stevenson's *Memorials of the Wesley Family*, p. 302. But in this matter Quiller-Couch's reconstruction seems much more likely. Once she had seen his true character and left him it is most improbable that she turned in that direction again.

the further fact that she had trusted a man against whom she had been repeatedly warned. Had he not told her even in the early days that the man was an 'unprincipled lawyer'? She had flagrantly disregarded his warnings and disobeyed his commands. An eighteenth-century father would put this as 'the most unkindest cut of all'. Under these circumstances he was not likely to understand her own bitter grief and loss, nor her inarticulate longing to have the wounds healed and to be comforted by her own. He did not look at the situation from Hetty's angle and ask what would be best for her. He sought to meet the claims of a forensic righteousness. He asked in what way the damage could be repaired and the least harm inflicted on his work and on public opinion. The demands of morality and society would be met if she married. She herself had confessed her readiness, and so when William Wright presented himself the Rector was willing to overlook all his imperfections.

No biographer of the Wesleys has failed to comment on the utter unsuitability of the match. The man was a travelling plumber and glazier who served his father in the family business at Louth. Even after he had married Hetty he was not able to start an independent business until Hetty under her Uncle Matthew's will inherited £200. This was in 1737, which was twelve years after their marriage. But his trade was his least disqualification. Even Samuel must have needed all his resolution to persevere with such a match in face of Wright's lack of breeding, education, and manners. More serious still were those flaws in character which only revealed themselves after the marriage. He was not vicious like Hall, nor selfishly unheeding like Ellison; but though, in a fuddled sort of way, he meant well, he had no strength of character. Once in his cups all decency and self-control seemed to leave him. At first he drank occasionally but it soon became a settled habit. In all our language no more poignant appeal has been made to an erring husband than Hetty's poem, *Address to Her Husband*. If I quote it fully it is not because of the poetry which is commonplace enough; but because it is a veritable *cri de cœur*. Here, better than any outsider, Hetty tells her own story. It is autobiography written in pain and sickness of heart. She knows herself still to be beautiful . She knows that she has not stooped to nagging and reproach but striven consistently to please him. And still there is the shameful record of tavern tipplings. In hope struggling against despair, she makes this last appeal out of her misery:

HETTY

*The ardent lover cannot find
A coldness in his fair unkind,
But blaming what he cannot hate,
He mildly chides the dear ingrate;
And though despairing of relief,
In soft complaining vents his grief.
 Then what should hinder but that I,
Impatient of my wrongs, may try,
By saddest, softest strains, to move
My wedded, latest, dearest love
To throw his cold neglect aside,
And cheer once more his injured bride?
 O thou, whom sacred rites design'd
My guide and husband ever kind,
My sovereign master, best of friends,
On whom my earthly bliss depends,
If e'er thou didst in Hetty see
Aught fair, or good, or dear to thee,
If gentle speech can ever move
The cold remains of former love,
Turn thee at last, my bosom ease,
Or tell me why I cease to please.
 Is it because revolving years,
Heart-breaking sighs and fruitless tears,
Have quite deprived this form of mine,
Of all that once thou fanciedst fine?
Ah, no! what once allured thy sight
Is still in its meridian height.
These eyes their usual lustre show,
When uneclipsed by flowing woe;
Old age and wrinkles in this face
As yet could never find a place.
A youthful grace informs these lines
Where still the purple current shines,
Unless, by thy ungentle art,
It flies to aid my wretched heart;
Nor does this slighted bosom show
The thousand hours it spends in woe.
 Or, is it that oppress'd with care,
I stun with loud complaints thine ear,
And make thy home, for quiet meant,*

The seat of noise and discontent?
Ah, no! those ears were ever free
From matrimonial melody;
For though thine absence I lament,
When half the lonely night is spent,
Yet when the watch or early morn
Has brought me hopes of thy return,
I oft have wiped these watchful eyes,
Concealed my cares, and curbed my sighs,
In spite of grief, to let thee see
I wore an endless smile for thee.
  Had I not practised every art
T' oblige, divert, and cheer thy heart,
To make me pleasing in thine eyes,
And turn thy house to paradise;
I had not asked, 'Why dost thou shun
These faithful arms, and eager run
To some obscure, unclean retreat,
With fiends incarnate glad to meet,
The vile companions of thy mirth,
The scum and refuse of the earth;
Who, when inspired by beer, can grin
At witless oaths and jests obscene,
Till the most learnèd of the throng
Begins a tale of ten hours long;
While thou, in raptures, with stretched jaws,
Crownest each joke with loud applause?'
  Deprived of freedom, health, and ease,
And rivalled by such things as these,
This latest effort will I try,
Or to regain thy heart, or die.
Soft as I am, I'll make thee see
I will not brook contempt from thee.
  Then quit the shuffling doubtful sense,
Nor hold me longer in suspense;
Unkind, ungrateful, as thou art,
Say, must I ne'er regain thy heart?
Must all attempts to please thee prove
Unable to regain thy love?
  If so, by truth itself I swear,
This sad reverse I cannot bear;

> *No rest, no pleasure will I see,*
> *My whole of bliss is lost with thee.*
> *I'll give all thoughts of patience o'er*
> *(A gift I never lost before);*
> *Indulge at once my rage and grief,*
> *Mourn obstinate, disdain relief,*
> *And call that wretch my mortal foe*
> *Who tries to mitigate my woe;*
> *Till life, on terms severe as these,*
> *Shall, ebbing, leave my heart at ease;*
> *To thee thy liberty restore*
> *To laugh when Hetty is no more.*

Wright was of too coarse clay to respond finely to this despairing cry. After drunken bouts in which he had struck her, he was capable of remorse. But the very fact that she could awaken a sense of shame in him only served to quicken his irritability against her and drive him to seek forgetfulness in the accustomed way. To this marital unhappiness was added the poverty and insecurity arising from his neglect of the business, and his self-indulgence. But Hetty had lived with poverty too long to be distressed by it. Two other circumstances filled to the brim her cup of suffering.

After she had entered her life-long servitude with Wright it might have been supposed that the family, if not the Rector, would consider atonement had been made and comfort her in her woes. When John Wesley returned to Epworth from Oxford in the summer vacation of 1726 he found his father was still unyielding and the family (Mary excepted) ranged behind him. Under these circumstances he preached a sermon in his parents' presence at Wroot Church on Sunday 28th August. He took as his subject, 'Universal Charity or the Charity due to Wicked Persons', and with great courage he enlarged on the Christian virtues of magnanimity and forgiveness. This was but the culmination of many attempts to bring his father into a better state of mind. Sermons are often acceptable when they apply to others but hard to receive when they speak to one's own condition. The Rector complained to Charles that John had argued with him many times about Hetty and now chose to remonstrate with him from the pulpit. The old man was deeply hurt and Charles sought out his brother to tell him so.

John was in a quandary. He loved his father and deeply respected him. He could not bear to be even the unwitting cause of pain. But he could not doubt that Hetty had been harshly treated and that now she needed help. It further bewildered him that so plain a course of action was not apparent to his mother and sisters. They believed that Hetty's penitence was assumed and it was in mild reproach that his mother said: 'You writ this sermon for Hetty. The rest was brought in for the sake of the last paragraph.' In this complex of emotions he sought out his father, assured him that he had intended no unfilial conduct and would never willingly give him pain. On the vital matter of the controversy he did not enter. On that subject he had spoken his full mind and farther argument would only exacerbate the Rector without promoting Hetty's cause. He therefore held out an olive branch by offering to write for him, and the Rector, in tears of joy, told him that he would employ him the very next day. Quiller-Couch regarded this as in some sense a capitulation on John's part, dimming the chivalrous gallantry of his previous attitude. That criticism seems quite unwarranted. John did not recant his own opinions. He only sought to bridge a widening rift between himself and his father. So much might be expected from any son.

Mary was always Hetty's champion, and the three brothers were likewise ready not only to forgive but to befriend her. Samuel, in the largeness of his heart and purse, gave what practical help and encouragement he could to Hetty. In a letter to John (6th January 1727/8) he said: 'One thing I am sure we ought to have a care of, that is, not to lay the cause of our misfortunes upon any person's fault so much as our own. I could say much, but I dare not write, and, indeed, *cui bono?*' Charles heard of his sister's arrival in London just as he was finishing his studies at Westminster. He did not hesitate to see her on every possible occasion, and then he wrote giving her address to John so that John might cheer her with a letter. In the course of his letter to John, Charles gave a vivid description of his visits (20th January 1728). 'Poor s[ister] Hetty! It grieves me almost to think how exceeding kindly she treated me, who am seldom so happy as to meet with bare humanity from others. 'Tis a shocking comparison! 'twas but a week before I left London that I knew she was in it. Little of that time you may be sure did I lose, being with her almost continually; I could almost envy myself the deal of pleasure I had crowded within that small space. In a little neat room she has hired did the good-natured, ingenuous, contented wretch and I talk over a few short days, which we both wished had been longer. As yet, she lives pretty well, having but herself and honest W. W[right] to keep, though I fancy there's another a-coming. B[rother Samuel] and s[ister] are very kind to her, and [I hope] will continue so, for I have cautioned her never to contradict my s[ister], whom she knows. The other person you'll hear something of when you come here, which I would advise you to do at summer, if you would have me survive next winter. I'd like to have forgot my s[ister Wright] begs you'd write to her, at Mr. W[a]lkden's, in Crown Court, Dean's Street, near Soho Square.'

But this brotherly kindness could not supply her father's lack of it. The letters which passed between brothers and sisters at this time reflect Hetty's sorrow at the Rector's hardness of heart. She had come to Wroot expressly to see her mother and Mary (Molly), but the Rector had refused the permission she sought. Molly, in a letter to Charles, put all that heartbreak in two sentences: 'My unhappy sister was at Wroot the week after you left us, where she stayed two or three days, and returned again to Louth without seeing my father. Here I must stop for when I think of her misfortunes, I may say with Edgar, "O fortune . . .".'

Back at Louth Hetty had to face the swarm of her husband's angry creditors and the immense darkness of losing her baby son when it was only two days old.

When two other babies had likewise lived but a few days, she wondered in her bodily weakness whether she lay under God's displeasure and whether that might not be removed if her father would forgive her. She pleaded for the sake of her children yet unborn for her father's intercession to stay God's wrath. She told him that her brothers would give a faithful account of her way of life and her struggle to redeem the past and she begged him not to withhold his forgiveness. Although Samuel's reply has been lost it was evidently unfavourable because Hetty was stung to reply with something of her old spirit:

[London] 3rd July 1729.

HONOURED SIR,—Though I was glad, on any terms, of the favour of a line from you, yet I was concerned at your displeasure on account of the unfortunate paragraph which you are pleased to say was meant for the flower of my letter, but which was in reality the only thing I disliked in it before it went. I wish it had not gone, since I perceive it gave you some uneasiness.

But since what I said occasioned some queries, which I should be glad to speak freely about, were I sure that the least I could say would not grieve or offend you, or were I so happy as to think like you in everything; I earnestly beg that the little I shall say may not be offensive to you, since I promise to be as little witty as possible, though I can't help saying you only accuse me of being too much so; especially these late years past I have been pretty free from that scandal.

You ask me what hurt matrimony has done me, and whether I had always so frightful an idea of it as I have now. Home questions indeed! and I once more beg of you not to be offended at the least I can say to them, if I say anything.

I had not always such notions of wedlock as now, but thought that where there was a mutual affection and desire of pleasing, something near an equality of mind and person, either earthly or heavenly wisdom, and anything to keep love warm between a young couple, there was a possibility of happiness in a married state; but where all, or most of these, were wanting, I ever thought people could not marry without sinning against God and themselves.

I could say much more, but would rather eternally stifle my sentiments than have the torment of thinking they agree not with yours.

You are so good to my spouse and me as to say you shall always think yourself obliged to him for his civilities to me. I hope he will always continue to use me better than I merit from him in one respect.

I think exactly the same of my marriage as I did before it happened; but though I would have given at least one of my eyes for the liberty of throwing myself at your feet before I was married at all, yet since it is past, and matrimonial grievances are usually irreparable, I hope you will condescend to be so far of my opinion as to own that, since upon some accounts I am happier than I deserve, it is best to say little of things quite past remedy, and endeavour, as I really do, to make myself more and more contented, though things may not be to my wish.

You say you will answer this if you like it. Now though I am sorry to occasion your writing in the pain I am sensible you do, yet I must desire you to answer it whether you like it or not, since if you are displeased I would willingly know it; and the only thing that could make me impatient to endure your displeasure is your thinking I deserve it.

Though I cannot justify my late indiscreet letter, which made me say so much in this, yet I need not remind you that I am not more than human, and if the calamities of life (of which, perhaps, I have my share) sometimes wring a complaint from me, I need tell no one that though I bear I must feel them. And if you cannot forgive what I have said, I sincerely promise never more to offend you by saying too much; which (with begging your blessing) is all from your most obedient daughter,

MEHET. WRIGHT.

But the Rector had chosen his way and nothing would deflect him. In a letter to John, Susanna concluded with a significant sentence: 'Dear Jacky, I can't stop now to talk of Hetty, but this—I hope better of her than some others do' (12th July 1731). Four years still remained to the Rector but Hetty waited for pardon in vain. The Rector has since discovered that an over-rigid moral rectitude can cause bitter and unnecessary suffering. There are sins of the good to lament as well as sins of the bad.

The second additional weight to Hetty's sorrow was in the loss of her many babies. Year by year they came and year by year they died. She needed them in those first years to win her husband back from careless living, and always she needed them for her own comfort and consolation. Her *Mother's Address to a Dying Infant* evidences once more her power of infusing genuine feeling into what otherwise is quite unremarkable poetry:

> *Tender softness! infant mild!*
> *Perfect, purest, brightest child!*
> *Transient lustre! beauteous clay!*
> *Smiling wonder of a day!*
> *Ere the last convulsive start*
> *Rend thy unresisting heart;*
> *Ere the long-enduring swoon*
> *Weigh thy precious eyelids down;*
> *Ah, regard a mother's moan,*
> *Anguish deeper than thy own!*
> *Fairest eyes! whose dawning light*
> *Late with rapture blest my sight,*
> *Ere your orbs extinguished be,*
> *Bend their trembling beams on me!*
> *Drooping sweetness! verdant flower,*
> *Blooming, withering in an hour!*
> *Ere thy gentle breast sustains*
> *Latest, fiercest mortal pains,*
> *Hear a suppliant! let me be*
> *Partner in thy destiny:*

> *That whene'er the fatal cloud*
> *Must thy radiant temples shroud;*
> *When deadly damps, impending now,*
> *Shall hover round thy destined brow,*
> *Diffusive may their influence be,*
> *And with the blossom blast the tree!*
> *September 1728.*

The 'deadly damps, impending now' was an allusion to her firm conviction that the death of her children was due to the fumes of the 'white lead' in Wright's paint factory. Another poem is entitled, *To a Mother on the Death of Her Children*.

One letter of William Wright survives to show the death of his children was a severe blow to him. Writing to John in a short ungrammatical note after the death of an infant he still awakens the reader's pity:

To the Revd. Mr. John Wesley, Fellow in Christ Church College, Oxon.

DEAR BRO: This comes to Let you know that my wife is brought to bed and is in a hopefull way of Doing well but the Dear child Died—the Third day after it was born—which has been of great concern to me and my wife. She Joyns With me In Love to your Selfe and Bro: Charles.
From Your Loveing Bro:
to Comnd—WM. WRIGHT.

PS. Ive sen you Sum Verses that my wife maid of Dear Lamb. Let me hear from one or both of you as Soon as you think Conveniant.

Hetty was deeply distressed by the death of Mary (Molly) in 1734, but she found a certain measure of peace and even a tired sort of happiness before she died. William Wright even at his best would leave her unsatisfied; the gulf between them was too great to be bridged merely by decent and sober habits. But at his worst he had the power to make her actively and intensely unhappy. It would seem possible that in her latter years he made some spasmodic and clumsy attempts to reform his ways. Quiller-Couch's explanation of a heavy fall which left him more docile may be true, but something ought to be credited to his own belated remorse and fuddled desire to do better. Hetty could never love him but she could find it in her heart to pity him and even to like him. Certainly she longed for his love and protection. And when she died the wretched man discovered his most bitter loss. Charles

Wesley writing to his wife about Hetty's death said: 'Last Monday I followed our happy sister to her grave. Her husband is inconsolable, not knowing Jesus Christ. I was much affected by his saying with tears, he hoped I should not forsake him now my sister was dead. He makes bold to send his love to you.'

Wright could not have been wholly beyond the pale of respectable people. Charles Wesley in another letter to his wife three years later[1] said that 'brother Wright and his sister salute you'. He then added laconically: 'Him I shall probably bring with me to Bath, but more probably Rob Windsor.' Two years later he told his wife: 'Was I Will Wright, you wd. soon die of a broken heart. He is better while I am near him.'[2] On 9th June in that year he addressed a letter to his sister, Mrs, Patty Hall, care of 'Mr. Wright, Plumber in Frith Street, near St. Anne's Church, Westminster', and he told her that in her difficulties over young Westley's education: 'Will Wright and you must keep this to yourselves.' For a time therefore Mrs. Hall stayed at the house of Wright. He made a second marriage of short duration and Charles, who hurried to the bedside and listened to the man's disposition of his money, felt that he had not settled sufficient upon his wife.

In his poor fuddled way Hetty had been his only love and he confessed his shame and penitence to his brother. Charles who had never ceased to visit and to help him was now the one he desired most to see. Hetty had struggled to help him in life and now in the dark hours of dying it was Charles who tried to bring him comfort. 'He is struck down by the dead-palsy; longed above all things for my coming; rejoiced and wept to see me. His stubborn heart was much softened by the approach of death. Now he is a poor sinner indeed, full of horror and self-condemnation, yet not without hope of mercy.'

Did he actually die then? It has always been assumed that he did. But a man does not always die when he thinks his end approaches. In December of that year Charles Wesley asked that his wife's letter should be addressed to him at Mr. Wright's, Plumber in Frith Street, Soho, Westminster, until further notice. On 8th March (1756?) Charles Wesley wrote to Mrs. Patty Hall a cryptic note: 'Desire W. Wright from me to pay you 2.10.0 on

---

[1] 16th April 1754. For these unpublished letters only recently discovered I am much indebted to the researches of the Rev. Frank Baker.
[2] Another unpublished letter dated 28th May 1755.

Lady-Day.' It was as late as 1759 (15th February) that Charles for the first time spoke of 'W. Wright's poor widow', and a little later he spoke of carrying Mrs. Venn to dinner at the house of Mrs. Wright.

The evidence is not convincing for either date, though on balance it is most likely that Wright lived a little longer in this new state of penitence. The point in any case is not important. It is sufficient that attempts to reform which he made before Hetty's death did not end when she was taken from him. His was a house the Wesley's could still visit and when he fell into a dangerous illness his repentance was genuine and complete.

But the slight easing of burdens in Hetty's last years did not come from William Wright's assistance. In her loneliness she had felt herself an exile from the family circle and the visits of Uncle Matthew could offer no adequate compensation. But when in the first flush of the Revival Susanna Wesley came to London, she found in her mother the comfort and strength she needed. When she visited her mother at the Foundery she must upon occasion have met her sisters. All five of them[1] were present at the mother's bedside and at her request they sang a hymn of praise after the tired spirit had gratefully slipped away from the over-fretted body.

After the blissful years of being in the same city as her mother, Hetty was left to the darkness of this further loss. But though she was deprived of her mother she did not return to her earlier misery. Her husband in gentler mood did not put any hindrance upon her religious practices nor did he any further impede her freedom of movement. She became a Methodist and eagerly attended the services at the Foundery. William Wright offered no objection to the visits of John and Charles Wesley and she found a fresh release from her dejection. In the *Journal* there are occasional references to John having tea with Hetty, principally in 1738 and 1739.

Through their help she was able in her growing weakness to visit Bristol and be tenderly nursed by Mrs. Vigor. She visited the Hot Wells and tested the curative properties of the springs. But no such medicine could give her more than passing benefit. In her last years she was virtually an invalid. So much is obvious from the brave and uncomplaining letter she wrote to brother Charles.

---

[1] Those alive at this time were Emilia, Susanna (Sukey), Hetty, Anne, and Martha. John was also present at his mother's death.

London: Frith Street, 4th October 1745.

Dearest Brother,—I received both your kind letters, and thank you for them, but am surprised you have heard no account of my better health, though I could not write myself, since many have seen me who I know correspond with you, and some of them are gone to Bath and Bristol lately, especially sister Naylor and Mrs. Wiggington. Indeed, I continue exceeding weak, keeping my bed except when I rise to have it made, and it is almost incredible what a skeleton I am grown, so that my bones are ready to come through my skin. But, through mercy, the fever that immediately threatens me (with a violent cough and some fatal symptoms) is gone off, and I am more likely to recover than ever; nay, if I could once get my strength I should not make a doubt of it. This ease of body and great calm of mind I firmly believe is owing to the prayer of faith. I think this support the more extraordinary, because I have no sense of God's presence, ever since I took my bed; and you know what we are when left to ourselves under great pain and apprehensions of death. Yet, though I am yet in desertion, and the enemy is very busy, I enjoy so great a measure of quietness and thankfulness as is really above nature. Hallelujah! Whether or no the bitterness of death is past, I am perfectly easy and resigned, having given up this, with dear Will's spiritual welfare and all other things, to the sovereign Physician of souls and bodies.

Dearest brother, no selfish consideration can ever make me wish your stay in this most dangerous, diabolical world; yet we must always say, 'Thy will be done'; and I am pleased still to think God will permit us to meet again, though I cannot say I desire life a minute longer, even upon these terms. Willy gives his love, and would be unfeignedly glad to see you. Pray join in prayer with me still that he may persevere. Molly too gives her duty and desires your prayers; neither of their souls prosper as I could wish them. Strange that though we know sanctification is a gradual work, we want our neighbours to go faster than we can ourselves; but poor Willy only waits for the first gift. I have not one fear for those who are truly in earnest.

If the nation is run stark mad in politics, though never a jot the wiser or holier, no wonder that the person you mentioned in your last is brimful of them, though she keeps within bounds, and does not talk treason, whatever she may think. I am glad the believers I know seem to run into no extreme about the present affairs, either of losing the one thing needful, by talking too much, or praying too little. The Lord give us a right judgement in all things.

My prayers, love, and best wishes attend all dear friends at Bristol, from whom I have received innumerable obligations: but, above all,

Mrs. Vigor and her family, who showed unwearied love in serving and humouring me; with my never-to-be-forgotten friend and sister in spirit, Sally Perrin, who, if possible, showed more kindness in the latter end than beginning. Give my particular love and humble service to Dr. Middleton; poor Nancy Perrot, my companion in misery; Mrs. Burdock and Miss, who were most wonderfully civil to me; and Mr. and Mrs. Wigginton; with Stephen and Betty Maxfield; poor sister Spear and Mrs. Williams, who spared no pains to serve me; and Sally Coltson, Sukey Peck, and Mrs. Halfpenny, with her daughter, who have all been very loving and obliging; and may our best Master reward their labour of love a thousandfold. It has been one of my heaviest crosses that I have been unable to write to them all; but if ever I recover I despair not of doing it yet, if acceptable from a novice. You think, perhaps, I may write to them as well as you; but, dear Charles, I write now in bed, and you cannot believe what it costs me. I trust to remember and bless you many times yet before I die; wishing we may have another happy meeting first, if it is best. So with prayers for the universal Church, ministers, assistants, and all mankind, I take leave to subscribe myself your most obliged and loving sister,

Mehet. Wright.

Our suffering, said the unknown writer of the Epistle to the Hebrews, seemeth grievous but afterwards it yields the peaceable fruit of righteousness. Hetty after all her afflictions was able to speak of ease of body and great calm of mind. She could go on to rejoice in 'so great a measure of quietness and thankfulness as is really above nature'. This was due not alone to altered circumstance at home, nor to the proximity of many members of the family, but to her newly-found religious experience. In a remarkable disclosure of her mind to John Wesley, she confessed that she had long desired to know one thing, Jesus Christ and Him crucified.

Stanmore, 1743.

Dear Brother,—Some years ago I told my brother Charles I could not be of his way of thinking then, but that if ever I was I would as freely own it.

After I was convinced of sin and of your opinions, as far as I had examined your principles, I still forbore declaring my sentiments as openly as I had an inclination to do, fearing I should relapse into my former state. When I was delivered from this fear, and had a blessed hope that He who had begun would finish His work, I never confessed so powerfully as I ought how entirely I was of your mind, because

I was taxed with insincerity and hypocrisy whenever I opened my mouth in favour of religion, or owned how great things God had done for me. This discouraged me utterly, and prevented me from making my change so public as my folly and vanity had formerly been. But now my health is gone I cannot be easy without declaring that I have long desired to know one thing, Jesus Christ and Him crucified, and this desire prevails above all others.

And though I am cut off from all human help or ministry, I am not without assistance; though I have no spiritual friend, nor ever had one yet, except perhaps once in a year or two, when I have seen one of my brothers or some other religious person by stealth, yet (no thanks to me) I am enabled to seek Him still, and to be satisfied with nothing else than God, in whose presence I affirm this truth. I dare not desire health, only patience, resignation, and the spirit of an healthful mind. I have been so long weak that I know not how long my trial may last, but I have a firm persuasion and blessed hope (though no full assurance) that in the country I am going to I shall not sing 'Hallelujah!' and 'Holy, holy, holy!' without company, as I have done in this. Dear brother, I am unable to speak or write on these things; I only speak my plain thoughts as they occur. Adieu! if you have time from better business to send a line to Stanmore, so great a comfort would be as welcome as it is wanted.

Your loving sister,

MEHET. WRIGHT.

John Wesley could speak with great plainness and in a letter to Patty (Mrs. Hall) he said: 'I have often thought it strange that so few of my relatives should be of any use to me in the work of God. My sister Wright was, of whom I should have least expected it, but it was only for a short season.' This is curt and almost unkind. In another mood he was prepared to modify its harshness. But its interest lies in its praise of Hetty. It is true he qualified this by limiting the time in which she helped him. But he could only have meant by this that Hetty came at the end of her life into the full possession of Christian truth, and that only a short period of service was possible to her.

She certainly fulfilled her brother's boast that Methodists knew how to die. When she realized that the homecoming was near, she said to a friend: 'I have ardently wished for death, because you know, we Methodists always die in a transport of joy.' Before the very end sheer physical weakness and pain robbed her of that ecstasy. Charles recorded in his *Journal* of 5th March 1750 that he prayed by his sister Wright, 'a gracious tender trembling soul; a bruised reed which the Lord will not break'. On 14th March she no longer had full possession of her spirit. In the frightening labyrinth of exhaustion and pain she was, he said, 'in darkness, doubts, and fears; against hope believing in hope'. But before her death, the sun had pierced the clouds and peace had come at last. 'On 21st March I called on my brother Wright, a few minutes after her (my sister's) spirit had been set at liberty. I had sweet fellowship with her in explaining at the chapel those solemn words: "Thy sun shall no more go down, neither shall thy moon withdraw itself; for the Lord shall be thine everlasting light, and the days of thy mourning shall be ended." All present seemed partakers both of my sorrow and my joy.

'26th March. I followed her to her quiet grave, and wept with them that weep.'

Hetty is remembered as a high-spirited lovely girl who suffered at the hands of her lover, her father, and then her husband, and whose gallant courage could not withstand the deadening effects of an ignorant man's weakness and petty vice. Such striking grace and beauty so rudely treated was a tragic theme to evoke a writer's art. It may be that in his superb tribute Quiller-Couch has thrown a bunch of everlastings on her grave.

Hetty was not alone distinguished in character and in personality but in her mental gifts. From the letters of Lady Mary Wortley Montagu and Fanny Burney, and from biographical details of Jane Austen and the Brontë sisters we know how hard has been the way of an English woman of letters. No one has shown more vividly than Virginia Woolf (principally in *A Room of One's Own*) the immense handicaps, in contrast with men, besetting the woman who craved artistic expression. Where the light had to be hid under a bushel, and even a written work had so often to be issued under a veil of anonymity; where a woman had to pretend to a genteel ignorance rather than to knowledge and her range of interests was so rigidly determined for her, it is remarkable that even a few could maintain their proper right and satisfy their urge to create.

Dr. Johnson in a celebrated *obiter dictum* said: 'Sir, a woman's preaching is like a dog walking on his hinder legs. It is not done well; but you are surprised to find it done at all.'[1] Much the same sentiment might be expressed of a woman in the

---

[1] Boswell's *Life of Johnson* (31st July 1763).

eighteenth century writing poetry. In particular this was true of Hetty Wesley who apart from the prime disability of sex, had an indifferent education and unceasing domestic worries. It could be said of her poetry that 'it was not done well'. But when she wrote, the age of Pope and Dryden was over and the Romantic Revival had not begun. In the absence of mountain peaks, even hillocks rise noticeably from the ground. Hetty's verses were not all published and many have been irretrievably lost. Whilst some were printed in the *Gentleman's Magazine* and at least one contemporary anthology, others were sent to members of the family and were printed at a later date in the *Poetical Register*, the *Christian Magazine*, and in the *Arminian Magazine*.

An unknown reader who read her manuscript poems was so impressed that he composed a poem which was a long pæan of praise in her honour. It must be said in justice that the praise is not so much lavished upon her poetry as upon her loveliness and her mental powers.

> '*Twere difficult with portrait just to trace*
> *The blooming beauties of her lovely face;*
> *The roseate bloom that blushes on her cheek;*
> *Her eyes, whence rays of pointed lightning break;*
> *Each brow the bow of Cupid, whence her darts*
> *With certain archery strike unguarded hearts;*
> *Her lips, that with a rubied tincture glow,*
> *Soft as the soothing sounds which from them flow.*
> *But oh! what words, what numbers, shall I find*
> *T' express the boundless treasures of her mind,*
> *Where wit and judgement spread their copious mines,*
> *And every grace and every virtue shines!*

After extolling the poetry of the Rector, and of Samuel, the eldest son, the author concludes:

> *... on the son the father's spirit fell:*
> *To these the daughter's equal flame subjoin,*
> *Then boast, O muses, the unrivalled line!*

The mysterious 'Sylvius' had contrived to write a panegyric without once committing himself to a serious criticism of the poetry itself. But the innocent Hetty was delighted and sent off the verse to the *Gentleman's Magazine* (1736).

When it appeared the gallant unknown added one last tribute.

> *Allowed by bright Granvilla to peruse*
> *The sprightly labours of her charming muse;*
> *Enraptured by her wit's inspiring rays,*
> *I chanted ready numbers to her praise.*
> *She, pleased, my unpremeditated lines*
> *To the recording magazine consigns:*
> *But would you be to best advantage known,*
> *Print not my verses, fairest, but your own.*

Despite this flattery Hetty's verses though often fluent and always sincere were not inspired. They were all infected by the melancholy of her own spirit and were largely concerned either with death or with its imminent prospect. There is, however, in one poem an echo of earlier days and it ought to be included as an indication that she had known a true and many-sided happiness.

> *Nay, to high heaven for greater gifts I bend:*
> *Health I've enjoyed, and I had once a friend.*
> *Our labour sweet, if labour it might seem*
> *Allowed the sportive and instructive scene.*
> *Yet here no lewd or useless wit was found;*
> *We poised the wavering sail with ballast sound.*
> *Learning here placed her richer stores in view,*
> *Or, winged with love, the minutes gaily flew.*
> *Nay, yet sublimer joy our bosoms proved,*
> *Divine benevolence, by Heaven beloved:*
> *Wan meagre forms, torn from impending death,*
> *Exulting blest us with reviving breath;*
> *The shivering wretch we clothed, the mourner cheered,*
> *And sickness ceased to groan when we appeared;*
> *Unasked, our care assists with tender art*
> *Their bodies, nor neglects the immortal part.*
> *Sometimes in shades unpierced by Cynthia's beam,*
> *Whose lustre glimmered on the dimpled stream,*
> *We wandered innocent through sylvan scenes,*
> *Or tripped like fairies o'er the level greens.*
> *From fragrant herbage decked with pearly dews,*
> *And flow'rets of a thousand different hues,*
> *By wafting gales the mingling odours fly*
> *And round our heads in whispering breezes sigh:*
> *Whole nature seems to heighten and improve*
> *The holier hours of innocence and love.*

*Youth, wit, good-nature, candour, sense, combined
To serve, delight, and civilize mankind;
In wisdom's love we every heart engage,
And triumph to restore the Golden Age!*

There is here no suggestion of a repressed and joyless girlhood. There were many golden hours spent in the Epworth Rectory, and in this poem, despite the stilted eighteenth-century manner, she can pleasingly recall it. Yet not in her poetry, but in the drama of her life, she refuses to lie quietly in her grave. Strangely and compellingly she forces herself upon the mind, and walks with her own grace along our common way.

Chapter Ten

THE FAMILY GROUP

THE FATHER had sacrificed much for his sons and indeed involved all his children in the same offering. It was natural therefore they should profoundly respect him for his qualities of character as well as his considerable scholarship. But the letters alone are sufficient evidence that they loved him, and when as in the case of Hetty, and later in the offer of the Epworth living, they felt bound to oppose his wishes, they did so with the greatest reluctance and with protestations of their regard for him. To Susanna they owed all their early education and her influence remained potent all their lives. On Samuel the eldest she had been willing to lean when the way proved difficult for tired feet. He was the special object of her regard and to his house she instinctively turned when her husband died. But she followed her three boys with sympathy, understanding, and a complete devotion. In the various stages of their career she gave them counsel and offered shrewd comment.

She could not have foreseen her Jacky's future greatness, but as she had not sought to restrain him from going to Georgia, so when the Revival broke out she did not oppose what she could not understand. Despite all the biting criticisms which distressed poor Samuel, her son, so much, Susanna kept an open mind. She was not to be burked by the prejudices of others. In those first years there was matter enough for alarm. The crowds were listening with curiosity if not with gladness, but the Bishops were suspicious and increasingly her sons were denied access to pulpits. And certainly for one who had been the wife of a country rector in the wilds of the Lincolnshire fens, preaching to people in the open-air and the overstepping of parish boundaries must have seemed strange and irregular proceedings. She had known from her husband of the religious societies, but these classes formed by John were noticeably different.

After Samuel's death at Tiverton she came to make her last home with John at the Foundery (1739), and with her amazing resiliency of mind she not only accepted the new doctrinal emphasis, but also the religious provision her sons were making for the Methodist converts. She attended the Preaching Services and the classes, and so far from restraining John she urged him to accept Thomas Maxfield as a preacher. So began the institution of lay preaching in the Methodist Societies. In the life of John it can be truly said that the greatest single influence was that of his mother.

The attitude of the daughters toward their parents was more complicated. They had to decrease that their brothers might increase. They could not fly from poverty and monotony to the excitement of school and university. Hetty in a poem to Emily, has given a vivid impression of a stale unprofitable existence to girls who craved so much from life.

> *Fortune has fixed thee in a place*
> *Debarred of wisdom, wit, and grace.*
> *High births and virtue equally they scorn,*
> *As asses dull, on dunghills born:*
> *Impervious as the stones their heads are found,*
> *Their rage and hatred steadfast as the ground.*
> *With these unpolished wights, thy youthful days*
> *Glide slow and dull, and Nature's lamp decays;*
> *Oh, what a lamp is hid 'midst such a sordid race!*

Hetty could go on to declare that Emily was 'in a noxious irksome den immured'. The others lacked Hetty's power of speech but she spoke for them all. In their letters the reader can peer through a window on to their life, 'cribb'd, cabin'd, and confined'. Frustration is a popular over-used word, but its meaning was fully known two centuries ago.

The bad husbandry of the Rector and therefore his unsuccessful coping with debts was more obvious to the daughters than the sons, and they could more easily see the wearing effect of it all upon Susanna. Mary (Molly) was best able to adapt herself to the daily round of rectory life, and quite unembittered, to find a mild happiness in it. She triumphed because she had won a greater victory in a harder struggle. The injury she received in childhood from a fall left her short in height and a cripple. Here was ample cause for self pity and a jealousy of others. But she refused to spoil her life by an unavailing bitterness, and accepted her limitations with complete poise of spirit. This meant that she was saved from the restlessness and discontent which so understandably, was apt to grip the others. She therefore had more patience with her father and a deeper appreciation of his nature. To the others he was, however unwittingly, a part cause of their misfortunes. And when he interfered with their love affairs, they had further cause for grievance. But Mary and her father understood each other. She was willing to help him in his work and was rewarded by his confidence and unstinted love. Hetty, on the other hand, was farthest removed from her father, not only because he baulked her desires and proved unsympathetic in her greatest need, but because there could be no understanding where there was no true affinity of spirit. The other sisters had their occasional grumble against their father,[1] and sometimes in their letters this was coupled with references to their mother's hard struggle against debts and poverty and unending toil. His devotion to the Parish, his love of books, and his preoccupation with his intended masterpiece, coupled with his engrossed interest in the boys, unfitted him to be a companion to his girls. To all this must be added the fact that the father in the eighteenth century did not seek, as in our day, to meet his daughters on a level of easy *camaraderie*. But they did respect him and though there was no demonstration of great love, they had a certain dutiful affection.

In the matter of their suitors it ought to be recorded that Susanna, so far as we know, shared the judgement of the Rector. The argument is one from silence, but is not therefore to be disregarded. Susanna did not hesitate to disagree with the Rector when occasion demanded, and from herself or from the daughters' letters we might reasonably have expected some scrap of evidence to show that her sympathies were with them. But no such hint has come down to us. Indeed, in the love affair of Hetty she did not show her daughter any encouragement. In a letter of John to his brother, Samuel, he said that his mother was persuaded that Hetty's penitence was all feigned. Doubtless it was only her intervention that prevented the Rector from sending Hetty away again after she had returned home from her ill-fated flight. Doubtless also she did not condone the Rector's later attitude to Hetty, but on the essential issue she shared her husband's views.

But the girls could come to their mother with their fears and hopes and longings in a way they could never approach their father. She had nurtured and trained them. They shared with her the labour of the house and bore with her the vexations of poverty and the restrictions of life in a remote Lincolnshire

[1] cf. Emily's letter to John, 7th April 1725.

THE FAMILY GROUP

Rectory. The boys could go to college and university and the Rector could make occasional visits to London, but mother and daughters could not share those privileges. In her ill-health she constantly needed them. Such letters as we still possess show that the relationship between them was warm and enduring. When the Rector died she went at once to stay at Gainsborough with Emilia for whom she had a special attachment. She was considered to be her mother's favourite. The MS. which Susanna wrote in 1711 is called *A Religious Conference between M(other) and E(milia)*, with the inscription: 'I write unto you little children of whom I travail in birth again until Christ be found in you.' In July 1737 she took up her abode with the Halls because Martha was also especially dear to her. 'My daughter', she said in a letter to Mrs. Berry, 'labours with as much duty and tenderness as can be expressed.' After she had removed to the Foundery upon the death of her eldest son, Martha came for a period to live with her, and the other daughters visited her as often as they were able. It was a great blow to her when Kezzy, the youngest, died at Bexley in 1741. But the others were sufficiently near to comfort her in those last months. Anne had come with her husband, Lambert, to live at Hatfield and it was she whom Susanna in her great weakness, asked specially to remain with her. Anne stayed on until the last hours of passing and wrote an account of her death to Charles. It was altogether fitting that at the close all the daughters, Emilia, Susanna (Sukey), Hetty, Anne, and Martha were gathered around their mother's bedside. If they were privileged beyond most in calling that wonderful woman their mother, she also was rich in the love of her daughters.

What was the relationship of the sisters to their brothers? It can be said in sweeping fashion that all were devoted to each other and that in the interchange of letters we can see how deeply grounded was their mutual love. But in any large family the brothers and sisters have their own special attachments within the harmony of the whole. Samuel, as the eldest, was in a special category as counsellor, benefactor, and untiring friend. He was, despite the excellence of the Rector and Susanna, almost *in loco parentis* to the family. Charles was his special protégé, but John benefited always from his advice and help, and even when they differed in opinion no shadow came between them. The sisters also never turned to him in vain. It was Samuel who took Hetty's part in the love affair and sought to secure money and tender dealing for her. His house at Westminster was open to her, and from him, as well as her uncle Matthew, she received comfort in those unhappy years when first she came to London. All the sisters visited him when they were in town and they found him more loving than his somewhat waspish wife. Martha, in a letter to John Wesley (10th March 1730) said: 'I sometimes go to Westminster, but I am afraid it will be impossible for me ever to make a friend of my sister. She fell upon me the last time I was there for "giving myself such an air as to drink water", tho' she told me "she did not expect that I should leave it". I told her if she could convince me that there was any ill in it, I would, and thank her for telling me of it; but I desired her in the first place to tell me what she meant by the word "air" which she did not choose to do; I believe for a very good reason; so our dispute ended. My brother said he would go to Oxford this Easter. I asked him if he would take me with him? He seemed pretty willing to do so, but I fancy his wife will hardly let him.' After her father had died Kezia (Kezzy) went for a short time to live with Samuel and his wife at Tiverton. He only let her go when other arrangements had been made for her happiness. But whilst he sought to help them all as they had need and whilst he wanted to be kept fully informed about the family happenings, his distance from them prevented anything in the nature of close and special likings. There is no clue to indicate a preference for any one of his sisters, and his wife was not sufficiently attractive for the girls to write ecstatically of their visits.

It was far otherwise with John and Charles. Although the girls had to suffer in education and prospects that the brothers might go through public school to university, it seems to have increased their sisterly pride and made them still more ambitious for their success. It was as though the very real sacrifice had given them a vested interest in the career of their brothers. They had no feeling of jealousy and no word of bitterness. Long and loving letters passed between them all. If any difference ever arose it was out of competition for the brothers' love and favour. They pined to know that as they loved, so an equal love was shown to them.

But within those firm bonds of mutual affection, there were special ties of regard. Charles was two years older than Kezia and throughout their lives they were closely united to each other. In all her letters to John there are references to Charles. She wrote in one letter (12th July 1729) of Charles' 'example of faith and patience' and wished she could follow it, but 'you know our sex have naturally weaker minds than yours, not that I bring this as any excuse in my particular case for I own I have been very defective in both faith and patience'. She asked in another letter that brother Charles should bring 'Prior' (the second part) when he came.[1]

When Charles called upon her at Stanton Harcourt during a visit she was paying to Miss Gambold he was able to help her in a great spiritual crisis. She longed 'to fathom the depths in religion and to know the love of God'. Despite his utmost endeavours he was not then able to bring her peace, for in a subsequent letter she wrote:

Bexley, 15*th November* 1737.

MY DEAR BROTHER,—Though I am very ill, yet nothing can prevent me returning my sincere thanks for your kind letter. You have not a friend in the world who will be more glad to be directed or reproved (in the spirit of meekness) than I shall be. I own it is a great fault, but my mind, and body too, are so much weakened with ill usage, that I cannot bear any roughness without either being angry or dejected. I have not heard from my mother this two months, nor have I had any letter or receipt from you. I cannot write to her, because I do not know how to direct. If you can still have patience, and retain any love and tenderness for 'a weak, entangled, wretched thing', you may, by your prayers and direction, add much to the happiness of your sincere friend and affectionate sister,

KEZIA WESLEY.

During the following year (1738) Charles fell seriously ill and Kezzy came from Bexley to nurse him. She watched over him for many days so assiduously that when at last he began to recover, she herself fell dangerously ill. It was at this period that she and Charles received Holy Communion together daily. The two hymns which Charles wrote on his recovery, he and his sister sang together. This was in March 1738 and in the May, Charles was converted. In July of that year at Stanton Harcourt he so pleaded with Kezzy to accept his new-found evangelical faith 'that she burst into tears and melted me into fervent prayer for her'. Many times after that he visited her, and two years later was present at her death. In her thirty-two years she had known much physical and spiritual suffering, but her almost reverent love for John,

[1] Matthew Prior was a favourite poet of the family.

and the complete giving of herself to Charles, were solid and lasting joys.

Both John and Charles were loved by all the sisters, and John in particular seemed capable of evoking their utmost devotion. Even Kezzy with her special preference for Charles told John that 'she loved him with more than sister's love'. She was hurt because for some time she had not received a letter and she proceeded to say how his words and actions had engaged her love and that 'love is a present for a mighty king'. Mary begged John to keep writing because his letters gave so much satisfaction 'to his loving sister'. Emily wrote of her unhappy life (1725) and begged John to be the repository of her secrets. 'Pray be faithful to me. Let me have one relation I can trust; never give any hint to anyone of aught I write to you, and continue to love your unhappy but affectionate sister, Emilia Wesley.' She begged him at Oxford to continue Leybourne's friendship and declared that this request ought to weigh with him more than anybody's except her mother. She ended by affirming that whilst life remained she would be his most affectionate sister (31st December 1729). In a later letter she laid bare her love even whilst she expostulated with him:

> Full well you know that even from our childhood you have been selected from all our numerous family for my intimate companion, my counsellor in difficulties, the dear partner of my joys and griefs; to you alone my heart lay open at all times, nor am I conscious of ever concealing my sentiments from your knowledge these many years, except in one only instance which has happened lately. Say, where slept your friendship, dear brother, when you could censure me so hardly for no offence? If I have since I came to Gainsborough swerved from that strictness which I practised for so many years at licentious Lincoln, if something here has gotten such hold of my heart as to draw me too strongly to this world, and to take up too much of my time, my thoughts, and affections; yet, suppose there is such an impediment in my way, as it is unknown to you, and every other, and ever will be, you can have no right to censure for secret faults. That is the privilege of Him only who is Omniscient. And here I cannot forbear speaking freely my doubts, or why has the good Author of our being given to us all such affections as we have. He cannot delight in the misery of any of His creatures: why shall it chance that through the whole course of life, whatever is liked, or say loved, shall certainly either be taken from us, or there shall such difficulties attend the enjoyment of it as cannot be surmounted by

human prudence? Is it purely to afflict? or is there not some further end? Is it not to show us that happiness must not be found on this side the grave, that we must not seek for rest here?—of which you have given me too plain, too sad a demonstration in the withdrawing of that love I held so dear. Yet whatever faults I have been guilty of in respect of God, to you I have been blameless, except loving you too well has been one; and considering you are a man I do too well love, that is the very thing which has disobliged you.—I am your affectionate sister,

EMILIA WESLEY.

In her great affection she could be virtually unreasonable. There had been a possibility of his coming to Gainsborough and he had chosen to visit the Moravians in Germany. It seemed in her disappointment a most unnecessary and reprehensible action to take, and she vigorously told him so. 'Pray write soon. Remember the natural affection you have always shown to your Emma and forsake her not in the day of her distress. Love to your sister in trouble is more pleasing in the sight of God and man than preaching to a thousand persons where you have no business. If you had come to me instead of going to Germany and laid out your money in travelling hither instead of visiting Count Zinzendorf you would have been, I dare say, as acceptable to our common Master. ... Had you the same, nay a quarter of the love to me I have for you, long since you would have been with me; it was in your power—you who could go to Germany, could you not reach Gainsborough? Yes, certainly, and had my soul been lost by self murder, my damnation would justly have been laid at your door' (24th November 1738).

It is by vivid words, such as these, that a long-dead person comes to life. In her fretfulness and worry, in her over-zealous love, in her sharpness of temper and asperity of tongue she suddenly stands before us. Emily, we know from many sources, was a most admirable person with gifts and graces, but until old age had mellowed her, she retained a certain caustic wit that was not easy to bear. On another occasion after she had reproached John for want of affection, he was goaded into a measured and unanswerable reply. He reminded her that she had been in his house and had been sustained by his money and that she had received concrete proofs of his attention. (30th June 1743.) Despite his hurt feelings he continued in his kindnesses and she remained a virtual pensioner on his bounty living in apartments at the West Street

Chapel. He not only supported her but also a maid to whom she was greatly attached. Whether John's letter showed that a man could be provoked too far or whether she grew more easy in mind by reason of his continual visits to London and therefore to her, the fact is that for nearly thirty years after that letter there was, so far as we know, unbroken calm. In a letter written to Martha (Patty) on 14th June 1761, John Wesley urged both Emily and her to even heartier approval of the work. He would have his sisters as single-minded as himself and at the time of writing he wanted to spur his two beloved sisters on to greater efforts. 'The day is far spent. What you do, do quickly. Life for delay no time will give!' Too much, however, can be read into this expostulation. He would whip up his dearest as he would whip up himself for ever greater zeal in the service of his Lord. Emily continued to attend the Services and share the life of the Society at West Street until she died in great peace about the year 1771.

When the Wesley sisters were nettled at John it was for the very natural and human reason that they loved him so much as to want more demonstrative affection than he could give to them. Their love occupied so much of their lives, and in scorn of logic and of facts, they desired that it should be true of him. There is an element of possessiveness in all human love, but John Wesley was not a man to be possessed. It was because no woman could hope for more than a part of his interest that he was the unwitting cause of so much heartburning to so many of them. His love affairs and his married life were all unhappy because since he had given himself so wholly to God, he could not give himself as he ought to any other. He was amongst those of whom Jesus said that they were eunuchs for the Kingdom of God's sake. God was the 'master light of all his seeing'. In brother Charles's language, God was all his happiness. Other men, with just as strong a sense of vocation, make necessary adjustments of their time for those who have a claim upon them. This John Wesley could not do. Even Generals are not always planning campaigns, but Wesley never ceased from working out a strategy for the advance of God's Kingdom, and at the same time the sword never slept in his hand. No wonder that women grew exasperated with him. He had the power to attract them and win their affection, but whilst they asked so much, he could give them so little. Temperament also played its part. There is no need to fly to psychology and look for a 'mother complex' to account for a certain diffidence and even shyness with women. Susanna and he were together all too rarely, and his relationship with her was most healthy and normal. But Nature had never cast him for the part of a bold and dashing Lothario. He had an ingenuousness which even contact with Hogarth's England could not eradicate. How much it would have helped him to have been a little worldly wise!

Now his sisters were spared the whirlwind of emotions which must have swept those women in his life who saw in him a possible husband. They had no need alternately to hope and despair, and they had no cause to be jealous of his work because it absorbed his energies. The relationship of brother and sister was a great simplification of the problem.

And yet even they, in their great love for him, had occasion for complaint. They had so much more time for letter writing and for thinking about him that his very understandable delays in replying, or his seeming lack of warmth, stung them to reproach or to pitiful entreaty. Those cries from the heart always bewildered John. He would make a reasoned reply pointing to his practical concern for them. He did not realize that in Pascal's words, 'the heart has reasons, reason knows not of'. Mary and Kezzy, Anne, Sukey, and Hetty, were less demanding because, whilst they loved him truly and assured him so continually, they did not feel they had any right to more love than he showed them. They were proud of him and grateful for all his kindnesses. Yet even they could write distressfully and beg him for the letters they desired so much.

Emily was by temperament less able to hide her feelings and in any case she felt she had a stronger claim upon John. She was twelve years older and could speak her mind more freely. She had watched over his growth with an elder sister's quiet satisfaction and her own strong and capable mind rejoiced in his mettle. She would fain have regarded herself as his favourite sister, dearer to him as she expressed it, than all else apart from his mother. Her acidulated remarks from time to time were only due to the excess of love. Happily good John Wesley knew his sister and she had her heart's desire when he provided for her later years, and brought her into closer contact with himself and his work.

But whatever Emily might think, it was Martha who, beyond question, was his favourite sister. She was three years younger and it is on record that even when she was a small child suffering from an illness, the sight of her beloved brother could cause her to forget her pain. We now know that it was Hetty and not Martha who addressed the heartbroken epistle from Kelstern in which she said she had been grieved at John's silence, and who yet confessed that her anger gave way to love as it always did when she chanced to be angry with him. In a true sense, however, the sentiments of that letter were unswervingly those of Martha. She, more than any sister, confided in him and sought in her own ill-fated union to be recompensed by John's sympathy and understanding. This attachment was mutual and extended from their earliest days. Dr. Adam Clarke, who knew Martha in her old age, probably heard from her own lips the fact that when other members in the Rectory conspired to play tricks on her and to overcome her 'philosophic steadiness' it was brother John who took her part against all the rest. Against the tricks which life was to play upon her, she needed in even greater measure, her own steadiness and John's support.

Her anger on another occasion might have blazed out, had John not written in the very nick of time. She confessed that the seducer, jealousy, had got her in its clutches. She supposed that his Varanese (Sally Kirkham) had made him forgetful, though she hastened to add that she had a vast respect for a woman 'so known, so loved'. But John's letter made all the difference and she applied to herself the words of Marcus:

> *Thou best of brothers and thou best of friends*
> *Pardon a weak distempered soul that swells*
> *With sudden gusts, and sinks as soon in calms.*

Then came the revelation of her own love and her desire to stand first in his esteem. 'I believe I need not tell you that when we love any person very well we desire to be loved by them in the same degree, and though I cannot possibly be so vain as to think that I do for my own personal merits deserve more love than my sisters, yet you can blame me if I sometimes wish I had been so happy as to have had the first place in your heart?'[1]

John could not help her in the wretched unhappiness of a union with the polygamous Hall but he sent her books and letters and visited her as often as he was able.[2] For a few years she found

---

[1] Written from Wroot, 7th February 1727.
[2] There are seven references to visits paid her in the *Journal* ranging from 1739–84. One of his best-remembered pieces of advice was addressed to Martha (Patty): 'Bear the Cross and it will bear you. The best fruit grows under the Cross.'

sanctuary at the Foundery only to be dragged away to Bristol by a husband who, though he deserted her whenever he chose, would not finally relinquish his hold upon her. For the better part of her married life she was dependent upon the allowance made to her by John, but the giving and receiving had no power to affect their love. When he died he left her a small legacy out of the sale of his books, but with his death she had no wish to live. In a few months the weary wheels of life stood still and the sister had followed her beloved brother.

Dr. Adam Clarke who knew them both intimately was always struck by their similarity in habits and in cast of mind. The likeness even extended to their appearance so that 'had they been dressed alike they might have been mistaken for the other' Boswell also commented on this astonishing likeness to John Indeed, since John taught her to write and later sent her copies to imitate, Adam Clarke was the first to notice that their very writing had striking similarities. Even in traits of disposition they were notably alike. Both had extraordinary poise of spirit so that even under the greatest provocation it was not possible to ruffle them. Both were generous to a fault, never seeing another in need without desiring to help. Martha indeed shouldered burdens when her own were mountains high and gave alms when she herself was well-nigh penniless. Her brother Charles said: 'It is vain to give Patty anything to add to her comforts for she always gives it away to some person poorer than herself.' Both had that unwearied patience and endurance which argues great resiliency of character; and so throughout long lives no adversity deflected them from the love of God and the service of man.

The evangelists, and Luke especially, speak of the ministry of women in our Lord's earthly life. They ministered to Him of their substance, but they followed Him with their love, and at the end when all others had fled, they stood beneath the Cross. It was they who came at the first streaks of dawn on the third day to perform the last sad offices, and one of them experienced the intolerable ecstasy of hearing her name spoken by One who so recently had been laid in a most quiet bed. On more occasions than one in Christian history the same has been true of His followers.

Those who have investigated Wesley's life have met all the women who attracted him, and his love affairs are public property. But it is not so readily recognized that there were other women who gave him of their substance and forwarded his work.[1] Nor is it remembered that throughout his life he had the undeviating love of his sisters. In his visits and correspondence with them, in the assurance of their sympathy and devotion, he was strengthened in his task. And of his sisters, the two he loved the best were most able to help him. Emily was associated with his work in London for thirty years, first at the Foundery and then at West Street Chapel. It is a strange coincidence that in the very year she died (1771) Charles Wesley removed from Bristol to London to take up permanent residence and superintend the Methodist societies. Thus without a break John had Emily and then Charles to be at the heart of the work in London. Martha (Patty) was always in a figurative sense at John's right hand and in her latter years in Bristol and in London she was especially close to him.

One must not therefore look on John as the leader, lonely and remote, who guided men, but dwelt apart. He was singularly fortunate in the love of his followers and his preachers. He was not austere and difficult, but easy and unforced in manner, and through a natural charm had friends in every walk of life. But most of all, both he and brother Charles, had the unequalled advantage of a richly coloured family life. They had such parents as Samuel and Susanna, and an outstanding scholar and wit like Samuel the Jacobite as their brother. Uncle Matthew was in London, rich, urbane, and hospitable. And they had seven sisters, all lovely and accomplished, differing in gifts, but one in their proud love of the brothers. When we speak of the influence of heredity and environment how shall we assess the importance of the Epworth family inheritance in the lives of the brothers? Moving against that spacious background, they were able to advance the more confidently to their great life work. When the villagers of Epworth gave their awkward and sometimes surly greeting to the members of the Wesley family, how could they know whom they were saluting? A salute today is given with greater understanding, for the Epworth Rectory has now its own impregnable place in the hearts of men and in the history of the world.

[1] Both the *Journals* and the *Letters* contain the names of many who shared this ministry.

A NOTE ON AUTHORITIES

FOR books dealing with the general history of the period, the reader may be referred to the classified sources of material in my *John Wesley and the Eighteenth Century*. In particular, the *Journals* (Standard Edition, 8 vols.); the *Letters* (Standard Edition, 8 vols.); the *Arminian Magazine* (1778 f.); and the quarterly *Proceedings* of the Wesley Historical Society.

The *Gentleman's Magazine* (1731–1816) was the most influential periodical of the day and contained many references not always favourable to the growth of Methodism.

The various works of Samuel Wesley, the Rector, have been quite indispensable to me in studying his character and influence. I have even secured a copy of the *Dissertations on Job*, but the fact that Samuel wrote it in Latin and that the subject matter is highly obscure has daunted me from anything more ambitious than a cursory turning over of pages. The *Poems on Several Occasions* of Samuel Wesley, Jun. (enlarged edition edited by James Nichols, 1862) I found absorbing. Here is an admittedly minor poet who yet by a wit and the facility for turning a striking line or verse can stimulate and delight his readers. Much of Susanna Wesley's written work and much information about her can be found in the *Wesley Banner* for 1849, 1851, and 1852.

The single outstanding life on the brilliant but unhappy Hetty is Quiller-Couch's book, *Hetty Wesley*. I hope I have indicated in the actual text how one may accept the known facts, but must treat his interpretation with great caution. His picture of the Rector is wholly distorted and must have given great numbers a totally erroneous impression of that good man. Susanna never comes to her full stature, and one can only claim for John and Charles that they have been inadequately but not unkindly treated. With all its defects, the book is still a work of genius.

There is no reliable book that deals with the relations of the members of the family to each other, and that assesses the influence of the sisters upon the brothers. Luke Tyerman's *Life and Times of Samuel Wesley*; Adam Clarke's *Wesley Family* (2 vol. edition); G. J. Stevenson's *Memorials of the Wesley Family* and his *History of City Road Chapel* are the chief sources. Whilst they are useful for reference, they must be treated with care because their approach is not always sufficiently critical. Eliza Clarke's *Susanna Wesley* is slight but shrewd, and a far better book than the verbose, sanctimonious life of John Kirk entitled *Mother of the Wesleys*. Mabel Brailsford's *Life of Susanna Wesley* is competent, but nothing more. Amongst the chief sources for our knowledge of the family is Joseph Priestley's *Original Letters by the Revd. J. Wesley and His Friends* (1791). It was freely used by Adam Clarke, but it is an original source, and contains letters by John and Charles Wesley, Samuel and Susanna Wesley, and Mrs. Hutton.

Any treatment of the Epworth family must involve a study of relevant sociological, educational, and philosophical books. Those to which I have been most indebted will be found especially in the chapters on the Rector and on Susanna. For a study of the family ghost, the books of Harry Price dealing with poltergeister are of especial value. Priestley's *Original Letters* and *The Epworth Phenomena collated by Dudley Wright. Introduction by J. Arthur Hill* give full accounts of the phenomena.

Through the courtesy of the Rev. Frank Baker, B.A., B.D., I have had access to information from unpublished letters of Charles Wesley. This has been of especial help in dealing with the later years of Hetty and events subsequent to her death.

INDEX

Anglesey, Earl of, 7
Annesley, Judith, 7
 Dr. Samuel, 1620–96, 6, 7, 46
 Samuel, jr., 15, 50, 96, 137
Arianism, 44f.
Arminian Magazine, 83, 87f., 95, 171, 187
Athenian Gazette, 8f., 11
Athenian Oracle, 44n.
Atterbury, Francis, 101, 115–18, 120, 125

Badcock, Rev. Samuel, 87n., 101
Baker, Rev. Frank, 12n., 165n., 188
Band Meetings, 146
Baptism, 41f.
Bayne-Powell, R., 62, 134
Benson, Joseph, 26
Berkeley, Bishop, 38
Berry, Rev. John, 126
 Mrs. (Samuel, jr.'s, mother-in-law), 80, 177
Bertie, Mr. 18
Blackwell, Ebenezer, 141
Body, A. H., 64
Borley Rectory, 94
Boswell, James, 170n., 185
Bourne, Vincent, 111f.
Bowen, Marjorie, 62
Brevint, Dr. Daniel, 43
Brontës, 12, 132, 170
Bunyan, John, 85
Burney, Fanny, 170
Butler, Bishop, 40f., 120

Calamy, Dr., 2
Calvinism, 40, 45, 76
Card-playing, 68
Carlill, Thomas, 9
Clarke, Dr. Adam, v, 31, 43, 71, 73, 87n., 135, 149, 185, 187f.
 Eliza, 7, 149, 188
 Samuel, 39
Class-meetings, 28, 84, 146n., 153, 175
Coke, Dr. Thomas, 10
Collins, Anthony, 39
Communion of Saints, 71f.
Congregational Churches, 44
Cowper, William, 101, 112
Curnock, Nehemiah, 37n.

Death-beds, 22, 83ff., 150, 153, 177, 182
Deeping, Warwick, 136
Defoe, Daniel, 8, 18, 27

Deism, 37–41, 43, 45, 69, 97f., 144, 148
Delamotte, William, 153
de Rougemont, Denis, 95n.
Dissenters, 2f., 6, 17f., 23, 27, 43, 143
Dove, John, 149, 152n.
Dryden, John, 10, 65, 118, 121, 148, 171
Dunton, John, 1659–1733, 6, 8f., 96, 125n.
Dyer, Mrs. Elizabeth, 101
Dymoke, 'Champion', 18

Earle, Mrs., 87n., 130
Education of children, 53–66, 133–5
Election, doctrine of, 44
Ellison, Richard, 141

Family prayer, 53, 68
Fires at Epworth, 14, 20, 68, 100, 103

Gambolds, 152, 179
Ganson, Sir John, 146
Gentleman's Magazine, 171, 187
Georgia, 29, 107, 110, 145, 151, 174
Grayston, Rev. Kenneth, 42

Halifax, Marquis of, 8
Hall, Westley, 78–81, 137, 148, 151f., 184
Harper, Robert, 135, 140
Harris, Howell, 83f.
Hobbes, Thomas, 39
Hogarth, William, 10, 183
Holland, John, 100
Holy Club, 35, 102
Hoole, Rev. Joseph, 88f., 104
Hume, David, 39
Hutton, Mr. and Mrs., 107

Inman, Mr. (curate), 53–6

Jacobites, 46f., 115–18
Job, Book of, 13, 25, 30–2, 104, 142, 147n.
Johnson, Dr. Samuel, 10, 64, 135, 150, 170

Kempis, Thomas à, 33, 68
Kingswood School, 66
Kirkham, Sally (Varanese), 184

Lambert, John, 145
Langton, Rev. Edward, 95n.

Law, William, 13, 65
Lay preaching, 81f., 175
Lely, Sir Peter, 7
Leybourne, Robert, 138f., 180
Liverpool Cathedral, 86
Locke, John, 38f., 64, 66f., 69
Love affairs, interference in, 139, 147f., 154ff., 176

MAXFIELD, THOMAS, 81f., 175
Messiter, 147
Methodist 'experience', 79, 107ff., 150, 168ff.
Middleton, Rev. Dr. Conyers, 45n., 125n., 168
Milton, John, 64, 135
Monarchy, the, 5, 12, 23, 47
Montague, Lady Mary Wortley, 133, 170
Moore, Henry, 14, 149, 152n.
Moravians, 65, 148, 181

NEY, MARSHAL, 130n.
Nichols, James, 112
Normanby, Marquis of, 8, 11
Northampton, Countess of, 17

OGLETHORPE, GENERAL, 29, 32
'Old Jeffrey', 47n., 87–99, 103, 154
Overseas missions, 29f.
Oxford, Earl of, 125

PARENTAL AUTHORITY, 136–9, 155f., 159f., 161–3, 176
Perfection, Christian, 73ff.
Phythian-Adams, W. J., 94
Piers, Rev. Henry, 81, 152
Podmore, Frank, 95
Poltergeists, 93–6, 155
Pope, Alexander, 5, 10, 37, 41, 118, 171
Dr. William Burt, 42n.
Predestination, 76
Presbyterian Churches, 44
'Pretender', the, 115
Price, Dr. Harry, 93n., 94f., 188
Priestley, Dr. Joseph, 87n., 92
Prior, Matthew, 118, 179
Prison visiting, 19, 34, 152

QUAKERS, 139f.
Quietism, 148
Quiller-Couch, A. T., 132, 136, 142, 148n., 154, 155n., 160, 164, 170, 187

RELIGIOUS SOCIETIES, 28f., 174
Reprobation, 44
Restoration, the, 40
Resurrection of the body, 72

Robertson, A. J. B., 95n.
Romantic revival, 171
Romley, Rev. John, 142, 147f., 154n.
Rousseau, J. J., 64f.

SACHAVERELL, DR., 24
Sacrament of the Lord's Supper, 41ff., 77
St. George's Hospital, 111
Satan, 95
Secker, Archbishop, 37, 43
Sharpe, Archbishop, 16f., 19f., 24, 49
Sitwell, Sacheverell, 94
Smith, Adam, 40
Smoking, 4f.
S.P.C.K., 19
S.P.G., 29
Society for the Reformation of Manners, 27
Socinianism, 44
Southey, Robert, 63, 96
Sprat, Dr. Thomas, 111, 115
Stapleton, Walter (Bishop of Exeter), 3
Steele, Richard, 103
Stevenson, G. J., v, 101, 147, 155n., 187
Stonehouse, W. B., 92
Superstition, 97f.
Swift, Dean, 8, 125n.

TATE, NAHUM, 8f., 122
Temple, Sir William, 8
Thorold, Sir John, 18
Tillotson, Archbishop, 11
Tindal, Nicholas, 39
Tiverton Grammar School (Blundell's), 113f., 125
Toland, John, 39
Toryism, 23f., 27, 51
Tyerman, Luke, v, 4, 7n., 44n., 87n., 132, 187

VULLIAMY, C. E., 97n.

WALPOLE, SIR ROBERT, 116, 119f.
War, 47
Warburton, Bishop, 32
Watts, Isaac, 85, 121
Wesley, Ann (Nancy), 1702–? (Mrs. Lambert), 145f.
and Charles, 83
and her mother, 68, 146, 177
and John, 145f., 183
and the Ghost, 88, 90f.
at Hatfield, 81, 177
marriage, 126, 145
Wesley, Bartholomew (John's great-grandfather), 1

INDEX

Wesley, Charles, 1707–88:
  and brother Samuel, 106–11
  and Hetty, 160, 164–70
  and his mother, 68, 78, 83, 85f.
  and Kezzy, 151, 153, 178ff.
  and Martha, 149, 165f., 185
  and Molly, 142, 167
  and Wm. Wright, 165f., 170
  Christian Perfection, 74f.
  like his father, 27
  poetry, 30, 36, 74, 85f., 118, 121, 133
Wesley, Emily, 1692–1771? (Mrs. Harper), 135, 138–41, 180–2
  and her mother, 68, 177
  and John, 135, 139f., 176n., 180–3, 186
  and the ghost, 87–96
  in London, 138, 140f., 182
Wesley, John, c. 1636–70 (grandfather of John), 1–3
Wesley, Mrs. John (grandmother of John), 100
Wesley, John, 1703–91:
  and Ann, 145f.
  and Brother Samuel, 106ff., 110f.
  and Emily, 135, 139f., 180–3, 186
  and Hetty, 105, 159f., 166, 169
  and John Whitelamb, 143f.
  and Kezzy, 135, 137, 151f.
  and Martha, 150, 169, 183–6
  and Molly, 142, 180
  and Richard Ellison, 141
  and the ghost, 87n., 88, 95–9
  and Women, 181–6
  Christian Perfection, 74
  deism, 45, 98
  education of children, 64ff., 133
  Epworth living, 22, 35, 104f., 107
  his wife, 48
  likeness to his parents, 67f., 81f.
  logic, 27, 33, 57
  mother's death, 83ff.
Wesley, Kezziah (Kezzy), 1710–41, 150–3, 178ff.
  and Charles, 178ff.
  and John, 135, 137, 151, 178, 183
  and Westley Hall, 148, 150ff.
  as a child, 60
  at Bexley, 81, 152
  at Tiverton, 101, 178
Wesley, Martha (Patty), 1707–91 (Mrs. Hall), 146–52, 183–6
  and Dr. Johnson, 135, 150
  and her mother, 34, 68, 146, 177
  and John, 150, 169, 182–6
  and Mrs. S. Wesley, jr., 131, 178
  and Richard Ellison, 141
  and Samuel (brother), 151
  marriage, 82, 137, 148–151, 184

Wesley, Mary (Molly), 1696–1734 (Mrs. Whitelamb), 142–5
  and Charles, 167
  and Hetty, 142, 155, 160f., 164, 167
  and John, 180, 183
  and the ghost, 88, 91
  her deformity, 137, 142, 175
Wesley, Matthew, surgeon (uncle of John), 1662?–1737, 2f., 24, 100, 134, 137, 141, 147f., 156, 166, 178, 186
Wesley, Mehetabel (Hetty), 1697–1750 (Mrs. Wright), 88–95, 133–7, 147, 154–73
  and brother Samuel, 105, 177f.
  and Charles, 160, 164–70
  and her mother, 68, 166, 177
  and John, 159, 166, 168ff., 183
  poetry, 140, 144f., 154–9, 163f., 171ff., 175
Wesley, Samuel, 1666–1735, 1–45
  and Dissenters, 3, 6, 17f., 23f.
  and Epworth living, 22, 24, 35, 104f., 174
  and his sons, 23–45, 49f., 101–6, 126, 174
  and his wife, 26, 46–56, 103
  and Samuel Annesley, jr., 15, 50ff.
  as farmer, 14f., 25, 52, 175
  Book of Job, 13, 25, 30ff., 104
  education of daughters, 132–5
  financial troubles, 14, 19ff., 24ff., 52, 56, 133, 175
  parental authority, 136–9, 147f., 176
  poetry, 4f., 8–11, 30, 34, 44, 48f., 171
  prison, 19, 34, 49, 103
  Toryism, 23f., 51
Wesley, Samuel, 1690–1739, 100–31
  and Epworth living, 104–7
  and his father, 9, 126
  and his sisters, 126, 139n., 141, 145, 151, 160, 177f.
  and Martha, 151
  and the ghost, 87, 94
  attitude to Revival, 79f., 107f.
  Blundell's School, 113f., 125
  his children, 130
  marriage, 126–31
  poetry, 115–31, 151, 187
  politics, 113, 115–20, 125
  Westminster School, 36, 100–14, 116
Wesley, Sarah, 1726–1822 (wife of Charles), 149
Wesley, Sarah (Sally), 1759–1828 (daughter of Charles), 149f.
Wesley, Susanna, 1669–1742, 46–86
  and child education, 57–62, 67ff., 75, 132–5

Wesley, Susanna—cont.
  and her daughters, 134, 146, 166, 175ff.
  and her husband, 15, 23, 26, 46–56
  and Methodism, 78–82, 174f.
  and the ghost, 87f., 96, 103
  and Thomas Maxfield, 81f., 175
  beauty, 7
  marriage, 6, 46
  her theology, 43f., 68–78, 102
  last days and death, 82–6, 166, 177
  letters to her children, 75–8, 101ff., 134
  poverty, 14, 20f., 25
Wesley, Susanna (Sukey), 1695–1764 (Mrs. Ellison), 141f.
  and her mother, 68f., 73
  and John, 183
  and the ghost, 88f., 91
  in London, 137
Wesley, Timothy, 1659–? (uncle of John), 100

Wesley, Ursula (*née* Berry), ?–1742 (wife of Samuel, jr.), 105, 126–31, 141, 161, 178
Wesley Historical Society, 69, 187
West Street Chapel, 140, 181f., 186
Westminster School, 36, 100f., 103, 106, 111f., 114ff., 178
Whichcott, Colonel, 19
White, John, 1574–1648 (father of Samuel's mother), 7n.
White, John, 1590–1644 (father of Susanna's mother), 7
Whitefield, George, 79f., 108
Whitelamb, John, 21, 29, 137, 142–4
Whiteley, Dr. J. H., 62, 133n.
Williams, Charles, 95n.
Witchcraft, 94, 97ff.
Wollstonecraft, Mary, 63, 133
Woolf, Virginia, 138, 170
Wright, William, 145, 156–61, 164–7, 170

ZINZENDORF, COUNT, 181

www.ingramcontent.com/pod-product-compliance
Lightning Source LLC
Chambersburg PA
CBHW071230170426
43191CB00032B/1227